THE PLACE WHERE YOU ARE STANDING IS HOLY

THE PLACE WHERE YOU ARE STANDING IS HOLY

A Jewish Theology
on Human Relationships

Gershon Winkler
with Lakme Batya Elior

JASON ARONSON INC.
Northvale, New Jersey
London

This book was set in 12 pt. Berkeley Oldstyle by Alpha Graphics, Pittsfield, New Hampshire, and printed by Haddon Craftsmen in Scranton, Pennsylvania.

Library of Congress Cataloging-in-Publication Data

Winkler, Gershon, 1949–
    The place where you are standing is holy : a Jewish theology on
human relationships / Gershon Winkler with Lakme Batya Elior.
        p.   cm.
    Includes index.
    ISBN 1-56821-218-6
    1. Interpersonal relations–Religious aspects–Judaism.   2. Jewish
way of life.   3. Covenants–Religious aspects–Judaism.   I. Elior,
Lakme Batya.   II. Title.
BM723.W55   1994
296.3'2–dc20   94-17362

Manufactured in the United States of America. Jason Aronson Inc. offers books and cassettes. For information and catalog write to Jason Aronson Inc., 230 Livingston Street, Northvale, New Jersey 07647.

We dedicate this book to
Joel Ehrlich and Priscilla Press,
who honor the work we do
and have given us the support we need to do it more freely.

CONTENTS

ACKNOWLEDGMENTS

We thank the Great Mystery, Who inspired us to find the words that felt best for communicating what we so wanted to get across. Certainly we take credit for writing this book, but it feels inauthentic to us to deny the spiritual inspiration we often experienced while searching for teachings and the sources that would support our premises, and while wrestling with the best ways to word them.

We also thank the Great Mystery for the gift of our marriage to each other and the Aliveness it has brought to us both. In fact, much of this book is an outgrowth of our willingness to make our marriage covenantal rather than contractual, and to test this way of doing relationship, which we believe is the thematic core of the Torah's message to humanity. Team-teaching this concept to audiences of varying spiritual paths and religious denominations has similarly nurtured the development of this book. And to both of these processes we are thankful.

In acknowledging the gift of our marriage, we need also to acknowledge Rabbi Dr. Zalman Schachter-Shalomi, whose mysterious karmic weavings brought the two of us together from the most incompatible backgrounds and circumstances. Through very different personal processes, each of us was attracted by the refreshing wisdom and authenticity of this colorful contemporary sage who then unknowingly set in motion a series of events that led to our marriage.

SPECIAL ACKNOWLEDGMENTS BY GERSHON WINKLER

I started out writing this book on my own, under contract with the publisher. Since I honor Lakme's wisdom and sensitivity, I asked her to review what I wrote at each stage. But Lakme ended up offering more than editorial critiques and spousal inspiration. She also added an enormous amount of her personal and professional insight, which eventually doubled the contents of this book. Moreover, as we started teaching this stuff together publicly I realized that Lakme understood the concept of Covenantal Relationship—about which I was trying to write—in ways that felt to me more concrete than my own understanding of it. Listening to her teach and reading her notes in the margins of my manuscript, I was struck by what I considered fresh feminine perspectives on what I was trying to express. It got to the point that I realized she was actually co-authoring this work with me. Gladly, then, do I share the credit and authorship of this book with this wise woman, whose contributions to the book rendered it more complete, balanced, practical, sensitive, and beautiful than it otherwise would have turned out.

I am very grateful to author Barbara Diamond Goldin for being my *shadkhan* (matchmaker) and recommending me to Jason Aronson, thereby making the publication of this work possible, and to Arthur Kurzweil, vice president of Jason Aronson Inc., who knows how not to badger a sluggish, delinquent writer, and who gave me only encouragement and respect throughout the writing of this book.

My thanks go as well to my incredible parents, Rabbi Menashe Zvi and Esther Rivka Winkler, who raised me in a Judaism that was warm, fun, and rich; and to my father's mother, who in her lifetime was affectionately known as "Fru Doktor." To this day I retain vivid memories of sitting on the lap of the rebbe I called "Mutti," while she introduced me to a gentle, personal, loving, and compassionate Creator.

I am also grateful to my many teachers, some of whom I suspect might cringe at portions of this work. Primarily, I thank my father who introduced me to the lesser-read classics of my tradition, nurtured my individuality by personal example, and taught me—as his father taught him—to question.

And I thank my *rosh yeshivah*, of blessed memory, Rabbi Ben Zion Brook, who would limp through the cold corridors of the crumbling *yeshivah* structure in a rather run-down section of Jerusalem, knocking gently on the fragile doors of our dorm rooms and chanting: "*Kumu, kumu, l'avoydas ha-boyrey*," yeshivish Hebrew for "Arise, arise, to serve the Creator." Although he often disagreed with my radical ways back then, and with some of my theological takes, he nonetheless treated me with an adoration and honoring that truly exemplified a covenantal relationship between teacher and disciple. In spite of our differences, he was the first to declare me Rabbi.

The second to declare me a rabbi was Rabbi Dr. Zalman Schachter-Shalomi, truly the grandfather of the Jewish renewal movement worldwide, who breathed new life into my personal theological evolution over the past decade. In 1982, when I took my first daring step out of the bounds of normative Judaic Orthodoxy, I secluded myself in primitive cabins across various mountain ranges from California to Colorado. The newness of my personal paradigm, theologically and otherwise, overwhelmed me and drove me like the prophet Jonah into the belly of America, working on remote ranches, living in the wilderness, and fleeing from my calling. It was Reb Zalman—through stubborn persistence and a series of warm-up processes—who dragged me kicking and screaming from my self-imposed exile and catapulted me back to rabbi-ing, pushing me closer in the process to the feasibility of an encounter with the woman I was eventually to marry. Thank you, Reb Zalman!

Last, but certainly not least, I thank the wild, scenic, fragrant forests that surrounded me as I wrote this book, both in West Virginia's Allegheny Mountains and, at this writing, the San Pedro Mountains of northwestern New Mexico. Admittedly, my wilderness surroundings quite often distracted me from the task of writing, but they also taught and inspired me at least as much.

PREFACE

My involvement in this book evolved over a period of about three years. Gershon was already working with the idea of compiling ancient Jewish teachings on relationship. And in my work as a therapist, as well as in the modalities with which I work, I had done a lot of learning about and teaching on many aspects of relationship with Self, Others, and spirituality.

Then Gershon and I started working together. We discovered that we team-teach well, balancing and augmenting each other. We were evolving in our work ways of applying the teachings of the Talmud that he was researching, and I would (of necessity) add my perspective on the way emotional and relationship issues are processed. Most of the time I found myself saying things like, "That's the way so-and-so works in teaching communication." "This is how that teaching might be put into practice." And as I thought about those teachings that seemed contradictory to my experience and philosophy, new and deeper understandings of the possible meaning of the ancient works spontaneously evolved, or rather erupted. I was always bringing them into the realm of the applied.

Also, Gershon and I were using all that we knew from any source to establish our marriage on the best possible footing. It worked. My knowledge and his dovetailed beautifully, both of us knowing many of the same things from different sources, our understanding and insight deepening from our bringing them into our everyday interactions. In a very essential way, the book came out of our living and teaching together.

Gershon did 95 percent of the actual writing and 99 percent of gathering the sources. Still, as he taught me many teachings from the Talmud, and certainly all that are contained in this book, I often made connections and interpretations that were novel and fitting. And I brought in some sources that he had forgotten about or not connected to the theme of this work. As he wrote each section, I would read it in detail, making suggestions (usually along the lines of "unpack this section") and writing a couple of paragraphs here and there. But the evolution of the ideas that went into the book, its basic organization—many of the "howevers" and juxtapositions—came synergistically from our teaching together and our living together. In this, the book is completely a joint project. We have lived it daily and continue to live it!

Lakme Batya Elior

INTRODUCTION

The Place where you are standing is holy.

—Exodus 3:5

We wrote this book because, after a combined sixteen years of teaching Judaica to both initiates and seekers, we realized that we had spent most of that time dealing with the way many Jews have become alienated by it. To some, Judaism constituted a scrolling preprinted list of what God required of them, all spelled out and nonnegotiable. To others, Judaism was filling out a synagogue membership application, raising money for Israel, and the puzzling memory of being sacrificed in their youth upon the *bar-* or *bat-mitzvah* altar following a year of excruciating lessons in a language totally alien to them so that they might be initiated into a way of life with which even their parents were fundamentally unfamiliar.

Judaism, however, is not about laws and not about blind obedience to some ever-demanding deity. Nor is it about supporting Israel, or belonging to a synagogue. It is about relationship-ing, and not just any kind of relationship-ing but a sort that allows for and encourages the fullest sense of Aliveness in each partner. What we felt was missing in the sharing of this rich millennial-old path of spirituality, then, was its very core teaching—the *covenantal* quality of relationship.

Humans are creatures of relationship. We are weavers, weaving our own experiences with those of others toward the creation of a tapestry that would represent the essence of the collective All without losing the individual Self. In much of religious teaching in general, however, the individual patch of the great cosmic tapestry is all too often downplayed if not outright dismissed. Rather, it is the collective garb of the "religion" that is set up as the exclusive focal point of the great weave. We live for religion, we die for religion, we love for religion, we hate for religion, we sacrifice for religion, and we kill for religion. Of course, we also add a "Thus saith the Lord" to religion to exempt it from accountability and lend it unquestionable credibility.

It is not religion per se that does all this: it is people who have done this to religion. Dr. Bahira Feinstein points out that not a single episode of the *Tanakh* (i.e., Old Testament) advocates blind, unquestioning obedience to human authority—any human authority. The classical mandate to adhere to religious authorities, for example, originates in the authorities themselves, not in the divine inspiration that seeded the religion. In Judaism, for example, the rule that you have to obey rabbis was invented by rabbis, and few Jews know that according to ancient Judaic law you do not need a rabbi for weddings, divorces, conversions, births, funerals, and other life-transition rites. Rabbis hold no religious authority other than the authority vested in them by their own communities, not by the religion, and not by God (see Maimonides' introduction to his *Mishneh Torah*, para. 5). The twelfth-century Rabbi Moshe Ibn Maimon (Maimonides) applied the biblical injunction of obedience to religious authority (Deuteronomy 17:8-11) solely to the ancient "Great Court" (*Mishneh Torah, Shoftim, Hilkhot Mamrim* 1:1-2). But even the so-called absolute authority of the Great Court was negotiable. First, you were only required to obey their decision if you asked them a question that you yourself were unable to resolve (*Mishneh Torah, Shoftim, Hilkhot Mamrim* 1:8). Second, if you felt that their ruling was wrong, you were not obliged to obey (Jerusalem Talmud, *Horayot* 1:1). There is a seemingly contradictory, oft-quoted rabbinic teaching that you needed to obey "even if they declared that right was left and left was right" (*Sifri* on Deuteronomy 17:11). But upon closer reading, the teaching does not intimate blind, unquestioning obedience. The wording is: "If it appears in your eyes that they are declaring right as left and left as right," which connotes uncertainty on your part. But if you are certain that their ruling is in error, you are not obliged to follow it, as stated in the Jerusalem Talmud.

Teachings like this, about individual rights in the realm of religious legislation, are not the subject of this book. Nonetheless, they reflect the more flexible *covenantal* versus *contractual* nature of the Creator's relationship with the Creation, and, in turn, the desired nature of our relationships with ourselves and with others. When we ignore this component of the Jewish religion, we miss its main point.

Throughout this book, we have quoted ancient rabbis whose often bold, nontraditional teachings remind us that there is a significant discrepancy between religion and God, between the mortally transmitted Word of God and what they believed to be the actual will of God. We have included such lessons in this modest book because so few of them are ever taught and are instead left buried beneath texts that more closely reflect the "party line"—whether traditional or progressive—rather than the heart and *kishkeh*. God, in turn, is often portrayed as a cosmic pinball machine into which we invest our blood, sweat, and tears for the hope of reward in the form of points in this world and a free game in the next. Wallace Black Elk, a Lakota Sioux medicine man, likens it to pouring quarters into a game machine for the sole satisfaction of winning. "But all we're actually winning are points," he says. "Meanwhile, we're losing quarters."

Performing "good deeds" and "divine imperatives" might accrue points, too, but how much of our precious essence are we spending in exchange? How much of the invaluable Self that is a gift to us from the Creator are we chipping away at under the illusion of "serving God"? How many of us fulfill our "religious obligations" out of fear or anxiety about some future reckoning? And what does our soul look like when it is nurtured into fruition through such emotional and psychical blackmail? As the third-century B.C.E. rabbi Antigonus of Soko taught: "[In serving God] be not like servants who tend to their master only because they will thus receive their rations" (Babylonian Talmud, *Avot* 1:3).

Our relationship with the Creator, Judaism posits, is personal and not mediated through any "authority." A religious authority might teach us the "correct way" to pray, for example, but God might prefer the haphazard, homebrewed gut way to pray we were accustomed to before we were taught the "religiously correct" way. The twelfth-century Rabbi Judah the Pious writes about an illiterate *kohen* (descendant of the ancient Jewish priests) who kvetched out the priestly blessings with so many gross mispronunciations that the rabbi of his synagogue, unable to take anymore, asked him to step down. In a dream that night, the rabbi was admonished to return the *kohen* to his station (*Sefer Hasidim*, no. 19): the *kohen*'s mispronounced prayers may have been improper by the standards of organized religion, but by the standards of the Creator, each unintelligible word was eternally precious, for "while the mortal looks at outward appearances, God looks into the heart" (1 Samuel 16:7). The *kohen*'s readings may not have been right, but his intentions were. And it is intent, Judaism teaches, that is important to the Creator, not accuracy. As an ancient rabbinic teaching goes: "A man who works for his father will do so with a joyous heart because he will say: 'If I don't do it just right, my father will not be angry with me because he loves me'" (*Tanchuma, Noah,* no. 19). Without intention there is no room for a viable relationship, and it is a living, breathing relationship, Judaism teaches, that the Creator seeks with us, not the impersonal protocol of sovereign and subject, master and serf. Likewise, it is a conscious, responsible relationship that we are encouraged to pursue with one another and with all creatures and with the earth.

This book, then, is about being in relationship—about how Judaism involves both doing and not doing religion within the living context of being in relationship with Self, God, and Other. It challenges us to be real with God and each other and to realize that as Creations of the Ancient Mystery we are not puppets but independent beings with the gift to make our own choices and to accept responsibility for them; the gift of voice, of having a say in life; the gift of Free Will; the gift of Covenant. In this book we will endeavor to introduce (or reintroduce) both the Judaically learned and the merely curious reader to the lesser-promulgated teachings of the ancient, medieval, and latter-day Judaic masters who understood Judaism to be a way not of blindly following but of actively challenging—of being in relationship with, rather than subject to, the Creator and the Creation.

On the surface, the path of the Torah may seem to be one more cache of religious rituals and ideological dogma, but a closer examination reveals that it challenges us to engage in relationship-ing rather than trying to whip us into some uniform order. Indeed the authentic Torah of Judaism is preceded by no "the" as in "the only"; it is fluid, living, breathing, ever-unfolding. We do not therefore consider this book the final version of what Judaism is "really" all about, because we believe there will never be a final version. As living beings we are creatures of change, and as a living Torah, Judaism is ever changing. Many of us are comfortable with the way it's been and the way it is, and many of us are not, but all of us need to remember that even the way it once was represented then a change from the way it was before then (see Babylonian Talmud, *Baba Batra* 120a: "What was practiced by the ancestors was not practiced by the descendants, and what is practiced by the descendants was not practiced by the ancestors"). Abraham and Sarah ate dairy and meat together, a no-no in later Judaic practice. Moses didn't wear a *yarmulke*, was married to a woman who wasn't Jewish, and had no problem with accepting the advice of his non-Jewish father-in-law about how to lead the Jewish people. King David played his harp on the Sabbath and Jeremiah never heard of Hanukkah and probably ate pasta on Rosh Hashanah instead of chicken and potato kugel.

Judaism, then, has always been changing. Always. Many traditionalists are in staunch denial about this, and just as many progressives are under the sad illusion that they are the first to pioneer change in a religion that has in actuality been shifting and changing from the moment it began. Whether changing or stationary, the survival of Judaism is contingent upon its Aliveness, its core nature of being a way of life that nurtures the practitioner only when she or he is in an authentic—not perfect—relationship with their Self, with Other, with the Creator. The doctrines, rituals, and dogmas are but the garments upon the body of Judaism; they are not its soul, not its essence.

Rabbi Shimon bar Yochai [second century] taught: "The text of the Torah is but the garment of the Torah. Woe onto those who consider this garment as the Torah itself. . . . There are indeed fools who, upon seeing a person covered with a beautiful garment, will look no further than that; and yet that which gives the garment purpose is the body. And what is even more precious than that is the soul [which is garbed by the body]. The Torah, too, has its body. These are the precepts, which one might call 'body of the Torah.' The ordinary narratives which are interspersed are the garments with which the body [of the Torah] is covered. Simpletons regard only the garments, or narratives of the Torah. . . . Those who are more learned pay no regard to the garment, but to the body which it encloses. Finally, the wise ones . . . are concerned only with the soul [of the Torah], which is the foundation of all else, and which is the authentic Torah." (*Zohar*, Numbers 152a)

What is threatening the survival of Judaism these days is not intermarriage or assimilation or the attraction of many New Age Jews to more meditation-centered paths like Buddhism and Hinduism. What is threatening the survival of Judaism these days is ignorance. And what is more dangerous than ignorance is when teachers of Judaism—from traditionalists to progressives—promulgate a particular "party-line" version of a way of life that is clearly broad enough and organic enough to embrace as many versions of doing Jewish as there are Jews to do it. This book, then, is not about any specific "right" way of doing Jewish or understanding Judaism, but an attempt to demonstrate how Judaism is more about relationship-ing than about religion; more about authenticity and effort than about performance and perfection; more about doing it than about doing it just right—"The Compassionate One says: Just do. And whatever you shall find to do, it shall be pleasing unto Me" (Babylonian Talmud, *Bekhorot* 17b).

Sensitive to sexism in language, we decided to employ the plural pronouns "they/their" instead of, for example, "he" or "she," even in the singular. We found that while it may not make for good grammar, it makes for smoother reading as opposed to constantly interrupting the flow with "he or she" or "he/she." We wrote this book with as many varieties of readers in mind as feasible, women and men, heterosexual and homosexual, married and single, those who believe in the Creator and those who do not, the mystical and the skeptic, from Orthodox Jews to what we call "Flexidox" Jews, and for peoples of all paths. Though it is impossible to please all, we still dare to hope that we have been sensitive to everyone, and insensitive to no one.

We pray to the Creator that the words on these pages will empower the reader with a sense of celebration of that priceless gift that is Life, that is Self, that is Other, that is God, that is the Planet, that is the Child. Being students of the Jewish path, we have written this book from the wellsprings of wisdom and experience that comprise Judaism, but there is no intent thereby of "selling" this way of being in the world over any other way. Judaism does not believe in a Jewish God, but in a Creator whose Spirit is embodied by all peoples, all creatures, all Life. And it believes that all paths—if but so much as directed toward the One—will lead to the One; that in the eyes of the Creator we are all the same, no one soul any higher or lower than any other, no one people more or less important than any other. Probably the most essential teaching in all of Judaism is that each of us is the most precious being in the entire universe. And it is upon this seemingly paradoxical principle that this book is based.

1

THE SANCTITY OF PERSONAL SPACE

Make for me a sacred space and I shall dwell amongst you.

—Exodus 25:8

In the creation myth of ancient Judaic mysticism, God creates the universe by a process dubbed *tzimtzum*, which in Hebrew means a sort of stepping back to allow for there to be an Other, an Else, as in something or someone else. The Judaic notion of a world of Free Will (Babylonian Talmud, *Berakhot* 33b) is deeply rooted in this concept, in the understanding that in creating life, the *Eyn Sof*, or the Endless One, subdued the omnipotent, all-embracing Divine Presence for the sake of the realization of the Divine Will that there be other beings (*Etz Chaim* 1:1:2). Our world, then, is the sacred space that the Great Spirit gave as a gift to us, a space in which to be as human as divinely possible, and as divine as humanly possible. A space to err, to fall, to believe, to doubt, to cry, to laugh. *Our* space, created by the simple motion of stepping back, the humble act of honoring the separate reality of an Other.

The Talmud–Judaism's largest literary body of Jewish law, lore, and philosophy, spanning the period between 200 B.C.E. and 400 C.E.–teaches that God claims only about four square cubits, so to speak, of human space, and that the rest is ours and ours alone (Babylonian Talmud, *Berakhot* 8a), into which not even God will enter without first knocking. This stepping back is true of the God-Acting-upon-Human-Affairs, and is partially true for the God-Dwelling, which is always present but might not always be experienced. However, it is not true that God-as-Love, the pure God-Essence out of which All is made, is ever anywhere absent. It is just that we, having been given the gift of free will (independent action and independent identity), may exclude some elements of the God-Presence from our lives simply by not extending the invitation. And, according to ancient teaching, it is the God-Will for the relationship between God and human that humans be free to experience independence from God. This will be borne out in the ensuing pages.

In fact, this seems to be a model for personal relationships in which there is a disparity of power. For example, the ancient rabbis taught that a man, then considered the "Head of the House," should not enter his home suddenly, without first announcing his arrival, lest he disturb, disconcert, disrupt the in-the-moment needs of other members of his household who might be inside bouncing about in their personal space (Babylonian Talmud, *Niddah* 16b).

However, God's "space" is also to be acknowledged with this level of respect. In the Bible, as well as in *Raider's of the Lost Ark*, it is the Tabernacle that demonstrates the sacredness of personal space. Approached by the wrong elements, or at the wrong time, or in the wrong context, it consumed anyone who dared to enter it (e.g., Leviticus 10:1-2; 2 Samuel 6:6). For just as the physical universe was the place that God had created for humans to dwell in the God space, the Tabernacle represented a place that we mortals had created for God to dwell in the human space. And as God honored our human space as ours, the God space of the Tabernacle had to be honored as God's. And if a mortal entered that space, he or she simply did not exist anymore, reabsorbed into the God space, the exception being the individual who was invited by the Dweller to share of that space, as was, for example, the high priest once a year, on behalf of the people. Even then, the Talmud teaches, he was humbled by his brothers prior to his entry (Babylonian Talmud, *Yoma* 18a-b), so that his earthly soul would not be extinguished in the God space due to a conceited heart or other such factors unwelcome there (Babylonian Talmud, *Sotah* 5a). Entering this space uninvited, unannounced, represented space invasion. Rather than a stepping back and an honoring of an Other's space and presence, it was an invasion. Rather than a subduing of Self to share space with an Other, it was a subduing of Other to make way for Self.

The Tabernacle is therefore called, in Hebrew, *mishkan*, which translates more accurately as "a mutual dwelling place," as in the related word *shekhunah*, which means "neighborhood" or "co-op." Likewise, God's immanent Presence in our world is called *Shekhinah*, because She dwells with us, the Talmud teaches, only when there is a sacred co-op-ing, a sacred meeting, be it between us and God, or between people joining in harmony (*Numbers Rabbah* 12:1), or joining in study (Babylonian Talmud, *Avot* 3:3), or joining in lovemaking (Babylonian Talmud, *Sotah* 17a). Perhaps that is why the tent in which the *mishkan* was housed was called *Ohel Moed*, which means "Tent of Meeting" (Exodus 40:2).

This ancient Judaic concept of mutual dwelling obviously connotes something very different from a free-for-all situation. *Mutual* does not mean license to march freely in and out of the Other's space whenever it suits you. It means a mutual honoring of that shared space, which means that those who share it must—every now and then—be prepared to step back to allow for the presence of the Other. And it is that honoring that makes the shared space a sacred place, whether that shared space be a sanctuary for the Divine Presence, or a home, or a relationship, or the environment, or the planet.

Post-Tabernacle Judaism teaches that when you retract Self momentarily to allow for an Other, when you subdue your own light to enable someone else to shine more brilliantly, when you avoid crowding someone, you thereby create a *mishkan*, a sacred place in the human space for all that is positive and wholesome (*Exodus Rabbah* 32:6, 36:3). Or, for the purpose of this book, you thereby create a special and beautiful setting for a healthy, loving relationship.

The *chupah*, or wedding canopy, is another element of this concept in the Judaic tradition. The canopy is suspended above the bride and groom throughout the ceremony. At the outset, only the groom stands beneath the canopy in anticipation of the bride's arrival. When the bride approaches, the groom steps out of his space to meet the bride and to escort her—not drag her—into his space. The bride, in turn, circles the groom to welcome him into her space.

The different ways in which the bride and groom create and share their respective sacred spaces with one another is reflective and respectful of the distinct reality structures within which women and men operate. According to ancient Judaic teachings, men, on the average, are more object-oriented and work with a more externalized sense of reality; women, on the average, are more subject-oriented and work with a more internalized sense of reality. Man *brings* and woman *holds*. He ejaculates, she reproduces. He brings her raw material and she creates from it (Babylonian Talmud, *Yevamot* 63a). He provides the abstract and she weaves it into reality. He shares his sacred space with her by inviting her into it. She shares her sacred space with him by encircling him (Jeremiah 31:22).

Beneath the *chupah*, then, the Canopy of the Sacred Space, both are to learn that while they now create a shared space that is sacred, the perpetuation of that sacredness is determined by whether they will *continue* to honor one another's personal sacred space. It should be noted that these dynamics can occur in same-sex unions as well.

The question is often asked where one would draw the line between personal-space rights and shared-space responsibility in a relationship. The question commonly involves religious observance. One partner might decide to adopt more stringent religious practices, while the other partner decides not to. Although both may be honoring the other's personal space so that both can be who they are and practice as they wish, eventually some of the newly adopted disciplines of one may at some point begin to affect the other. This is most often the case when the issue centers on sexual intimacy and involves restraints that leave the other partner feeling deprived on the mutually shared level of their relationship space. At the same time, however, the partner practicing the restraints certainly feels entitled to their personal space as well, disciplines and all. And so, again, the question is, where does one draw the line between personal-space rights and shared-space responsibility?

There is a discussion of a similar sort of case in the Babylonian Talmud, in the tractate of *Baba Kamma* (60a, 61b), which discusses ancient legislation on property damage and personal injury. A man was innocently barbecuing in his own backyard when a mischievous wind suddenly came along and blew some sparks onto the adjoining property of his neighbor, causing a fire. The rabbis ruled that he was liable for the damages caused by his fire.

But why should he be liable? What happened to personal space? Isn't he entitled to do whatever he wants on his own property, whether it be to light a fire or to blast his boom box? Yes, he is. But only so long as it doesn't interfere with the welfare of someone else, of an Other; as long as what one does in their private space does not chip away at the private space of someone else.

That is where the line might be drawn. For then it is no longer an issue of personal space but of shared space. So if a couple shared a relationship, and one of them wanted to practice a strict discipline of sexual restraint, a personal issue, they are so entitled because they are entitled to their individual space in the world. Indeed, the Talmud obliges everyone to declare that the whole world was created for them personally (Babylonian Talmud, *Sanhedrin* 37a). But they are also responsible for the ramifications of their personal-space actions as they affect others—as they affect their partner—no less than in the case in the Talmud where the man was responsible to tend his fire in his own backyard so that it would not blow across the fence and burn down the private space of his neighbor.

There is also the talmudic issue of *mechzei k'yehura* (Talmud, *Berhakhot* 17b), a term applied to an individual whose excessively pious practices might appear to others as "holier-than-thou" theatrics. The eighteenth-century mystic and moralist Rabbi Moshe Chaim Luzzatto comments that if you wish to adopt religious stringencies above and beyond normative practice, you are certainly entitled to, as long as you draw the line at the point where your personal practice becomes an imposition on others (*Mesulat Yesharim*, chap. 20). In other words: We don't owe it to anyone to fashion our personal lifestyles after social norms and live our personal trips apologetically. Each of us is entitled to our personal modes of expression, of being, of happening. And others can think of us as they wish, and can, as they say, like it or lump it. Nevertheless, we are also responsible to see to it that what we do in our personal space does not impose upon others against their choosing; does not violate the personal or shared space of others; does not cause harm to anyone, or needlessly cause others to harm us.

Space invasion, then, is not just the stuff of science fiction, it is a real-life phenomenon of everyday human relationship. It is not uncommon that one partner will superimpose their presence over the other and behave with total disregard for the personal-space needs of their partner. In a vampirelike fashion, they gradually drain them of their self-esteem and personal identity, leaving them with a feeling of having been psychically violated. All the spaces in their heart and mind read *occupado*, occupied by their omnipresent partner. There is no room for them, and the only sense of space they can truly call their own is the commode.

It is not surprising, then, that close to 80 percent of rapes in this nation alone occur in the course of relationship, court-ship, and matrimony. A society bearing such statistics needs to be admonished that there is no moral or legal qualifica-tion for imposing one's will or person on another. Every in-dividual needs to be honored as an Other, as a distinctive personality with a particular set of feelings, of likes and dis-likes, of moods and desires, and with a distinct sense of tim-ing and pace.

Martin Buber, a noted Judaic philosopher, wrote exten-sively about what he called the I–It/I–Thou gauge for rela-tionship-ing (*I and Thou*). *I–It* is like relating to someone or something as devoid of any personality, unworthy of any regard or special importance; unconscious of their indepen-dent existence and value as who or what they are; talking *at* someone or leaning against a tree without any acknowledge-ment of the tree. *I–Thou*, on the other hand, is like relating to someone or something with the consciousness of their otherness, their separateness from you and your need of them, as well as of their relationship with you in the moment.

So if some of the people with whom you are relationship-ing are trying to override or replace your reality set with their own, stop them dead in their tracks. But don't place the entire blame on them. Each time you allow them an inch of your space without invitation, you become an accomplice, a col-laborator with the invader. To paraphrase Julius Caesar in the motion picture *Cleopatra*: No one can take from you what you will not relinquish. Love is not a partnership of Give-and-Take, but rather of Share-and-Receive, wherein each person shares of their love and nurturing willingly, as op-posed to feeling obligated to "dish it out" on demand; and wherein each receives from the other as one receives a gift, as opposed to taking it by force, taking it for granted, as if collecting on some kind of emotional IOU.

The ancient rabbis made it clear that marriage was no special kind of license for two people to use or abuse one another, and that it was forbidden to engage one's partner in sexual intercourse when they were unwilling (Babylonian Talmud, *Eruvin* 100b; *Pesachim* 49b; *Yalkut Shimoni* on Prov-erbs, no. 959). Men and women, they taught, needed to honor one another as two distinct "nations" (Babylonian Talmud, *Shabbat* 62a) with very different sets of physical and psychical needs and ways of fulfilling those needs. What might be considered trivial to a man, they taught, could be of vital importance to a woman (Babylonian Talmud, *Shabbat* 62a; see also Rashi on Babylonian Talmud, *Yevamot* 62b), and vice versa; each needed to honor the otherness of their partner. And marriage, it was understood, was a sacred context in which this was to be exercised most consciously rather than filed away with the *ketubah*, the marriage contract.

No wonder, then, that the Talmud urges a man to "love his wife like himself, but to honor her more than himself"

(Babylonian Talmud, *Yevamot* 62b; *Sanhedrin* 72a). We cannot like anyone any more than we like ourselves, because how we think of ourselves gauges how we think of others. As one second-century rabbi put it: "If you notice a blemish in your friend, contemplate first whether it might not be your own" (Babylonian Talmud, *Baba Batra* 15b; *Kiddushin* 17a; *Arakhin* 17b). Or as another rabbi of the same period taught: "The standards by which you measure [others] are the standards by which you, too, are measured" (Babylonian Talmud, *Sotah* 8b; *Shabbat* 127b). Thus the wording of the highest biblical commandment of the Jewish faith is "You shall love your fellow human as yourself" (Leviticus 19:18; *Torat Kohanim* on same). Hopefully you will endeavor to think well of yourself first, because, again, how well you think of yourself will reflect how well you think of another. So we are only capable of loving another as much as we love ourselves. However, when it comes to honoring, we can, in honoring another, go beyond our own standards of what might be considered honorable for us, personally. We can and are taught to elevate the standards by which we honor others beyond the standards by which we ourselves might wish to be honored. This teaching, once again, is a teaching about the distinctiveness of another human being, that no two of us are alike, and therefore what is OK for you might be uncomfortable for someone else. The classical teaching "What is discomforting for you, do not to another" (Confucius, in *Analects* 5:11 and 12:2; Tobit, in *Apocrypha* 4:15; Hillel the Elder, in Babylonian Talmud, *Shabbat* 31a) seems to ask us to transcend what *we* might be OK with in the sense of not allowing that to become the standard by which we determine what would be OK for others. It is safer *not* to do something to another that I myself find disconcerting, than to *do* something to someone else that I do enjoy, and thereby risk hurting them because, it may turn out, they *don't* happen to enjoy

it. So if I love being tickled, and I pounce upon an unsus-
pecting friend and tickle them, perhaps they would find it
excruciating. If I *don't* like being tickled, it will be one less
assumption I'll be making about someone else's wishes. It
will mean that much more of the Other's space that I will be
honoring. Every time we make an assumption about what
someone might or might not want, or what may or may not
be beneficial for someone, we trespass on yet one more inch
of their personal space, and violate the sacredness of Other.

The sanctity of space operates on all levels, not only at holy
shrines or during religious services. For there is also the
sacred space that we create for one another by allowing for
each person's individuality, their quirks (in Yiddish, their
meshugaas), their distinct paths and paces of growth and
realization, their personal opinions, tastes, and preferences.
This space is so easily violated by judgments, assumptions,
and intolerance. There is no better example of the honoring
of Other than the sacred space that God created for us by
allowing us to be so totally human.

2

COVENANTING WITH GOD

The Bible is more than the word of God: it is the word
of God *and* man; a record of both revelation and response; the drama of covenant between God and man.
　　　　　　　　　　　　　　　–Abraham Joshua Heschel
　　　　　　　　　　　　God in Search of Man, pp. 260–261

Judaism is not about ways of how to be Jewish, but about
Jewish ways of how to be. The root principle of these ways
is the concept of *Brit*, which means "covenanting"– covenanting with Self, Other, and God. This path is not a one-way
street; it is an ongoing dialogue, an ongoing interaction, in
which your opinions have voice, your feelings count, and
your right to be in this world is honored.

When we view our relationship with God as Contract, we
are left with an arrangement that is nonnegotiable and with
the consequence of having to sever the relationship if the
contract is breached. Such a perspective, however, leaves little
breathing space between God and Humanity. We are allowed
no ifs, buts, or maybes, and our margins of error are reduced
to the half inch or so of white page framing the text of the
Bible. Yet, when we examine the Judaic teachings on the relationship between God and the Human, we find anything

11

but the sense of claustrophobia too often portrayed in the picture of Divine Covenanting. Judaism does not teach that when we err, when we breach the Covenant with God, the proverbial lightning will strike us down in the moment. Nor do we experience this. Rather, we are taught that God will wait patiently for us to own up to our actions and change our ways—what is known as *repentance*. In Hebrew, the word for "repentance"—*teshuvah*—means, literally, "return."

> God follows the *khotte* [one who has become distant from right being] all through the marketplace, waiting patiently until there is an inclination to return. (*Pesikta D'Rav Kahana* 163b)
>
> . . . for God is gracious and compassionate, patient and abundantly merciful. (Exodus 34:6; Joel 2:13)
>
> Have I any pleasure at all in the death of the wicked? And not rather that they return from their ways and live? (Ezekiel 18:23)
>
> Even unto old age am I [God] the same; and even unto hoary hairs will I carry you for I have made you and I will bear you; yea, I will carry and deliver. (Isaiah 46:4)
>
> It is analogous to the son of a king who distanced himself from his father a journey of one hundred days. His friends urged him, saying, "Return unto your father." Said he to them, "I am unable to!" When his father heard of this he sent to him and said to him, "Walk toward me as far as you are able and I shall meet you the rest of the way." Likewise does the Holy Blessed One say to us: Return unto me and I shall return unto you [Malachi 3:7]. (*Pesikta Rabati* 184b-185a)

This is Covenant. Unlike Contract, Covenant is compassionate; it takes into account much more than merely the technical act of breach and considers the broader situation of human frailty. Covenant recognizes the whole of the individual and does not coldly or judgmentally dissect and separate any part of the fullness of their being. God does not judge our action separate from our intention, or vice versa. While certain emotional and physical consequences easily arise from our actions irrespective of what we intended, or what we thought we were doing, "God judges us by the intentions of the heart" (Babylonian Talmud, *Sanhedrin* 106b; *Megillah* 20a).

> People judge by outward appearances, but the Lord looks upon the heart. (1 Samuel 16:7)
>
> It matters not whether you do a lot or whether you do a little, as long as your heart is directed toward God. (Babylonian Talmud, *Berakhot* 17a)
>
> If you thought of doing a *mitzvah* (a good deed, or the fulfillment of a religious precept) but were prevented from actually doing it, the Holy Blessed One considers it as if it was done. . . . An evil thought, the Holy Blessed One does not consider it as if it were carried out; a positive thought, the Holy Blessed One considers as if it were carried out. (Babylonian Talmud, *Kiddushin* 40a; *Berakhot* 6a; *Shochar Tov* on Psalm 30)
>
> Everything is contingent upon the intentions of the heart. (Babylonian Talmud, *Megillah* 20a)

Teachings about how God is more concerned about what's in our hearts than whether we performed a religious act with accuracy is emphasized even in such heavily moralistic writings as *Mesulat Yesharim* ("Path of the Just"), by the eighteenth-century mystic Rabbi Moshe Chaim Luzzatto: "And thus did our sages teach, that 'The Compassionate One desires the heart' because the Blessed Master is not satisfied with deeds done merely in a spirit of obedience to a command. Rather, what is most important before God is that the heart be pure toward the intention of earnest service" (end of chap. 16, *Midat HaTaharah*). Or, as the fifteenth-century Rabbi Yossef Albo writes: "The most important thing [in the performance of religious duty] is the intention. As King David

said, 'O God, create for me a pure heart' (Psalms 51:12)"
(*Sefer HaIkkarim*, 3:25, toward end).

The teachings are clear, that even if you thought of doing
a *mitzvah*, a positive deed, and you ended up not doing it
because of circumstances beyond your control, your thought,
your intention, has already performed it as far as God is concerned: "If you decide to give [to the poor] and you give, God
rewards you for deciding and for doing; if you decide to give
but then discover that you have not the means, God rewards
you for deciding in a manner equal to the reward for giving"
(*Sifri* on Deuteronomy 15:10). The ancient rabbis tell of a
woman who brought a handful of flour for an offering. The
priest turned her down, admonishing her, "What kind of an
offering is that? What is in there that is worth sacrificing or
eating?" In a dream that night, the priest was told this: "De-
spise her not. But consider it as if she had brought herself as
an offering!" (*Leviticus Rabbah* 3:5). And we find the same
attitude again regarding prayer: "The Holy Blessed One says:
'When you pray, pray in the synagogue in your city. But if
you cannot pray there, then pray in your field. And if you
cannot pray there, then pray in your bed. And if you cannot
pray at all, then be still and meditate in your heart'" (*Shochar
Tov* on Psalm 4). Or: "Rabbi Chiyya said in the name of Rabbi
Safra, 'Concentrate on all the words of the prayers. If you
can't, then concentrate on at least one word'" (Babylonian
Talmud, *Berakhot* 34b).

Throughout, the ancient teachings of the Judaic tradition
emphasize heart, intention, effort. We are judged not by how
much or how correctly or how precisely we perform a *mitzvah* but by our motivations, and by how hard we *try* given
the limitations of our circumstances. The first-century Rabbi
Tarfon taught: "The work is not upon you to complete,
though neither are you exempt from trying" (Babylonian

Talmud, *Avot* 2:16). The second-century Rabbi Yishmael said it even more directly: "Accept not upon yourself to complete the whole Torah, but neither are you at license to abstain from her" (Babylonian Talmud, *Avot D'Rabbi Natan* 27:2). Or, as paraphrased by Rabbi Yishmael's disciples: "Let not the Torah be upon you like an obligation, nor shall you abstain from her" (Babylonian Talmud, *Menachot* 99b).

Then there are the more radical teachings about intention, such as: "Greater is a transgression intended for the sake of Heaven, than a *mitzvah* with no intent. . . . Others say they're equal" (Babylonian Talmud, *Horayot* 10b). In other words, even if your deed turned out to be a serious transgression, like the daughters of Lot who committed incest with their father (Genesis 19:31-32), or like Tamar's illicit union with the patriarch Judah (Genesis, chap. 38), but your heart was sincerely in the right place, as were the intentions of these women in their actions, then, again, it is not the nature of the act that God considers but the quality of the intention. Lot's daughters thought there was no man left in the world after the fall of Sodom and Gomorrah, and Tamar believed she was destined to bring forth the seed of the Messiah through the patriarch Judah (Babylonian Talmud, *Horayot* 10b; *Nazir* 23b). In the end, both these illicit unions did indeed result in the messianic seed of the Davidic dynasty, via Ruth, who descended from Moab, the offspring of Lot's eldest daughter (Genesis 19:37, Ruth 1:4), and via Boaz, who descended from Peretz, the offspring of Tamar (Genesis 38:29, Ruth 4:18-22).

It is clear from these and countless other teachings like them that neither God nor Torah are as judgmental and as demanding of us as we are of ourselves and each other. We're asked to do what we can, not what we can't. The Torah was given to mortals, not to angels (Babylonian Talmud, *Berakhot*

25b). Whatever it is that God asks of us, it is asked for in accordance with our abilities, not any superhuman divine abilities (*Numbers Rabbah* 21:22).

> The son serves his Father in Heaven with joy, saying, "Even if I do not succeed entirely [in doing the divine will]—still, as a loving father, He will not be angry with me." On the other hand, [one who sees himself as] a hired servant is always afraid he might not fulfill the commandments just right and therefore serves God in a state of constant anxiety and confusion. (*Tanchuma, Noah,* 19)

> Do not be afraid of [God's] judgment. . . . Do you not know Him? He is your relative! He is your brother! And what is more, He is your father! (*Shochar Tov* on Psalms 118:5)

According to the Talmud, the Jewish people did not observe Yom Kippur (Day of Atonement) during the year King Solomon's Temple was inaugurated because the people were so euphorically engaged in joyous celebration over the consecration of the House of God. Later, though, the people felt really bad when they realized they had failed to observe the holiest festival of the year. But then a *bat kol,* a heavenly voice, was heard, saying: "All of you are destined for the World-to-Come!"—an assurance that their failure to perform the observance of Yom Kippur was not lost on a God Who considered it no less holy that they had gotten caught up in their rejoicing (Babylonian Talmud, *Mo'ed Katan* 9a). As the third-century Bar Kappara summed it up: "Which is the shortest sentence in scripture that includes in it all of the most important principles of the Torah? It is, 'In all your ways acknowledge God, and He will direct your paths' (Proverbs 3:6)" (Babylonian Talmud, *Berakhot* 63a).

True, according to biblical text, unintentional sinners had to bring a sin-offering (Leviticus 4:2). However, the Torah is referring to someone who transgressed a "Thou shalt not," and the ancient teachers go through great pains to make it clear that the sin-offering, brought only for unintentional wrongs, applied exclusively to the transgression of a *lo-taaseh*, a no-no, and not to an *asseh*, a "Thou shalt" (*Sifra* on Leviticus 4:2).

And while those who transgressed a "Thou shalt not" unintentionally did indeed bring an offering, it was more for the peace of mind it gave by resolving the person's own sense of conflict and failure, not anything God required:

> To what purpose is the multitude of your sacrifices unto Me? —saith the Lord. I am full of burnt-offerings of rams and the fat of fed beasts. And I delight not in the blood of bullocks, or of lambs, or of he-goats. ... Who has required this at your hand, to trample my courts? Rather, seek justice, relieve the oppressed, judge the orphan, plead for the widow. (Isaiah 1:11-17)

> Thus saith the Lord of Hosts, the God of Israel: "Add your burnt-offerings unto your other sacrifices, and eat ye the meat thereof yourselves. For I spoke not unto your ancestors, nor commanded them in the day that I brought them out of Egypt, concerning burnt-offerings and sacrifices. But this is what I commanded them: 'Listen unto My Voice, that I may be your God and you may be My people; and walk in the way that I teach you so that it may be well with you.'" (Jeremiah 7:21-23)

> O Lord! Open Thou my lips, and my mouth shall declare Thy praise. For Thou delightest not in sacrifice, or else I would give it. Thou hast no pleasure in burnt-offering. The sacrifices of God are a broken spirit; a smitten and contrite heart, O God, Thou will not turn away. (Psalms 51:17-19)

> To do righteousness and justice is more acceptable to the Lord than sacrifice. (Proverbs 21:3)

Ritual sacrifices in general were believed by both ancient and medieval rabbis to have been a "kosher" way of weaning the ancient Israelites from the then prevalent and powerful universal urge to sacrifice to spirits and other life forces (Leviticus 17.7, *Leviticus Rabbah* 22:5; Maimonides' *Guide to the Per-*

plexed, Book Three, 32:46). In an era ruled and intimidated by rampant and often abusive sacrificial cults, the Torah suddenly limited sacrifices only to specific species of animals, and only for certain times, and only in one solitary spot on the face of the planet. In Jerusalem, but not anywhere, only on Mount Moriah; and on Mount Moriah, but not anywhere, only in the Holy Temple; and in the Holy Temple, but not just anywhere, only in the Holy of Holies; and in the Holy of Holies, but not just anywhere, only in a certain sacred spot, upon a modest altar constructed of acacian wood and plated with gold. The sacrificial rite outlined in the Bible, then, represented an intermediate phase of teaching humanity to let go of the idea that divine approval and grace could be bought. It was a step toward fading out humanity's tendency to perceive of God as impersonal, and reachable only by bribes and through the mediation of priests and prescribed rituals. It was a way to gently ripple the unfolding of a new understanding of God as personal and immanent. It was an introduction to the God of Covenant.

Unfortunately, some of the dogmatic manifestations of Judaism and its offshoots continued to perpetuate the very perception of God they were supposed to have gotten us away from. The scriptures speak of covenanting, but religion, it seems, pushes contracting, resulting in centuries of dysfunctional personal and interpersonal relationship dynamics and immobilizing syndromes of guilt. The Old Testament, however, is pretty much a story of the elasticity of Covenant, wherein God's relationship with us never breaks, only stretches. Yet, as compassionate and as flexible as a Covenant might be, it also takes that much more effort to keep it alive.

For example, God never asked Adam and Eve, condemningly, "What have you just done?" but "Where are you now?" (Genesis 3:9). This is the question of a Covenantor. The contractor asks, "What have you done?!" The Covenantor asks,

"Where are you at?" If Adam and Eve would have understood this, they would never have cowered in the bushes and concealed their genitals with fig leaves. They would have allowed themselves to be cradled in the loving, nonjudging Grace of God. When we don't see God this way, when we hide shamefully from the One Who Knows our deepest parts (Psalm 39), it is not God Who condemns us, Who judges us and sentences us, it is rather we who do so, to our selves, to others, even to our most beloved ones. "Am I the one they anger? . . . rather, is it not they themselves for their own shame?" (Jeremiah 7:19). When it seems that God has turned from us, it is actually we who have turned to hide from God: "And they have turned their backs to Me" (Jeremiah 32:33); "You cast Me behind your back" (1 Kings 14:9); "Your sins have hid God's face from you" (Isaiah 59:2); "Return unto Me, and I shall return onto You" (Malachi 3:7); "Let [the sinner] return onto God, and God will have compassion upon them . . . and will abundantly pardon" (Isaiah 55:7). Our sense of unfathomable distance from God at times is just that–a sense. But actually: "God is as near to you as your ear is to your mouth" (Jerusalem Talmud, *Berakhot* 13a).

In Covenant, then, each looks upon the Other, not just at what they have or have not done or what they should have done or would have done or could have done, but at the whole of the Other's being, the weaknesses, the strengths, the love and understanding that had led to the place of covenanting to begin with. However, we are not to look for rationalizations when we hurt each other, or to find justification for what hurt has been done to us by the other, because co-dependence is not at all synonymous with covenanting. Rather it is the deeper honoring of otherness, the striving –in that moment of feeling victimized–to emulate the model of relationship-ing through Covenant set forth in the Torah and played out by God throughout history, collectively, and throughout our lives, individually. And if we find ourselves feeling resentment at being coached to transcend our humanness and emulate God, we need remind ourselves that there is nothing necessarily divine about not doing unto others what is uncomfortable to ourselves, as Hillel the Elder taught (Babylonian Talmud, *Shabbat* 31a). We must keep in mind that if it were us breaching the relationship, if it were us perpetrating the betrayal, the hurt, we would wish for our partners to muster that Godlike strength of forbearance and to hold us supercompassionately with all our faults, all our demons, and to cradle lovingly our individual and mutual wholeness of being—everybody's anger and hurt intact.

In the prevalent mind-set of marriage, for example, infidelity frequently results in an almost instantaneous termination of the marriage, for there has been a blatant violation of a contract. If, however, marriage is Covenant, the breach would not be so automatically and narrowly confined to one of violation; there would be a sacred space in the covenantal context in which the parties to the relationship could hold what has occurred and cradle it toward mutual healing even if divorce becomes the path of that healing. Covenant allows for holding the hurt, the betrayal, the confusion, the shame, the shattered trust—whatever the breach has wrought—and to treat it as a shattered vessel of creation rather than of destruction.

Sound paradoxical? contradictory? It is! Because we mortals are comprised of both paradox and contradiction. We expect God to know that and accept that about us, and we expect others to know it and expect it of us, and we ought therefore also to expect this and know this of others, especially those with whom we relationship. Deep down, then, we might ask whether the human quest in relationship-ing is not really to Covenant, rather than to Contract; and which of the two is closer to home, closer to who we are; which of them presumes our nature to be organic rather than static.

Covenant then would not preclude divorce in a marriage, for instance. Bottom line, it would create a sacred space between wounded partners to heal, and therefore to separate with dignity and in peace with one another, or to renegotiate respective definitions and expectations of marriage, and reinforce the foundations and ever-expansiveness of their Covenant. Contracts break. Covenants stretch. Nonetheless, while there are times when stretching improves circulation and general well-being, there are also times when it reaches threshholds of discomfort that no one, despite the noblest of intentions, deserves.

In Covenant, your wholeness as a being is more important than the form of the agreement. God does not desire our obeissance and sacrifices at the expense of our spirit, of our aliveness:

> "With what shall I come before God? And bow myself before God on high? Shall I come before God with burnt-offering? With calves a year old? Will the Lord be pleased with thousands of rams? With tens of thousands of rivers of oil? Shall I perhaps give my firstborn for my transgressions? The fruit of my body for the sin of my soul?" It has been told you, O Human, what is good, and what God *does* ask of you: Only to do justly, and to love mercy, and to walk humbly with your God. (Micah 6:6-8)

To those who feel that the definition of Covenant put forth on these pages is sacrilegious, we ask: Is it not, rather, sacrilegious to describe God as some kind of psychotic deity foaming at the cosmic mouth? some kind of divine version of Henry VIII? As the third-century Rabbi Shmuel ben Nachmani said: "Woe to those who turn the [divine] attribute of mercy into the attribute of judgment" (*Genesis Rabbah* 73:3).

Is it not, rather, sacrilegious to declare ourselves more loving and compassionate than God? Are we rather to presume
that we are capable of at least conceiving a patience, forgiveness, and forbearance which far outdoes God's? Or, perhaps
more appropriately, is it not time we supplanted the false god
we had worshiped for so long at the cost of so much death
and humiliation with the real God who asks for life and dignity: "Behold I set before you today Life and Death, the Blessing and the Curse. And you shall choose life" (Deuteronomy
30:19). How we choose to live is up to us, but God implores
us to "choose life" and to see our God as a no-strings-attached
God of Life, a God of Good.

> Customarily, when people appear before a mortal court for judgment,
> they approach in morbid clothes and unkempt hair, in trepidation
> of the outcome of the judgment. . . . Not so, however, when the day
> of [divine] judgment begins [Rosh Hashanah, the Jewish New Year],
> for the Jews then are clad in white and groom their hair; and they eat
> and drink and rejoice in the conviction that God will do wonders for
> them. (Jerusalem Talmud, *Rosh Hashanah* 57b)

It is we who condemn, not God. When God summons
Adam and Eve after the "fall," why presume it is for judgment of breach of contract? Perhaps it is rather to help them
heal and to re-Covenant. God does not bellow: "What have
you done?!" but rather calls out: "Where are you?" Parties of
Covenant do not jab their beloveds with the guilt pangs of
the irreversible past by demanding "Where *were* you?" But
in the compassion and holding of the moment they call out,
"Where *are* you?" In the moment. What *is* needed? What can
we *do*? They do not ask what *should* have been done or *could*
have been done, or what should the Other *not* have done?
Conversely, Adam's reponse is a reactionary tirade of de-
fensiveness, which in no way addresses the question and
which frames a perception of God as impersonal and intru-

sive, rather than personal and immanent; which neglects the special sacredness of Covenant and instead lowers the relationship to Contract. "I heard your voice in the garden," Adam replies, "and I became afraid because I was naked; and so I hid" (Genesis 3:10). It is Adam and Eve's *perception* of their relationship with God as Contract versus Covenant that is the "fall." And in the context of this understanding, God's response—which we customarily read as curses and punishment—actually sounds more like this:

> "If you see yourselves as no longer in relationship with Me just because you goofed, then this can no longer be a garden. And if you cannot let Me come to you in your place of mistakenness or feelings of need and guilt, if you break your link with Me and see yourselves as objects of My Power and not beloved extensions of My Being, then you limit your capacity to experience the fruition of My partnership with your lives. You also limit your access to healing and forgiveness, fencing in your very life, and thereby becoming mortal. Having relinquished your sense of your own power, you will have difficulty exercising it in your newly created reality. It will be uneasy to wield your creative powers over the earth now. And there will be much work needed to heal the confusion of your sense of your powers in relationship to one another, as well. Each of you will be inclined to fear rather than to honor the other's power, and in turn each of you will be inclined to remove power *from* the other, or once again to relinquish your power *to* the other. You will, in turn, also experience resistance in other arenas where I have empowered you, such as your human creativity, whether in farming, industry, science, arts, or technology. It will be a challenge for you to let go, to believe in yourself and in your creative potentials, and to bring them to fruition. In turn, it will also be a challenge to release your power of bringing forth new life. You will do so with hesitation and uncertainty, often with striving and great discomfort. Moreover, you and your children will also have fear and loathing of what the serpent will come to represent as a result of your severing yourselves from Me. You will crush beneath your heels any feelings of inadequacy and brokenness, and they in turn will bite you; you will be poisoned by them. Do you understand yet the magnitude of the consequences of your hiding from Me?"

Adam and Eve probably did understand the magnitude of the consequences but somehow not the act of covenanting, and therefore felt *driven* from the garden. As the fourth-century Rabbi Channina Bar Yitzchak taught: "When Cain wandered the earth [after having unintentionally killed his brother Abel], he encountered Adam the First Human. Said Adam: 'And what, pray tell, was the result of *your* judgment?' Replied Cain: 'I acknowledged the wrongfulness of my action and I was forgiven.' When Adam heard this, he cried: 'Woe! So great is the power of *teshuvah* [turning back], and I did not know about it!'" (*Leviticus Rabbah* 10:5; *Pesikta D'Rav Kahana* 160b). The ancient rabbis even believed that Adam and Eve could have actually gone right back into the Garden of Eden after they were thrown out, had they only believed in a God of reconciliation (*Genesis Rabbah* 25:10).

Our mistakes, and our own reactions to them, are what makes God seem hidden from *us*, wrote the prophet Isaiah (Isaiah 59:2). But we are never hidden from God: "Is it I who have turned My face from you? It is rather you who have turned your faces from Me" (*Shochar Tov* on Psalm 13). God exists in all of Creation equally, and certainly no place exists where we can leave God behind. The Garden of Eden is not a "For Members Only" kind of place. It is not just in the realm of perfection and shadow-less light—but exists wherever we are.

The eighteenth-century Rabbi Pinchos of Koritz once visited the home of a disciple who had suddenly absented himself from the rabbi's weekly discourses. He found the young man secluded in his bed chamber, disheveled, melancholic, and unkempt. "Where are you?" the rabbi called to him. The disciple, shocked by the presence of the holy master, warned him to stay away: "Do not approach me, Rebbe, for I am in the darkest of places, the lowest of abysses, and, in fact, at the very final gate of ultimate defilement! Stay away or you will be contaminated!" When the rabbi heard these words, he broke into joyful excitement and seized the hand of the "fallen" man, exclaiming: "The darkest place, you say? The lowest of all abysses, you say? The very final gate of ultimate defilement, you say? Please let me join you! For I, too, want to see the Face of God!" (Heard from Rabbi Shlomo Carlebach)

"There are forty-nine gates of defilement," wrote the nineteenth-century Rebbe of Gur, "but in truth, the fiftieth and ultimate level is completely holy. For at that level there exists no duality, only goodness. Because on that very plane dwells the Source of Unity" (*Sefat Emet*, p. 181).

Even if we read the Adam and Eve story as saying that God literally chased them out of Eden, we might understand it as analogous to a lover who insists on the departure of a beloved following a betrayal, hoping to provoke the beloved to counterinsist on remaining steadfast and working out the issues that may have led to the betrayal. It is no different from God saying to Moses after the Golden Calf incident, "Step aside and I shall destroy these people and make another people out of you instead" (Exodus 32:10), thereby creating an opportunity for Moses to argue down such an action, which he does (Exodus 32:32). It never occurred to God to judge the entire people for the actions of the three thousand or so involved. God's respone to Moses' daring demand that he be blotted out of the God Book, too, is: "Whosoever *sinned against Me* will I blot out of My Book" (Exodus 32:33), as if to say: "Moses, think not that I was about to wipe the people from memory before you stood up for them so boldly. I wasn't going to do a thing about them, to begin with, I was only going to deal with those who were guilty. But I would have been sorely disappointed had you not stood up for them as you did; had you related to me as if I were any one of the nonnegotiable deities being worshiped by the Canaanites and the Hittites."

Similarly does God challenge Abraham's perception of God's relationship with the human by informing him of the impending destruction of Sodom and Gomorrah. First the narrative has God saying: "Wait! I have made a covenant with Abraham of partnership in human-ing—a covenant of compassion, benevolence, and justice with all the peoples of the earth! Shouldn't I go to him as a partner now, too, and tell him about what I am about to do?" (Genesis 18:17-19). Abraham responds appropriately by challenging the divine decree, thereby demonstrating his perception of, and relationship with, God as a deity who is negotiable and who is welcoming of feedback and wrestling (Genesis 18:20-23) and whose glory fills not only heaven but also earth (Isaiah 6:3):

> And Abraham drew near, and said: "Will You indeed sweep away the righteous along with the wicked? Perhaps there are, say, fifty righteous people within the city. Will You actually sweep them away and not forgive the place for the fifty righteous that are there? It would be very unlike You to do such a thing, to slay the righteous with the wicked, to treat the righteous the same as the wicked. Far be it for You to do such a thing! Shall not the judge of all the earth do justly?" And the Lord said: "If I find in Sodom fifty righteous people, I will forgive all of the place for their sake."
>
> And Abraham answered and said: "Behold, I have now taken it upon myself to speak unto the Lord—I, who am but dust and ashes. But perhaps there might be forty-five righteous people. Will You destroy the entire city for lack of five righteous ones?" And God said: "I will not destroy it if I find forty-five there." And he spoke unto God again, saying: "What if there shall be found only forty there?" And God said: "I will not do it for the sake of the forty." And he said: "Please do not grow impatient with me, O Lord, and I will speak further. What if there are only thirty?" And God said: "I will not do it if I find thirty there." And he said: "Behold now, I have taken it upon myself to speak unto the Lord. What if there were to be found only twenty righteous ones there?" And God said: "I will not destroy it for the sake of the twenty." And he said: "Oh, let the Lord not be upset with me, but I will speak only once more. What if only ten righteous ones were to

be found there?" And God said: "I will not destroy it for the sake of
the ten." (Genesis 18:23-32)

The biblical Book of Judges recounts how an angel of God
appeared to the warrior Gideon and told him, "The Lord is
with thee." Gideon throws aside the honor and instead takes
the opportunity to voice the frustrations of his people who
were constantly fighting off attempted invasions by enemy
armies:

> And Gideon said to the Angel: "Oh, my lord, if the Lord be with us,
> why then is all this befallen us? And where are all God's wondrous
> works of which our ancestors told us, saying, 'Did not the Lord bring
> us up from Egypt?' But now the Lord has cast us off, and delivered
> us into the hands of Midian." And the Lord turned towards him, and
> said: "Go in this power of yours [to stand up on behalf of the people
> (*Tankhuma, Shoftim*, para. 4)], and save Israel from the hand of Midian.
> Have I not sent you?" (Judges 6:12-14)

God, the ancient rabbis mused, enjoys being "defeated"
at the hands of those who intervene on behalf of others: "I
seek to be conquered: when I win, I lose, and when I am
defeated, I win" (*Shochar Tov*; Psalms 103:9). The ancient
teachers heaped roses and confetti upon the prophets who
"placed the honor of the children [the Israelites] before the
honor of the parent [God]" (*Mekhilta* on Exodus 10:3; *Tanchuma, Shoftim*, para. 4).

Furthermore, when the prophets—including the most
lauded defenders—spoke harshly to the people, they were
admonished for it. A rabbinic tradition has it, for example,
that Moses was not allowed entry to the Promised Land
because he had raised his voice to the people and called them
"infidels" (Numbers 20:10, 12), and that Isaiah the Prophet
was reproved for calling them "a people of unclean lips"
(Isaiah 6:5, 7). The prophet Elijah, too, was met with disin-

terest when he sought God's help by elucidating the sins of
the people against God:

> Said Elijah: "I am jealous on behalf of God, the Lord of Hosts, for the
> Children of Israel have abandoned Your covenant!" Replied God: "My
> covenant, not yours." Said Elijah: "But they have desecrated your
> altars!" Replied God: "My altars, not yours." Said Elijah: "But they have
> slain your prophets by the sword!!" Replied God: "They are *my* proph-
> ets, so what concern is it of yours?" Said Elijah: "I alone remain! And
> they seek to take my soul, too!" [God then responds to his cry and
> directs him out of his conflict]. (*Song of Songs Rabbah* 1:39, based on
> 1 Kings 19:14-15)

Interestingly, God is here portrayed as responding to Elijah's
supplication only after Elijah has stopped using the sins of
others as leverage for his personal prayer and shares straight
out with God what it is he, personally, needs. For God does
not only wish us to stand up for others, but also for ourselves.
In Moses' argument with God at the Burning Bush, he does
not readily accept the divine command to go down to Egypt
and negotiate the freedom of the slaves. Rather, he stands
up for himself, sharing with God his fears, his doubts, his
vulnerable places—until God assures him that his brother
Aaron will assist him and serve as his spokesperson (Exodus 4:1-15).

Covenant, then, forges a framework of mutual relationship
that welcomes disagreement and negotiation, but that also
allows for whatever space is necessary for the preservation
and honoring of the individual Self, within—and in spite of—
that relationship. Even though the human is integral with,
and inseparable from God, for example, God nonetheless
honors us as Other. Every moment of our lives we are being
granted our personal space to be by the very source of our
Being, by the One Who knows us more intimately than our
closest friends or relatives ever can. God covenants with us

in the *tzimtzum*, the stepping back, so to speak, giving us the gift of space and pace we need to do our human processes.

Once [during a discussion about the application of *halakhah* (Jewish religious law) to particular circumstances], Rabbi Eliezer attempted to convince his colleagues on the validity of his ruling. But the rabbis refused to concede to his arguments. Said Rabbi Eliezer: "If the *halakhah* is as I rule it, let this carob tree prove it!" The carob tree flung itself a hundred cubits. Some say it moved four hundred cubits. The rabbis said to him: "We do not derive proof from a carob tree." Said he to them: "If the *halakhah* is as I say, then let this stream prove it!" The waters of the stream flowed backwards. Said they: "We do not deduce proof from a stream of water." Said he to them: "If the *halakhah* is as I say, may the walls of the House of Study prove it!" The walls of the academy began to crumble when Rabbi Joshua rose and rebuked them [the walls], and said to them: "If the learned ones are disputing the *halakhah*, what has it got to do with you!?" In honor of Rabbi Joshua, the walls did not buckle completely, and in honor of Rabbi Eliezer, neither did they straighten, and they remain contorted to this day. Then said Rabbi Eliezer: "If the *halakhah* is as I say, may it be so proven from Heaven!" A Heavenly Voice instantly declared: "What do you want from My son Rabbi Eliezer? Do you not know that the *halakhah* is as he rules it in every situation?" Rabbi Joshua rose to his feet and replied: "It is written '[The Torah] is not in Heaven' [Deuteronomy 30:12]." What did Rabbi Joshua mean by this? Rabbi Jeremiah said: "[He meant that] the Torah was given to *us* at Sinai. We therefore pay no attention to a heavenly voice. After all, the Torah we received at Sinai states: 'By a majority shall you decide' [Exodus 23:2]." Later, Rabbi Nattan encountered [the spirit of] Elijah the Prophet and asked him whether he was in the heavens during that period [when Rabbi Joshua challenged God]. Said Elijah: "Yes, I was present." Asked Rabbi Nattan: "What did God do about it?" Said Elijah: "God laughed, and said, 'My children have defeated Me! They have defeated Me!'" (Babylonian Talmud, *Baba Metzia* 59b)

Challenging God is as much a part of Judaism as is praising God.

There are of course statements throughout the Bible that

describe God as angry, vengeful, threatening, and foaming at the cosmic mouth, and certainly no one you'd want to dialogue with. Nonetheless, Judaism reminds us that God is not mortal (Hosea 11:9) and is thus void of all these mortal emotions. More appropriately, then, biblical portrayals of God exhibiting human emotional outbursts are our ascriptions to God rather than our descriptions of God. As the ancient teachers put it: "The Torah speaks in the language of the Human" (Babylonian Talmud, *Berakhot* 31b). For lack of a better handle—of a more vivid way of expressing ourselves about experiences we believe reveal "the Hand of God"—we are often left with no choice but to resort to human metaphor (Maimonides, *Yad, Yesodei HaTorah* 1:11; *Guide to the Perplexed* 1:54; Rabbi Yossef Albo in *Sefer HaIkkarim* 2:15:16). When we experience "God's wrath," then, it is our own wrath we're feeling at ourselves: "Is it Me that they anger? Is it not themselves that they anger, by their confusion and shame?" (Jeremiah 7:19). Abraham Joshua Heschel put it this way: "Prophecy is superior to human wisdom, and God's love is superior to prophecy" (*God in Search of Man*, p. 261).

It was asked of Wisdom: "What is the punishment for a sinner?" Replied Wisdom: "Evil shall pursue the sinner" [Proverbs 13:21]. It was asked of Prophecy: "What is the punishment for a sinner?" Replied Prophecy: "The soul that sins shall die" [Ezekiel 18:4]. It was asked of Torah: "What is the punishment for a sinner?" Replied Torah: "Bring a sacrifice and be atoned" [Leviticus 1:4]. It was asked of the Holy Blessed One: "What is the punishment for a sinner?" Replied the Holy Blessed One: "Return unto Me and I will receive you" [Jeremiah 3:1]—for it is written: "Good and just is God; therefore does God show the way for the sinner" [Psalms 25:8]. (Jerusalem Talmud, *Makkot* 2:6)

Comments the sixteenth-century Rabbi Judah Loew of Prague:

It is analogous to a mortal king who gave one of his subjects a royal vase to keep for him and to watch over. But the man later dropped it and it shattered. Pained over the tragedy and fearful of what the king might do to him, the subject sought the counsel of a wizard. The wizard told him that it would be a disgrace to the king to return the vase to him in its damaged condition. Dissatisfied with the wizard's counsel, he went to inquire of one of the king's relatives, figuring they would know better how the king would react. But the relative, too, advised him not to dare return the broken vase to the king, and that it would be far better to get rid of the vase completely than to return it in that condition. At his wit's end, the man then brought the vase to a repair shop, but was told that the damage was irreparable; that the pieces could be mended together but that the cracks would still show. Said the man: "I will never be free of what I have done, so I may as well just go directly to the king himself, and face whatever consequences he will mete out to me." When he brought the broken vase to the king, the king simply said: "I shall make good use of this broken vase. And the others, who gave you erroneous advice, did so because of my honor and dignity, not because of the way I actually conduct myself. But I will make good use of it just the way it is."... And this is what is meant by "It was asked of the Holy Blessed One: 'What is the punishment for the sinner?'" and the Holy Blessed One replies: "Return and be forgiven." (*Netivot Olam: Netiv HaTeshuvah*, chap. 1, para. 3)

In the biblical Book of Numbers (*Bamidbar*), there is a fascinating story of five sisters who were among the Israelite people who journeyed through the Sinai wilderness following the exodus from Egypt: Makhla, Nowah, Hoglah, Milkah, and Tirzah. Moses has just spoken forth the law regarding inheritance as revealed to him by God: "All family inheritance was to go to the male survivors." The sisters, whose father, Zelaphchad, had died, step forward and challenge the law: "What about us, whose father passed on leaving no sons, only daughters?" they ask. Moses takes their complaint to God, who replies: "The daughters of Zelaphchad are right!"

and the law gets changed in midair to include women with no brothers (Numbers 27:1-6).

"Not like the compassion of flesh and blood is the compassion of the Holy Blessed One. The compassion of flesh and blood is upon males more than upon females, but the compassion of the Holy Blessed One is equally upon all" (*Sifri* on Numbers 27:1). Prophecy, Judaism then teaches, is not infallible, is not immune to the physical and emotional circumstances of its mortal recipient. There is no doubt that Moses himself was aware of this. His reaction to the challenge by the five sisters is not, "How dare you challenge what God has commanded?" He does not overlook the possibility that perhaps he misinterpreted what had come down to him from the divine, and so he "brought their question before the Lord" (Numbers 27:5).

According to an ancient rabbinic interpretation of the story, God's response to the sisters' proposed reinterpretation of the law is: "So, too, is it written in front of Me" (*Sifri* on Numbers 27:1)—meaning that the sisters' challenge to Moses' rendition of the law brought it more into harmony with the way God had intended it than had Moses' revelatory prophecy.

The ancient rabbis did not feel they were committing blasphemy by acknowledging the finiteness of even the highest of the prophets. Rather, they acknowledged that what the infinite Spirit speaks and what the finite mortal hears are not always completely compatible. That just as the divine revelation of wheat calls out for human consumption, so, too, the divine revelation of Word remains incomplete until it is processed. The Word requires creative interpretation, and as such is subject to human subjectivity: "The Holy Blessed One gave us the Torah only as if it were wheat from which to derive fine flour, or like flax from which to make a garment" (*Tanna D'Bei Eliyahu Zutta*, chap. 2). The fourth-century Rabbi Avin taught that the biblical text is but "an incomplete image of Heavenly Wisdom" (*Genesis Rabbah* 17:7).

> I testify before the witness of Heaven and Earth that the Blessed Holy ~~Key~~
> One did not instruct Moses [after the Golden Calf incident] to tell
> the people "Thus saith the God of Israel: All who are for the Lord ~~See~~
> join [Moses] . . . and take everyone his sword and slay his brother ~~p 25~~
> [who has sinned]!" Rather, Moses reasoned with himself as follows:
> "If I order the people to slay the Golden Calf worshipers, they will
> protest, saying, 'Have we not been taught that the court which passes
> a death sentence upon a single person even so much as once in sev-
> enty years, is considered a murderous court? How can you then sen-
> tence to death three thousand persons, and in one day!?'" Therefore
> did Moses attribute the command to the honor of the Above, and
> proclaimed: "Thus saith the God of Israel. . . ." (*Eliyahu Rabbah* 4)

When King Hezekiahu became ill, the Bible quotes God as telling Isaiah to instruct the king to set his house in order because he was about to die. The way Isaiah comes across with the message is: "Thus saith the Lord, 'Set thy house in order for you shall die and not live'" (Isaiah 38:1). The ailing king, however, refuses to accept the prophet's message as absolute, because he believes in a God who is negotiable, and sure enough, after asking God for an extension, is awarded fifteen more years of life (Isaiah 38:5). The ancient rabbis were taken aback by Isaiah's choice of words and could not imagine that God would actually have communicated the message to Hezekiahu as crudely as Isaiah spoke it. As a result and with some justification, they came up with this remarkably bold as well as amusing speculation of what the king's reaction might have been:

> Said the king: "Isaiah, usually when visiting the sick, one says, 'May
> God have mercy upon you.' And when the physician arrives, he will
> say, 'Eat this, and do not eat that, or drink this, but do not drink that.'
> Even if he sees that the patient is near death, he would not say to

him, 'Set your house in order' because it might upset him. You, however, come here and tell me, 'Thus saith the Lord: Set your house in
order, for you shall die and not live.' I refuse to pay any attention to
your message, nor will I listen to your counsel. I hold on to nothing
else than what my ancestor [King Solomon] taught: 'For through the
multitude of dreams and vanities there are also many words, but you
need only heed God'" [Ecclesiastes 5:6]. (*Ecclesiastes Rabati* 5:4)

Should we then rewrite the text when it comes across too
harshly? Or at least declare it "primitive"? Perhaps not, for
as our Cosmic Teacher, God relates to us within the framework of our human reality and our experience of relationship. When the Torah describes God as being angry or jeal-
ous, or threatening destruction, it is depicting God in the
human mode so that we can interpret the passage in a way
that leaves us ample room to relate back to God in forms
that are closest to home. Otherwise, we would be left in the
experiential dark, striving to become too transcendental, and
less human, in our quest for relationship with the divine. Not
only would we be left with no handle on experiencing God
from the human place, but we would also be incapable of
responding to God. The prophet Jeremiah could then never
have shouted at God: "The Lord has become like an enemy"
(Lamentations 2:6) and gotten away with it. Rather, we can
expect God to appreciate our perspective and to recognize
that expression is not always synonymous with fact. As the
third-century Rabbi Levi has God saying to the reluctantly
repentant: "Did I not write in My Law, that I will set My face
against [idol-worshipers] and cut them off from among their
people? (Leviticus 20:6). But have I actually done so? No, I
have not caused Mine anger to fall upon you 'for I am mer-
ciful and do not bear eternal grudges' [Jeremiah 3:12]"
(*Pesikta D'Rav Kahana* 165a).

How much more clearly can Judaism sound the message
of a Personal God? And how much more understandable,

then, is it that the Jews of Paul's time were not impressed by the notion of a Personal God? For although the concept was perhaps new to Paul and his Greek-influenced upbringing, it was certainly not new to those Jews who had been living and breathing it for thousands of years through both the literal and interpretive teachings of their forebears. Judaism understands God to be not only personally concerned with each and every one of us, but also personally accessible to us all in that God relates to everyone of us where we are, and in such a way that we can relate back in the most comfortable way we know how—as humans, rather than as celestial angels (Babylonian Talmud, *Berakhhot* 25b; *Yoma* 30a; *Kiddushin* 54a; *Me'ilah* 14b). It is not that God limits the divine Essence down to something that a human can grasp, but rather that God encourages us to relate however we can. In fact, when Moses on Mount Sinai asked to see God's Glory, the Totality of the God Presence, God said: "You cannot see My Face, for a human being cannot see [all of] Me and live." And God showed Moses a limited view of the God-Presence and Moses lived (Exodus 33:18-23). "When God gives, God gives according to God's ability. When God asks of us, God asks of us according to *our* ability" (*Numbers Rabbah* 21:22).

The Judaic concept of covenantal relationship is very basic to its theology of Free Will. If I do not have the freedom to choose and pursue that which is right for me, that which fosters my aliveness, then there is no *me*. And if there is no *me*, then there is no possibility of relationship, not with a friend, not with a horse, not with God. The gift of Free Will is God's allowing me a place in the universe where I can be as human as divinely possible, and as divine as humanly possible. This gift is the cosmic teaching of the honoring of the space of an Other, of—again—*tzimtzum*, or God stepping back, so to speak, in order that there be space for the created world to breathe and flourish. Yet, though God steps back, God is always right there: "as near to you as is your ear to your mouth." Covenanting is then the dance of partners stepping back to further and foster each other's aliveness and uniqueness—stepping back, yet always being present.

In his classic *You Shall Be as Gods*, Erich Fromm intimates that God loses power by giving us free will, that it involves a sort of a relinquishing of power. But the Judaic tradition teaches that the gift of free will and a relationship with creation that is covenantal rather than contractual does not involve a weakening of the absolute and all-encompassing power of God but is rather a fulfillment of the will of God. For it is God's will that there be an active and conscious relationship with the creation, which can only unfold in the mutual, sacred space of Covenant. Again, the Bible is filled with examples about how God interacts with human choice to create situations that draw forth this kind of conscious relationship-ing. For example, God telling Abraham about the impending doom of Sodom was intended to draw out arbitration, and likewise with God telling Moses that a new nation would be forged out of his seed to replace the rebellious Israelites, and so on. The Bible is sort of an EKG monitor, where for pages spanning generations of history there is a steady horizontal, until, every now and then, someone like a Moses or a Gideon will come along and talk back to God, and take God personally, intimately, who will veto divine counsel when it feels incompatible with the immediate human experience and treat the Covenant as dynamic rather than static. By contrast, those who had the opportunity to negotiate but didn't are met with disapproval (Babylonian Talmud, *Pesachim* 87a-b; see *Midrash Tanchuma*, *Shoftim*, para. 4, for reference on praise for those who stood up to God on behalf of others):

> Said the Holy Blessed One to Hosea: "The Israelites have sinned."
> Hosea should then have protested: "But they are your children! They

are the descendants of those [whose faith in You] have been proven! They are the children of Abraham, Isaac, and Jacob! Turn your mercy upon them!" It is bad enough that Hosea did not thus protest on their behalf, but worse, [it is as if he had said]: "Master of the Universe! The entire world is yours! Exchange them for another nation!" Said the Holy Blessed One: "What shall I do unto this elder [to teach him a lesson]?" Therefore did God say to him: "Marry a prostitute and establish a family with her" [Hosea 1:2] for God intended to wait until after he had children with her and to then tell him to leave them [to see whether he would protest]. Said God: "If Hosea will send away his family, I, too, will send away the Israelites from before My Face." Hosea did as God bid him and when the woman bore him two sons and a daughter, God said to him: "Hosea, should you not have learned from your teacher Moses who, since I began speaking to him, separated himself from his wife?" Replied Hosea: "Master of the Universe! I have had children with her! I cannot separate from her, nor can I send her away!" Said God: "You cannot separate from a wife who might have been unfaithful to you, nor from children who may therefore not even be your own—and yet you tell Me I should exchange My children for another nation?" When Hosea realized his shortcoming, he rose and asked God to have mercy on him. Said the Holy Blessed One: "Before you seek compassion for yourself, seek it also for others." Immediately, Hosea rose to the occasion and prayed that God judge the erring people with compassion and avert any ill decrees destined upon them. And he blessed the people, saying: "And the number of the Children of Israel shall be as the sand of the sea, which cannot be measured nor numbered; and it shall come to pass that, instead of that which was said unto them: 'Ye are not My people [Hosea 1:9],' it shall be said unto them: 'Ye are the children of the Living God' [Hosea 2:1]." (*Yalkut Shimoni* on Hosea 1:2)

Covenant, then, allows for the space necessary for negotiating divine ideal into cosmic real. Before you are born, taught the third-century teacher Rab, God decrees who your mate will be (Babylonian Talmud, *Mo'ed Katan* 18b). When you are actually in the world, however—added Rabbi Shimon ben Lakish, a contemporary of Rab's—the direction you choose in your life might bring you to circumstances that will lead you nowhere near your divinely intended, predetermined soul mate but rather someone altogether different from the one who was intended in the realm of the ideal (Babylonian Talmud, *Sotah* 2a). The one you might be drawn to instead thus becomes ideal in the real. This becomes possible only because of the covenantal nature of God's relationship with Creation, which is not a consequence of the gift of free will, as Fromm intimates, but rather the very intention of it: "Let us make the Human in our image . . ." (Genesis 1:26).

Covenant, then, is the act of *tzimtzum*—constriction—performed mutually by the parties involved, where each steps back to allow for the Other to shine fully as the Other they are or are in the process of becoming, in light and in shadow, without fear of being struck by lightning. As we saw, God does not ask Adam and Eve, "What have you done?" but, "Where are you?" as if God wishes to open up a dialogue for reformatting the Covenant: "OK, so this is not working, telling you to stay away from the Tree of Knowledge of Good and Evil, this protecting you too much. So maybe I need to step back even more, and let go of My parental inclination toward excessive precaution, and allow you to make your own mistakes and deal with the consequences yourselves." Perhaps all God was asking in the great "Where are you?" was something like: "What do you need now from this relationship, from this Covenant? Where are you in all this?"—the sort of question we should be asking one another in intimate relationships every several years, or perhaps months, but certainly whenever one of us has been moved to partake of mutually agreed upon forbidden fruit, whenever one or both partners are finding the relationship stifling rather than nurturing of their aliveness and their rightness of being.

With covenanting sounding so elastic and compassionate, where do we put evil? What do we do with the seeming paradox of a compassionate Creator of a world where evil runs rampant? Where is the Covenant when a typhoon hits an island and destroys life? Or when a tyrant annihilates a people? Or when someone abuses a child or threatens a life in the relative safety of one's own home?

To tackle this problem we need to examine some of the givens in the Judaic understanding of God's relationship with Creation, with some of the "fine print" in the Covenant and in the meaning of our being here to begin with. We also need to distinguish right off between the evil that comes about because of human error and misunderstanding, or the evil that just happens—like an earthquake or other disasters commonly labeled "acts of God"—and the evil of deliberately perpetrated atrocities: what we might call "sinister acts."

The Free-Will factor discussed above is both a blessing and a curse. The blessing is that we have the freedom to make choices that are our very own and that forge our personal aliveness and rightness in our own lives and the lives of those around us. The curse of it is that we also have the freedom and the power to make choices of the kind that impede rather than further our own aliveness and that of others. Nor is the curse component of free will restricted to the sinister choices. Ninety-nine percent of illnesses, the ancient rabbis suggested, are due to our own recklessness. Ninety-nine percent of deaths, too, they held, are due to human choices and carelessness (Babylonian Talmud, *Ketuvot* 30a; *Leviticus Rabbah*, chap. 16; Jerusalem Talmud, *Shabbat* 43a). Contemporary statistics bear this out, as well—though not nearly as dramatically as the Talmud—that, even barring sinister mortal choices of war and home-front assaults, most deaths and illnesses occur because of human recklessness, from drunk or incompetent driving to destructive diets and lifestyles.

As in any relationship, there is a tendency in Covenant to hold the Other responsible when something goes wrong: to attribute personal tragedy to God's work, to blame God for either commission or omission. But before we react to tragedy by asking, "Where was God?" we might rather first ask, "Where were we?"

The bottom line, though, is that there is good and evil in life, and that their push-pull dynamics—at any intensity less than that at the atrocity level—are akin to the inhale-exhale dynamics of breathing in that, together, they generate life on this plane. Judaism teaches that good and evil are both creations of the One God (e.g., Isaiah 45:7; Proverbs 16:4; Lamentations 3:38), yet they have no existence of their own other than the forms we give them by the choices we make. For example, God does not create donuts, only wheat and sugarcane. Donuts are created by the choices we make about raw wheat, about the dormant potentials of life's givens, of life's possibilities. Likewise, God created the *capacity* for good and evil—their possibility. But it is we who make the choices that give form to either one, for better or for worse:

> All the masters of Torah believe that God created all in His wisdom, and did not create anything repulsive or unseemly. If we were to say that sex is repulsive, then we blaspheme God who made the genitals. . . . Hands that write sacred writ are honored and ennobled and exalted, whereas hands which rob or perform other evil deeds become tainted and repulsive thereby. . . . So with all the other faculties of the human body, that whatever repulsiveness there is in them comes from how we use them. . . . All organs of the body are neutral; the use made of them determines whether they are holy or unholy. . . .
> (twelfth-century Rabbi Moshe ben Nachman in *Iggeret HaKodesh*, chap. 2, beginning)

Good and evil, therefore, are set up so they can be determined only by the Free-Will choices of human reasoning and grappling. Good is not always the better. Evil is not always the worse. It is evil to lie, and it is good to tell the truth. But if telling the truth would endanger an innocent life, is it still good? And would lying then still be evil? As absolutes they have no footing on this plane. They come alive only in dance, only when animated by the relative nature of human experience. They then become seeds of potential, which bear fruits of one or the other according to the intentions that forge our choices.

Sinister evil, or intentional atrocity, aside, there is also the kind of experience that can go either way, depending upon subjective interpretation. A single experience can to one person seem evil, and to another, good. A medicine may be poison to one and a sure cure for another. Roses are attractively colored and scented, but they are also surrounded by painfully annoying thorns, and some people are terribly allergic to them. In addition, an experience may seem bad initially but in the end be understood as good. The dentist's drill is painful and a very "bad" experience, yet it is also "good" in that its end purpose is to repair decaying teeth and thereby prevent the development of far more painful consequences.

Opposites, we are taught, are dual phenomena only in relationship to subjective human perception, but to God all opposites are unified (Psalms 139:12) and serve a common divine purpose: "This, too, opposite the other, did God create" (Ecclesiastes 7:14). Evil, for example, can compel the good to surface. It can also be harnessed toward good ends. The Judaic concept of Satan is described in this context. The mythic archangel of evil—called *HaSatan* in the Hebrew, or "the one who obstructs"—is portrayed as a force of opposition not to God but to humans, assigned the role of proving our soul-deep convictions by challenging the credibility of the "good" of which we boast, or by bringing its latency to fruition. In the biblical Book of Job, for example, the satan brings tragedy to a righteous and innocent Job only after consulting with God and receiving divine license to do so toward the purpose of validating Job's piety (Job 1:6-12):

And the Lord said to the satan: "Have you considered My servant Job,
how there is no one like him on the earth, a whole-hearted and up-
right man, who is God-conscious and who shuns evil?" And the satan
answered the Lord, and said: "Does Job honor the Lord for nothing?
Have You not a hedge around him, and about his house, and about
all that he has, on every side? You have blessed the work of his hands,
and his possessions are increased in the land. But if you were to put
forth Your hand now, and afflict all that he has, he will surely blas-
pheme You to Your face!" And the Lord said to the satan: "Behold,
all that he has is given into your power: only do not put forth your
hands upon his self." And the satan went forth from the presence of
the Lord. (Job 1:8–12)

Then there is the tragic experience of chaos in the world,
of earthquakes, volcanic eruptions, genocides, famines, random slayings, ritual abuse, and fatal epidemics; of either
humanity or nature gone berserk and slipping backward
across the line of Creation into the chaotic abyss of Genesis,
the primal cauldron in which life and death churn and fer-
ment in the seething mixture of paradox, and where life and
death are easily confused for one another, the boundaries
between them blurred and deceiving. It is an unpredictable
form of evil, void of any definitive pattern, subject to chance
and circumstance, indiscriminately striking both the righteous and the wicked, the guilty and the innocent alike
(Babylonian Talmud, *Baba Kamma* 16a). It is the terrifying
sense of helplessness, of hopelessness, of being flung without choice and without control into a whirlwind of sense-
lessness and incomprehensible torment. It is the stuff of
nightmares experienced by survivors of holocausts, child
abuse, rape, and of other terrors. It is what makes us call out
at times: "Where is the God of justice?!" (Malachi 2:17), and
which—according to one legend—drove the eighteenth-century Rabbi Mendel of Kotzk to blow out the Sabbath candles
one Friday night, after a number of Jews had been massa-
cred by anti-Jewish marauders, and declare to his astonished

disciples: "There is no judge and no justice!" It is the Mendel-of-Kotzkian cry most every one of us has experienced at one time or another when there were no answers, not even imaginary ones; when nothing made sense; when it so vividly seemed that God was absent, or even completely nonexistent. It is the encounter with the Life Force that emanates from what the ancient Jewish mystics called *Sitra Achra*—"the Other Side." For when we make our choices and commit our actions far from the clarity of the God-Light—of the God-Will that there be life and joy—we risk crossing the Line of Life and slipping ever so gradually into the Other Side; we risk losing our Selves in the realm of the *Sitra Achra*, where everything is one great undiscernible glob, void of distinction. There, the boundaries that mark life and death, right and wrong, are confused, and our mortal manifestation of soul becomes distorted, mistranslating the cries of our tormented spirits into twisted exhilaration in our now out-of-control bodies. There, our pleas to desist sound like demands to *per*sist.

There is indeed that possibility in life, for the human—in fact, any one of us—to fall so far from the God-Light that we would perpetrate cruelty, whether in the name of what is "politically correct" or some other rationalized cruelty toward others, or upon ourselves. When we are the victims of such evils, we cry out from where we experience the pain—our bodies; and often our hearts and souls. And when we are the perpetrators we cry out as well—from our souls, which, too, languish in torment. While the Bible tells of the wicked deeds of the people of Sodom, for example, it also alludes to their spiritual torment. The victim suffers in many ways, and the abuser suffers spiritually:

> And the Lord said: "Behold, the cry of Sodom and Gomorrah is exceedingly great, and their sin is tragic. I will go down and see whether

they have done altogether according to the cry of it which is come unto Me, and if not, I will know." (Genesis 18:20-21)

Reading this verse one can either envision God as what Rabbi Zalman Schachter-Shalomi calls a "Cosmic Cop" preparing to execute judgment on the guilty, or as a compassionate shepherd venturing into the hills to retrieve some desperately lost and confused sheep. These people went too far. They crossed the line. They slipped so deeply into the abyss of the *Sitra Achra* that they badly needed to get out. And so the fire and brimstone that followed needs perhaps to be understood beyond the image of "punishment" spewing forth from a wrathful God, but rather as a cleansing, a mass recall of malfunctioning souls. Likewise, perhaps, can we understand the global flood in Noah's time. Things had gone too far, and God *had* to step in and weave those shattered souls back into the God-Light. There was no waiting around for them to return on their own. Too many innocent others were bearing the consequences. The moment we begin to cross the line, God begins to draw the line. We can take it just so far and no more, for our sake and for the sake of those we might hurt along the way.

Even the sadistic smile of a coldhearted abuser, then, veils the intense sadness of a shattered soul engulfed within the whirlwind of chaos and confusion. This does not excuse the evil committed nor the person behind the deed. But the Judaic understanding of evil seeks to penetrate the surface level of its experience to grasp the heart of it; to break through the seemingly impregnable bulwark of this intimidating energy, which often seems more powerful than we are, and disassemble it piece by piece; to follow it to its very end in order to discover even there—God:

In the prophet Ezekiel's vision, he saw "a stormy wind sweeping out of the north, and a great cloud, with brightness around it, and with fire flashing forth from it continually" [Ezekiel 1:4]. . . . The "great cloud" represents the force of destruction in the world and it is called "great" on account of its darkness which is so intense that it conceals and renders invisible all sources of light, and thus overshadows the entire world. The "fire flashing forth" alludes to the fire of stern judgment that is attached to it. "With brightness around it" means that although it is in itself the very arena of ultimate defilement, it is nevertheless surrounded by a particular degree of light. . . . It possesses an aspect of the holy and should therefore not be altogether regarded lightly, but should rather be allotted some degree of space in the arena of holiness. (*Zohar*, Exodus, pp. 203a–203b)

When God created the world and wished to reveal that which was concealed in the depths and to disclose the light out of the darkness, they were all merged with one another, and therefore did light emerge from darkness, and also did the profound come forth from the mystery. Each came from the other. Thus from Good can come Wrong, and from Mercy can come Stern Judgment. All are intertwined, the good as well as the evil impulse. . . . For each was interdependent, one upon the other. (*Zohar*, Leviticus, p. 80b)

There is nothing of the Other Side which does not also have a spark of the divine light in it. . . . All things cleave to one another, the pure and the impure. There is no purity except through impurity. (*Zohar*, Exodus, pp. 69a–b)

It would seem from these teachings that, as the eighteenth-century mystic Rabbi Abraham Azulai wrote, "It is the very spark of holiness present even in evil that maintains its existence" (*Or HaChamah*, vol. 2, p. 218a), and that without it, evil would be but illusory and powerless and fade into oblivion like a threatening thundercloud looming momentarily before dissipating into nothingness. This concept is certainly an enormous challenge to anyone who has suffered by the evil choices and actions of others: an actual spark of the God-Light even in the most sinister nightmares? Is God really present and with us even in the moment of a tragic experience, of our being victimized? How can we reconcile the seeming contradiction of a God who would instruct us "not to stand idly by the blood of another human being" (Leviticus 19:16) and not to turn away when someone needs help with so much as their donkey! (Deuteronomy 22:3-4), and who yet often seems guilty of both?

Welcome to the Garden of Paradox. Here, there is no light without the accompanying background of darkness, and no good without the possibility of bad to define it. Everything defines its opposite by its contrast:

> God has also set one thing opposite the other; the Good opposite the Evil, and the Evil opposite the Good; Good from Good, and Evil from Good; the Good defines the Evil and the Evil defines the Good. (*Sefer Yetzirah* 6:4)

While evil and suffering are certainly not necessary prerequisites for the existence of our world, it is nevertheless only in a realm of opposites that free will can flourish, for where there are opposing options there are also opposing choices. The capacity for opposition is as vital to the human spirit as is oxygen to the human body. It is the psychic and spiritual atmosphere necessary for us to thrive as humans, as conscious beings capable of individual choices and distinct relationships. Opposition, then, does not automatically connote wrongness, except to the subjective experience of those with whom we might disagree in a discussion, for example. However, the Garden of Paradox has ample room for disputation, as we have illustrated from the teachings of the Bible itself; and God, it was shown, desires it of us because—if for no other reason—it is a real-time exercise in covenanting, in the realization that our feelings count, our opinions matter, and that our individual aliveness is not only God's gift, but our right.

In a universe endowed with Free Will, it is hardly obvious to us whether a particular tragedy occurs by divine directive or is just one of those vague, random things. For example, if we were to run across a busy intersection blindfolded and suddenly find ourselves atop the hood of an oncoming pick-up, random carelessness would be a more educated guess than either divine directive or random evil. If, however, we walked cautiously out into that intersection, looking both ways, and suddenly got hit on the head by falling chunks of concrete that had broken loose from an adjacent building, something we could absolutely not control, then we might guess that it was possibly an Act of God, but only possibly, because, again, this world is a world of Free Will. And in order to allow for that Free Will to be, God may not consistently manifest conspicuous Presence or Guidance. Otherwise there would be no room for doubt, and therefore no place for faith; no room for error, and therefore no place for rightness; no room for question, and therefore no place for knowledge; no room for failure, and therefore no place for growth. If all were clear-cut, black and white—if only the guilty suffered— there would be no choice but to believe in and draw close to God effortlessly, meaninglessly, purposelessly, like puppets or robots rather than humans, by compulsion rather than by personal choice and conviction. If all were Light, we would be as incapable of seeing anything as we would if all were Dark. Together, the opposites dance a choreography of iso-metrical push and pull and can only maintain their balance so long as both remain organic and continue to weave up as well as down, right as well as left, forward as well as back-ward, each step and movement playing out the choices and actions of the Human on Earth under the observation and guidance of the Great Cosmic Dance Instructor who watches from afar but who is yet as "close to you as is your ear to your mouth."

In the Time To Come, the Holy Blessed One will display the Evil Force before the righteous and the wicked and shall destroy it in front of them. To the righteous, it shall appear as a huge mountain, and to the wicked it shall appear as a single strand of hair. Both the righteous and the wicked will then weep. The righteous shall weep out of joyous amazement, and exclaim: "How did we overcome so great a power?" And the wicked shall weep out of intense shame, and exclaim: "How could we have succumbed to such a weak force?" (Babylonian Talmud, *Sukkah* 52a)

Therefore, free reign is given erratically to circumstance, as in hurricanes and earthquakes, as in plans that don't work out, as in prayers that aren't answered, in order to preserve free will in the world and thereby ensure the perpetuation of opportunities for personal growth. But whether by carelessness, Act of God, or natural circumstance, we cannot always know which is which, and must take each pain in life as an opportunity to grow and to improve. If we hurt ourselves through obvious neglect or carelessness, we need to learn to be more careful. Then, not unlike a cardiac patient, we need to reevaluate our lifestyle, the direction we are taking, and attempt to make some appropriate adjustments. We might then consider the experience as an attempt to protect us from an even greater calamity, whether on the physical or spiritual plane of existence: "For whom God loves, does God reprove, as a parent its child" (Proverbs 3:12).

If we hurt due to circumstances beyond our control, we might salvage what we can of the lessons that can be extrapolated from the rubble of the experience, although we should certainly not allow the gift of the life lesson to justify the tragedy. We could learn, for example, how Free Will is more than a gift: it is a serious responsibility, no less than a loaded pistol. When misused, when exercised from the *Sitra Achra* place, it can empower human beings to damage others, and to thwart the flow of Free Will from other human beings. We could also know much more vividly how this world is but a means toward a higher end; the imperfections of the material world will at times remind us of this. We are not obliged, however, to take the blame for what happens to us, to always attribute death and sufferings to wrongness on our part.

"There is death and suffering even without sin," taught the second-century Rabbi Shimon ben Elazar (Babylonian Talmud, *Shabbat* 55b). And if a person who has been the victim of natural disaster or sinister assault is able somehow to reclaim their free will piece by piece and to turn the experience around a little or a lot—if that person can heal, can wrest gifts out of a tragic situation and end up functional, or OK, or even stronger than before—the credit belongs to them, and them alone, *not* to the disaster and *not* to the perpetrator. Nevertheless, Judaism teaches that God would much rather we did not test ourselves (Babylonian Talmud, *Sanhedrin* 107a), or try each other with suffering, nor relate to God as punisher and disciplinarian, but rather as teacher and friend: "Do you not know God? God is your Relative! God is your Sibling! And what is more, God is your Parent!" (*Shochar Tov* on Psalms 118:5).

However we might suffer, and for whatever reason, it can be an opportunity for growth, for self-transformation, for sensitivity attunement. We are here to learn, to self-actualize, and like any seed that is planted we need to undergo fertilization in order to become organic, sometimes by the pleasantness of sunshine, sometimes by the mediocrity of rain, and sometimes by detestable manure. As the nineteenth-century Rabbi Samson Raphael Hirsch wrote:

> The evil which God at times seems to tolerate actually serves to discipline man by helping to strengthen his moral fiber and to ennoble him. The wrong which a man must endure is part of that training course of suffering which will refine him through discipline, a discipline to which God subjects only those who are capable of improvement and ennoblement. . . . Thus we see that suffering is not reserved for the most wicked on earth. . . . (*The Psalms*, vol. 2, pp. 167–169)

Then, again, as a second-century rabbi put it: "I prefer neither the suffering nor its rewards" (Babylonian Talmud, *Berakhot* 5a).

As human seedlings, we are planted on different soils of circumstance to effect fruition, each according to our particular constitution. Every person's disposition in life is therefore as distinct from that of the next as are their respective fingerprints, and so are their trials and tribulations.

Classical Judaism therefore also suggests that some tragedies may at times occur as a kind of "last resort" coaxing toward badly neglected opportunities for personal unfolding, or as a consequence of failing to utilize them. For, since they are part of the process of life-realization, spiritual life is threatened by their neglect as is physical life by the neglect of any of the physical processes, such as breathing, blood circulation, and digestion. The physical game of life and its highly honored rules and regulations are but mirrors of the spiritual dynamics of life, and both deserve at least the same respect. And as there is a science for one, so is there a science for the other, the difference being that while the physical laws are cold and unbending, the spiritual laws are compassionate and flexible.

But no one is automatically protected from any form of wrong in this world, whether it be a flat tire, a malfunctioning zipper, or an automobile accident. And no one can ever know for certain whether his or her particular experience of suffering is due to some divine providence, plain carelessness, or random circumstance such as being caught in the crossfire of war or the flying debris of an earthquake.

The question, "Why do some wicked prosper and some righteous suffer?" (Jeremiah 12:1) supposes that life as we know it is the be-all and end-all. But the discontentment that we might experience every now and then, whether we are naughty or goody-goody, and whether by our own failings or the erratic disharmony of life's circumstances, serves to remind us that this is not the place of paradise but rather the road to it, fraught with imperfection to allow for the attainment of perfection. And, when we overcome it, suffering demonstrates to us that the human spirit exists separate from and in spite of the limitations of the body and the physical reality.

Ultimately, we might take solace in the faith that, if God designed a reality that allows for randomness, then that very randomness, too, is a part of the God-Will, and therefore one can find God even where God "isn't." And therefore is God with us always, through every experience, although we can only see God when we look beyond the givens of circumstance; and all prayers, too, are answered, but not always in the illusory forms assigned to them by our subjective expectations.

The Bible's proverbial Blessing-and-Curse package should therefore be understood beyond the common notion of reward and punishment. Rather, Blessing connotes the human experience of God's conspicuousness in life through the gifts of contentment and prosperity, of peace and well-being. Curse, on the other hand, implies the experience we have of God seeming absent or distant, such as in times of tragedy or when things aren't working out the way we want them to, personally, socially, or economically. When it feels like God is present and tending to our needs, as in: "I will give you rain in its proper time" (Deuteronomy 11:14-15), then we label it God's Blessing; and when it feels like God has abandoned us, as in "the heavens will shut up and there will be no rain and the earth will not give forth its produce" (Deuteronomy 11:17), then we label it God's Curse. Blessing, therefore, is when we experience God as cradling our welfare in the palm of the divine hand, so to speak, and Curse is when we experience God as having left us to fend for ourselves, placing us at the mercy of the unnegotiable laws of nature and random probability. Sometimes the weather is nice, sometimes catastrophic. Sometimes global events go smoothly and peacefully, sometimes they erupt into chaos and war. Sometimes the rain falls, sometimes it does not, leaving millions to starve and thirst. And sometimes the rain will fall but with such abundance that it will erode precious soil and wash away entire communities.

In fact, the nineteenth-century Rabbi Samson Raphael Hirsch taught that the original Hebraic word used in the Bible for "curse," *arror*, is related to the biblical Hebrew word for "barren," *arriri* (*The Pentateuch* on Genesis 3:17). Curse, then, implies barrenness, or a sense of absence—in this case, the absence of Blessing. When Curse is in effect, then, it does not mean that God has withdrawn, only hidden, as in "I will hide My Face from them" (Deteronomy 32:20). But, again, God only seems hidden from us when we hide from God (Isaiah 59:2), as in the biblical story of the original curse of Adam and Eve. The Curse—the sense of God-Absence—did not take effect the moment Adam and Eve ate of the forbidden fruit but the moment they acted out their own presumptions about the repercussions of their trespass by hiding from God (Genesis 3:8-10). The concept of curse, like that of the "wrath of God," is, again, an illusory reality map drawn by people, not God. It reflects the guilt and trepidation that humans experience when they misbehave, reinforced and overly dramatized by ideological and ritual dogma of organized religion.

Sin, too, is not so much the transgression of divine will or the failure to live up to what we are taught are God's expectations of us. Sin is not so much what we believe we have done against God—quite an arrogant presumption at best. Rather, Sin is more about wronging ourselves and others; it is more about self-compromise, belittling ourselves for our vulnerabilities, apologizing to God for being human—sort of like Pinocchio apologizing to his inventor for being made of wood. When we hide from God, then, whether out of guilt or out of spite, God, in turn, will appear to be hidden from us, for that then becomes our choice of relationship with God; of the kind of cosmic choreography we create with God. We are the ones who then break the Covenant, which means to break with the covenantal nature of God's relationship with us and to declare a contractual one instead: "Is it I who hide My face from you? Rather, it is *you* who hide your faces from Me" (*Shochar Tov* on Psalm 13).

Nevertheless, even a casual reading of the biblical text would make one wonder whether the consequences of tres- passing the Covenant—of hiding from God—far outweigh the benefits of its fulfillment; whether what we perceive as divine retribution is a more severe penalty to pay than banishment to the mercy of chance and circumstance. But closer exami- nation of the history of both forms of consequence reveals the fallacy of such an assumption. As King David said to Gad the Prophet, "I am deeply distressed; let us rather fall into the hands of God, for God's mercy is abundant, and into the hands of humans let me not fall" (2 Samuel 24:14). David realized that the laws and actions of mortals are as whimsi- cal as those of the random probabilities of, say, a major earth- quake, resulting in indiscriminate and unnegotiable catas- trophe. God, however, bears no grudge, is void of the human emotions of hatred and vengeance (Jeremiah 3:12, 7:19; Hosea 11:8-9) and executes judgment with the compassion of a parent/teacher, deliberate and measured, purposeful and educative (Deuteronomy 8:5; Proverbs 3:12; Babylonian Talmud, *Berakhot* 5a, 60b). The proverbial Covenant of God and Israel, in other words, was not just a form of security but a framework within which even random evil could be- come an opportunity for personal or national refinement rather than a meaningless experience of senseless tragedy.

In the Jewish experience of covenanting with God, then, whether prayers were answered in the way people had hoped for them to be or not, the Covenant was always there; it was always present, always encouraging, always breathing new hope into shattered lives and fresh idealism into broken dreams. It was an unspoken understanding between God and a people, from the time God appeared to their ancestors Sarah and Abraham, promising them a land of plenty and a progeny of multitudes, and then leading them instead to a land that was as barren as they were. Yet, Abraham and Sarah carried on not because of their expectations of God but in spite of them, with the faith that God does indeed come through with the fulfillment of yearnings and prayers, though not always necessarily in the particular forms we mortals might choose to envision them.

As God steps back from God-ing to allow us our space to be human, they taught, so must we step back from our human expectations and definitions and presumptions to allow God the space to be God in our lives. This is the quality of covenanting, being in an I–Thou relationship, in a partnership that certainly has mutual benefits, but that is not solely dependent upon them or demanding of them, and also has ample room for each member to be themselves as fully as possible. And that means that every now and then, when the Aliveness or Selfhood of one of the parties is being chipped at or drained, they can in that moment renegotiate a *tzimtzum*, a withdrawing from otherwise shared mutual space into personal I-Am space. This might or might not result in the shattering of the expectations, preferences, or flow of the Other. Nevertheless, such situations demand that the Other be honoring enough of the imminent needs of their partner to match their partner's *tzimtzum* of withdrawal with their own *tzimtzum* of letting go. And it is in this honoring that covenanting takes place. And it is thus with God, too. Sometimes

God seems present, right where we want God to be, and sometimes God seems to have withdrawn from us. Likewise, sometimes we seem so present to God, so very conscious of God, and other times our thoughts of God are totally withdrawn deep into the recesses of our minds. In a noncovenantal context, it would imply abandonment and the termination of relationship. In a covenantal context, however, it is nothing more than the breathing dynamics of the Life of a relationship; the exhaling and inhaling, the weaving in and out of the kind that furthers the developing fabric of the relationship; the dancing of the kind where the partners take turns at leading and holding, and at being swept up and held. Covenant is the choreography of power in a playful mode rather than of a power struggle; wherein each endeavors not to *take* from the Other, but to receive from them; wherein each is free of the fear of being usurped; and, wherein each becomes empowered not by dismissing or downplaying the Other's power, but by appreciating and acknowledging it.

It is important to note here that the theology that the ancient Jewish teachers developed around the Covenant principle did not confine this special relationship form to Jews alone. Special, personal, or direct relationship-ing with God is not the exclusive domain of any one chosen people. Rather, any nation or individual may choose to forge such a Covenant with God as the Universal Creator of the Personal Soul. In King Solomon's prayer at the inauguration of the First Temple in Jerusalem more than 2,700 years ago, he asked that the Creator hear the prayers and accept the offerings not only of the Jewish people but of any people (1 Kings 8:41–43; 2 Chronicles 6:32–33). The God-Presence, Judaism teaches, feels just as much at home with any human being who seeks a relationship with God, and/or whose way of being in the world reflects a conscientious honoring of fellow human beings and other creatures (*Tanna D'Bei Eliyahu Rabbah* 9; *Zuta* 20; *Yalkut Shimoni* on Judges 4:4; *Shochar Tov* on Proverbs 17:1. Note, too, the commentary on this by Mahari Kohen [the sixteenth-century Rabbi Yitzchak HaKohen Katz]). For all of us are created in God's image (Genesis 1:27), and God's concern is for the welfare of all peoples (e.g., Isaiah 19:20–25; Jonah 4:11).

The biblical principle of the Covenant, then, which in the scriptural mind-set was established between God and the Jewish people, is, for all practical purposes, but a microcosmic teaching applicable to all. Noah was not Jewish, yet God established a Covenant with him as well as with all of humanity and the whole planet (Genesis 9:9–17).

To choose a covenantal rather than a contractual relationship with God is up to each individual, just as it was Abraham's choice to engage God in such a way that God, in turn, chose him and established with him a Covenant (Genesis, chap. 17). As the Talmud puts it: "The form in which you personally choose to relate to God and the universe will mirror the form in which God and the universe will relate back to you" (Babylonian Talmud, *Megillah* 12b). God chose Abraham and Sarah only after they had chosen God, had imaged a framework of relationship with God, which, in turn, meant some kind of commitment and compromise, but certainly not *self*-compromise, as God demonstrated to Abraham in the story of the near-sacrifice of Isaac (Genesis, chap. 22). Such forms of compromise, or sacrifice, were invented by humans, not God:

> Will the Lord be pleased with thousands of rams? With tens of thousands of rivers of oil? Shall I give my firstborn for my transgression? The fruit of my body for the sin of my soul? It has been taught you, O Human, what is good, and what the Lord does require of you: only to do justly and to love mercy, and to walk humbly with your God. (Micah 6:7–8)

Nor did Sarah and Abraham commit to a Covenant with ulterior motives of personal gains or privileges, for they were informed spontaneously that covenanting with God did not guarantee a trouble-free destiny (Genesis 15:18). Rather, they accepted the Covenant out of their profound sense of love for God and responsibility to the universe, engaging a commitment that would charge them and their descendants with the difficult but noble task of "circumcising" their world, removing the "foreskin" of fear, superstition, and ignorance that obstructed the intellectual and spiritual potentials of human ennoblement (Isaiah 42:6; Maharal [sixteenth-century Rabbi Judah Loew] in *Tiferet Yisrael*, end of chap. 19). God, in turn, is envisioned as promising to remove them from the mercy of chance and circumstance, from the laws of nature and astrology, transplanting their welfare and destiny instead into the realm of divine providence: "No longer shall your names be called Abram/Sarai, but your names shall be Abraham and Sarah" (Genesis 17:5, 15). For, according to the stars, or the disposition of natural circumstance, Abraham and Sarah had been unable to bear children together, but now, released from subjection to these nonnegotiable laws and replaced within the flexible, compassionate providence of God, they were able to transcend biological and astrological limitations (Babylonian Talmud, *Shabbat* 156a). Nor did covenanting with God require any negation of Self. Although God changed their names, the alteration was minimal, leaving intact the roots and foundations of their original names, their Selves, adding but a single letter, *heh*, to each of their names, but requiring no changes in who they already had been, and who they were now becoming in the moment. In human partnering, too, we might want to change our names a little, or resituate the furnishings of the space we share, but if we are covenanting, we want to go no further; we want to draw the line at the point of demanding change in individual aliveness; we do not want to end up re-creating the Other in our own image, or we slip from I-Thou to I-It.

The Jewish people, its theology further taught, were to be moved by God alone, not the stars and not the directives of nature or history. According to the biblical account of the Jewish people, it worked out pretty much that as long as they maintained their part of the covenantal relationship with God, they successfully overcame some of the ill effects of their surrounding cultures and circumstances, morally and politically. But when the covenantal consciousness was abandoned, so were they, abandoned to fates no different from those suffered by the Canaanites whom they replaced (Deuteronomy 29:22) or by other nations. Yet, even through such periods, the story of Judaism teaches, God never forsook them or rejected them.

Translating this microcosmic theology to its broader application, we come away with this: Nobody's perfect, and nobody's expected to be, and all is forgiven, for unlike a contract, Covenant is negotiable:

> And yet for all that, when they are in the land of their enemies, I will not reject them, nor will I abhor them, to destroy them utterly and to break My Covenant with them; for I am God their Lord. But I will for their sakes remember the Covenant of their ancestors [i.e., the pure and altruistic intent with which the Covenant was originally engaged]. . . . (Leviticus 26:44-45)

> For God your Lord is a merciful God; God will not fail you, neither destroy you, nor forget the Covenant of your ancestors. . . . (Deuteronomy 4:31)

> The One that scattered Israel does gather it as a shepherd does his flock. (Jeremiah 31:10)

> For a brief moment did I forsake you, but with great compassion will I gather you. In a little wrath I hid My Face from you for a moment; but with everlasting kindness will I have compassion on you, says God your Redeemer. (Isaiah 54:7-8)

3

COVENANTING WITH SELF

Each and every person is obliged to declare:
"Because of me was the universe created!"
—Babylonian Talmud, *Sanhedrin* 37a

To devote a chapter to the importance of Self might seem to some as New Age stuff, as one more diatribe on self-importance, self-growth, self-improvement, self-empowerment, and so on. Then let it be so. Self is important, needs growth, can always stand improvement, and is often in dire need of empowerment. It is not unusual for us to become so hopelessly entangled in Other-ing that we lose sight of Self-ing.

It is true that religion tends to deemphasize Self and to stress instead God, creed, and community as the primaries of life. And it is also true that this kind of thinking and teaching has led countless people to lead constricted lives void of the fullness and expansiveness that is otherwise available to the human spirit. Many of us in our zeal to "do what is right" for God and country end up doing what is wrong for our personal aliveness and spiritual well-being. For centuries, the organic human spirit has, to a considerable degree, been held captive by static government and religion. Judaism as most of us know it is no exception to this tragic rule. Blessed as it is with teachings that encourage the blossoming of the individual Self in all its fullness, Judaism, too, suffers from the fact that its codifiers and canonizers have harvested mostly from the more dogmatic teachings that keep the masses intimidated, ignorant, and in check, though in most cases also blissfully happy. The Marxist aphorism that "Religion is the opiate of the masses" is not far off track. It can be just that— an alternating blissful and hypnotic anesthetic with the promise of Eternal Reward if the operation is successful, and Eternal Punishment if it is a failure. However, with little room remaining for error or divergence, there is little room for a Self. And, in turn, any communal body comprised of such stunted Selves becomes itself diminished.

Any ism can be an "opiate of the masses." Any societal or religious ideology that seeks out of fear or greed to subjugate the individual for its own perpetuation is anything but godly. For God is not a collective or a "cause"; God is not a political party or a religious denomination. Rather, God is One, which implies an Ultimate Self, indeed the most fully realizing and individualizing Self. Only a God so optimally One can be the Creator of so much diversity and the God of so many multitudes of varieties of creatures and multitudes of varieties of spiritual paths. It is from the divine Self place, then, that God can be the One God of All. If God's sense of Self were limited, so would the variety of creation be limited, as well as the capacity of the human spirit for diversity and, therefore, individuality.

Creation is, after all, a mirroring of the God-Self, its variety but a finite reflection of the infinite attributes of an infinite Creator. How can a being actualize its potentials if it does not trust its own capacity to actualize? At the same time, a wholesome sense of Self—aware of its capabilities—as that personified by the Judaic teachings about God, is not driven to absoluteness and possesses also the capacity to consciously hold back on self-unfolding at times so that an Other might shine, might become thereby more present. God—capable of infinite creation—at some point chose to say, "Enough," and to step back some to allow humans the space and opportunity for co-creation. In fact, one of the God-Names, *Shaddai*, was interpreted by the third-century Rabbi Shimon ben Lakish as "the One who said *'dai'* (enough)" (Babylonian Talmud, *Chagigah* 12a).

How blind we are when we read verse after verse in scripture and in liturgy of the glory of God, praises to God, God pronouncing God's own uniqueness and power—God's "I"-ness (e.g., Isaiah 33:10, 42:8, 43:11, 44:6, 45:12, 45:18, 45:21-22, 46:5). The God of Judaism is a Self-ing God, who therefore has that much more to offer an Other. If we are to emulate God, then we need to learn how to emulate God's unashamed expression of God's Self as well. Our constant affirmation and reaffirmation of God's Self ought to have taught us the lesson of the preciousness and uniqueness of that gift of being that is Self, a gift we have far too often sacrificed on the altars of the very God who gave it to us in the first place. "Shall I offer up the fruit of my body?" we ask. "Shall I sacrifice my Selfhood unto God?" "No," responds the prophet Micah (6:6-8), "just walk humbly with God." But what does humbly mean if not the surrender of our Self-ness; if not the demeaning of our worth? What it means is that we emulate God Who—as the ancient rabbis taught— exercises a humility that is simultaneous with greatness. As the third-century Rabbi Yochanan taught:

> Wherever the Bible mentions the greatness of God, there, too, you will also find mention of the humility of God. It is written: "For the Lord your God is God of all gods and Lord of all lords, the Great God, the Mighty and Awesome God Who does not favor any one person over another and does not accept reward." And alongside this

it is written: "God does execute justice on behalf of the orphan and the widow, and loves the stranger, providing them with food and clothing" [Deuteronomy 10:17-18]. In the Books of the Prophets it is said: "For thus says the High and Lofty One Who inhabits eternity, Whose name is Holy, 'I dwell in the high and holy place,'" And alongside this it is written: "I am with the one who is of broken and humble spirit, to revive the spirit of the humble, and to revive the heart of the remorseful ones" [Isaiah 57:15]. In the Books of Writings it is said: "Extol God Who rides upon the heavens!" And alongside this it is written: "A father of the fatherless, and a judge on behalf of the widows, is God in God's holy dwelling place" [Psalms 68:5-6]. (Babylonian Talmud, *Megillah* 31a)

We might add some more: "Though the Lord is on high, the Lord regards the lowly" (Psalms 138:6). "Thus says the Lord: 'The heavens are My throne, the earth My footstool, but I look to the person who is poor and of a contrite spirit'" (Isaiah 66:1-2). "[God] Who made the heavens and the earth, the sea and all that is in them . . . Who executes justice for the oppressed . . . gives food to the hungry . . . frees the imprisoned . . . opens the eyes of the blind . . . straightens those who are bent over . . . upholds the orphan and the widow . . ." (Psalms 146:6-9).

Humility, Judaism teaches, is not antithetical to greatness. On the contrary, the greater we feel we are, the less self-conscious we need to be, the less pretentious, the less driven to pursue glory, or to feed and defend our otherwise vulnerable and insecure ego.

The biblical King Saul, for example, humbly fled the honors of kingship when Samuel the Prophet first dangled the crown before his eyes (1 Samuel 9:21), but in the end he slaughtered his own people when his nobility so much as *seemed* threatened (1 Samuel, chap. 22). In actuality, it was not at all threatened, because David, who was to become his successor, continued to revere him as king and as "the anointed of the Lord" (1 Samuel 24:7-11, 26:15-20). On the other hand, David—humble enough that his countrymen considered him a nobody (1 Samuel 16:10-11, 17:28)—wasted no time seizing the occasion when warriors were sought to challenge Goliath (1 Samuel 17:32-37). And in contrast to Saul's reaction, when David's own nobility was threatened, he did not at all take it personally and, following a failed coup attempt, spared the lives of those who posed a threat to his rulership (2 Samuel 16:5-11).

Obviously, David's sense of self was solid enough that he had no need to flaunt his powers and be a "somebody"; but when those powers were needed, he went all out in bragging about his exploits as a warrior. Being in a place of self-appreciation and self-honoring, there is little or no urge to advertise oneself, which is nothing but a disguised act of looking for one's apparently absent Self. But being present, there is no need to flaunt oneself—to get definition from outside. One is content with both anonymity and exposure. It is as if David is saying: "I am aware of my strengths and weaknesses, and I am at peace with them. So I do not need to flaunt the one or to conceal the other. Yet, when I am needed, I will be there in full regalia, in the fullness of my Self."

> And David said unto Saul: "Your servant is a keeper of his father's sheep, and when there would come a lion or a bear, and take a lamb out of the flock, I would go out after them and deliver the lamb out of their teeth. And when they would attack me, I would catch them by the mane and slay them. Your servant has smitten both the lion and the bear, and so this uncircumcised Philistine [Goliath] shall be as one of them, seeing he has taunted the armies of the Living God." (1 Samuel 17:34-36)

Conceit, in Judaism, would be a conscious preoccupation with one's Self that leaves little or no space at all for an Other: "Be careful lest your heart lift above you and you then forget the Lord your God" (Deuteronomy 8:14). Of such a one, the ancient rabbis taught, God says: "This one and I cannot dwell in the same world [as in: This town ain't big enough for the both of us]" (Babylonian Talmud, *Sotah* 5a). In the same breath, then, Judaism teaches us both to feel like the entire world was made just for us (Babylonian Talmud, *Sanhedrin* 37a) and that the mosquito preceded us in the order of Creation (Babylonian Talmud, *Sanhedrin* 38a). In other words, be proud of yourself and feel big—but don't let it get to your head; don't let it swell you into numbness; don't let your heart float up, up and away. It belongs at home with you. If you therefore deliberately pursue greatness, the ancient teachers taught, then greatness will elude you; and if you elude it, greatness will pursue you (Babylonian Talmud, *Eruvin* 13b). If greatness is something you do not feel within your Self, and therefore you deliberately look for it outside of your Self, it will elude you because it is already inside you. If you do not attempt to find it outside of you, then it will become known to you within your Self.

> Once a disciple sought audience with his rabbi, and the rabbi noticed instantly that he was distraught. "Please share with me the frustrations of your heart," the rabbi said. "Well," the disciple replied, taking in a deep breath, "I have learned from the holy books that if you pursue greatness, greatness flees from you, but if you flee greatness, greatness runs after you. Master, I have for many years now been running away from greatness, but to my utter disappointment, greatness has still eluded me!" The rabbi draped his arm around the disciple's shoulder and sighed. "That is indeed a serious predicament. But I don't think the discrepancy is in the teaching. I think the problem might be as follows: When you are running away from Greatness, my son, Greatness is indeed running after you. However, every now and then you stop dead in your flight from Greatness and you turn around to see whether Greatness has been pursuing you. Greatness then sees you stopping and turning toward it and so it assumes you are about to pursue *it*, and so it eludes you!" (Heard from Rabbi Shlomo Carlebach)

David's speech to King Saul in the Goliath episode therefore represents an essential Judaic teaching about a form of humility that is not self-debilitating but rather honors the Self in all its capabilities while also maintaining ample space for the recognition of an Other. He brags about his accomplishments as a bear wrestler, but at the same time attributes the success of his personal efforts to the Great Spirit who inspires us with courage and empowers us with determination and strength.

> And David said: "The Lord Who delivered me out of the claws of the lion, and out of the claws of the bear, will deliver me out of the hand of this Philistine." (1 Samuel 17:37)

David's wholesome sense of Self—one that leaves room for Other—is further dramatized when in a moment even of vulnerability and passion he is able to step down from the role of nobility and set aside patriarchal power play to listen to the wife of his archenemy request that he not go after him. The story of David is, then, a story of a man who was fully Present in his Self place, and who was able, therefore, to perceive others as Present to him, rather than as haphazard peripherals, or "objects in the way."

> And David said to Abigail: "Blessed be the Lord, the God of Israel, Who sent you today to confront me. And blessed is your discretion, and blessed be you that you have kept me this day from shedding blood with my own hands just to placate myself. For as the God of Israel lives, had you not held me back by your haste in coming to confront me, there would surely not have been left unto [your husband's] house so much as a single male survivor by the time morning light would have come. . . . Go then in peace to your house, for you see now that I have chosen to listen to your voice, and that I have accepted your Person [I-Thou]." (1 Samuel 25:32-35)

David did not feel the need to live up to the image of an infallible king, nor, therefore, to persist on a course of action that was shown to him to be wrong. And while he in no way so much as entertained any doubt about his authority as king, he nevertheless treated Abigail with the dignity she so obviously possessed in her Self.

Yet, perhaps the most stunning example of David's honoring of his Self place is when he transgressed it; and the greatest example of his Presence in his Self place is when he became absent from it—in the episode with Batsheva. In a moment of intense passion, David has an affair with Batsheva, who is married to one of his army officers, Uriah, who is stationed at the front. Batsheva later informs David that she is pregnant. David, in an attempt to conceal the incident, summons Uriah back from the front and suggests he spend some time at home in the hope that the pregnancy will then be attributed to Uriah. Uriah declines, insisting his place is with his men at the front. Desperate, David sends Uriah back to the battlefront and issues covert orders that Uriah be directed to the most dangerous spot of the battle and then abandoned so that he will stand a good chance of getting killed. This is what happens, and David then takes Batsheva as his wife (2 Samuel, chap. 11). Subsequently, in chapter 12 of the second book of Samuel, Nathan the Prophet employs the delicate instrument of parable to bring David to his senses, to return him to his abandoned Self. And when David then realizes how wrong his actions have been, he grieves exceedingly over them, acknowledging them before the nation, and does penance. But thereafter he does not throw off his crown and run off to the bushes to hide from God as did Adam and Eve. Rather, he reaffirms his selfhood in full and remains as king! Once again fully Present in his Self place, he reestablishes, reconstructs, the broken pieces of that place, and instead of negating himself and joining a monastery of ascetics in the Judean hills, he heals himself and resumes his being in Life. When the healing has been completed, he and Batsheva have a child, Solomon, the one who built the first Holy Temple in Jerusalem, and whom God named "Beloved Of God" (2 Samuel 12:25) and "My son" (1 Chronicles 28:6), and from whom springs the lineage of the Messiah. God receives David's penance (1 Chronicles 28:13) at no expense to David's Self place, leaving his career and life-flow intact. Where Adam and Eve fall, David rises.

How sad it is that many *baalei teshuvah*—Jews who have turned from secularism, or from any of the liberal denominations of Judaism, to Orthodoxy—have felt or been made to feel that they needed to squelch themselves, demean themselves, subjugate their precious Selves in order to become "religiously correct." How sad that they are often misled into a life of abstention from what once nourished their Selves, and are instead taught that their pre-Orthodox form of self-nourishment was poisonous to their souls. Many of them are even told to switch professions and to give up careers in show business, for example, or in modeling, or in the arts or other professions held not to be conducive to a religious life. In many more instances, *baalei teshuvah* are urged to leave behind the luxury and financial security they once enjoyed and to live in conditions that are abusive to their Self place, to what had once nurtured their aliveness. Worse, those who have walked a spiritual path other than Orthodoxy are made to feel that they have "sinned," though it was the only path they knew, and though there was not anything innately wrong in it. Consequently, they are directed to undergo intensive programs of penance. But God, Who is nondenominational, was certainly as near to them then as in their newfound Orthodoxy. How blatantly contradictory is all this to the tenets of a path that teaches about a God Who knows us not by our labels but by our intentions; a God Who is described as the highest possible Self! If God truly wished that we subdue our own Selves so that we might know no other

Self but the God-Self, then that is precisely what we would call selfish! Rather, the God of Judaism is a God Who remains ever that much more aloof, so to speak, and silent, the more we try to discover our wholeness in the God-Self by rejecting the gift of our own Selves. In religion's zeal for each of us to foster our humility, it has nearly destroyed our greatness. Neither extreme, the ancient Jewish teachers taught, is the preferred one (see Maimonides' *Mishneh Torah*, *Sefer HaMadda*, *Hilkhot De'ot* 1:2–4, 3:1). In fact, a case can be made, as in David's example in contrast with Saul's, that true greatness and humility augment each other synergistically, and are not, as religion often posits, at odds with one another.

The most important precept in the Torah, taught the second-century Rabbi Akiva (*Sifra D'Bei Rav* and *Yalkut Shimoni* on Leviticus 19:18) is the biblical injunction to "love your fellow human as yourself" (Leviticus 19:18), which teaches that we need that tabooed Self stuff to set the pace for our relationship with others; that if I love myself, I can love others, and if I don't, then I can't; that how I am with others will be determined largely by how I am with my Self.

Without a wholesome sense of Self, there can hardly be a fully developed sense of Other. If we are not authentic with and honoring of our Self, then we run the risk of becoming absent from life and, therefore, from an Other, who can then likewise seem to us equally to become absent. Perhaps that is what Hillel the Elder (first century B.C.E.) meant with his mysterious teaching, "If I am here, then everyone is here; and if I am not here, then no one is here" (Babylonian Talmud, *Avot D'Rabbi Natan* 12:11)—in other words, if I make space for my true self to be present, then I will in turn experience those around me as present, and if I do not make space for my true self to be present, then I will not experience those around me as present.

Self-importance, then, is not selfishness. It is rather an honoring due our station as creations of the Ancient One. "How beloved is the Human that they were created in the Image of God," taught Rabbi Akiva (Babylonian Talmud, *Avot* 3:14). "But how much more beloved," he continued, "that the Human was so informed" (Genesis 9:6). The gift of being alive is synonymous with the gift of being your own Self, not the Self molded by who you think you are supposed to be, but by who you actually are in the moment.

To declare "I Am" is not an act of conceit but an act of love that comes out of the experience of *being* loved, of being aware in that moment of the gift of one's selfhood and of its uniqueness. After all, "I Am" was the declaration of the divine in the revelatory cloud that hovered over Mount Sinai more than three thousand years ago (Exodus 20:2). More importantly, it continues to be the declaration of the divine in each and every one of us this very instant. When God said "I Am," it resonated in the Self place of all who heard, so potently in fact that their Selves lifted from their bodies, from the place of their environmental influence, and joined as one with their Creator, with the ultimate cosmic selfhood of God (*Song of Songs Rabbah* 6:3). According to the ancient rabbis, it was the only word the people actually heard from the remaining words of the Ten Commandments: "*Anochi*"— "I Am" (*Song of Songs Rabbah* 6:3). It was the most powerful word of the decalogue, the one word that was itself the very revelation that forged the Jewish people and the path we know as Judaism. "I Am" was more than a declaration of the God-Self; it was a reminder to these former slaves that each and every one of them was a unique and precious "I." For more than two centuries these people had been subdued and stepped on, their dignity and sense of individuality all but demolished. The resounding Sinaic "I Am" was then a calling forth, a resurrection and reaffirmation

of their deeply buried I's, which had gotten lost in the mas-
sive glob of an anonymous "we."

"I Am" is also the God-Name revealed to Moses at the
Burning Bush: "Tell them *Ehyeh* (I Am) has sent you" (Exodus 3:14), from the broader God-Name of *Ehyeh Asher Ehyeh*
(Exodus 3:14), which means simultaneously, "I Am What I
Am" and "I Will Become What I Will Become." God, then, is
the great cosmic I Am, unfolding and becoming, so to speak,
in each of our own unfoldings and becomings. For the individual aliveness of each one of us pulsates in our every breath
of the life force that God breathes into our souls. Each of our
I Am's is enlivened by the God-Breath and therefore *is* the
God-Breath. Likewise, the biblical Hebrew word for our tran-
scendent Soul-Self is *Neshamah*, which means literally
"breath," as in: "And God blew into [the Adam's] nostrils
Nishmat Chaim—the Breath of Life" (Genesis 2:7). In each of
us, then, is a breath of God, an echo of the divine "I Am."

As with any idea, Judaism does not teach about the sacredness of Self to the exclusion or neglect of Other, nor vice
versa, but rather encourages us to find a workable balance
between both. While Jewish law requires that we give at least
one-tenth of our income to the needy, it also discourages us
from relinquishing more than one-fifth (Babylonian Talmud,
Ketuvot 50a). Think of others, in other words, but honor your
own needs as well. "If you have lost something and your parent or teacher has also lost something, the search for your own
loss takes priority" (Jerusalem Talmud, *Horayot*, toward end).

In a hypothetical discussion about two men lost in the
desert in which only one of them has water, and only enough
water for his own survival, the ancient rabbis concluded that
"your life takes precedence over the life of your companion"
(Babylonian Talmud, *Baba Metzia* 62a), which means that
the one with the water is morally allowed to keep it for his

own survival. Certainly they did not mean to imply that one is morally forbidden to share the water even at the risk of death (Babylonian Talmud, *Baba Metzia* 62a). Rather, the lesson is that the one with the water is obliged, morally, to save him- or herself; that we don't owe anyone their life any more than we owe ourselves our own (Maimonides' *Mishneh Torah, Sefer HaMadda, Hilkhot Yesodei HaTorah* 5:7). On the other hand, if someone threatens you with your life unless you murder another, then to save your own life by deliberately taking the life of another would be immoral (Babylonian Talmud, *Pesachim* 25b). Throughout Jewish law the principle remains steadfast that every individual life is infinitely precious and cannot be weighed against or in favor of the life of another: "Do you suppose that your blood is any richer than that of your fellows'?" (Babylonian Talmud, *Pesachim* 25b). If an entire community is threatened with death by an enemy unless they surrender a single innocent person from among them for execution, the law holds that they are forbidden to surrender the one to spare the many (Maimonides' *Mishneh Torah, Sefer HaMadda, Hilkhot Yesodei HaTorah* 5:5). For all life is infinitely precious and cannot be added up; quantitative valuing of Self-ness is antithetical to its absolute, qualitative essence. And, again, the blood of one person is no more or less valuable than that of another (see *Tosefot* on *Pesachim* 25b: "*Af Naarah*").

Tragically, during the Holocaust of World War II there were rabbis and community leaders who decided to allow the surrender of the few to save the many when the Nazis ordered Jewish communities to relinquish certain numbers for the slaughter in the beginning of the nightmare. In the end, however, the rationale behind such decisions wilted into ashes as eventually everyone was ordered onto the cattle trains (Lucy Dawidowicz, *The War against the Jews*, pp. 383–

385). We are indeed responsible for our selves, but we may never, Judaism teaches, sacrifice another in the name of that responsibility. I need to do what is necessary to save myself, and if I have only enough water for myself I may drink it. But I cannot seize you in a battle zone and use your living person as a shield against incoming rounds in order to preserve my life. Likewise, I have a moral obligation to intercede on your behalf if you are being pursued (Leviticus 19:16; Karo's *Shulchan Arukh, Choshen Mishpat* 426:1), but, again, not if there is certain risk to my own life. My life is my priority, but not actively at the expense of your life, for Selfhood is interconnected with the welfare of Others in the collective fabric of the One Creator of all.

> Hillel the Elder taught further: "If I am not for my Self, then who will be? And if I am solely for my Self, what am I? And if [I am not for my Self] in the moment, then when?" (Babylonian Talmud, *Avot* 1:14)

Covenanting with Self then means that there is an honoring of your separateness from everyone else, your individual distinction from all Others, and at the same time a recognition of your connectedness to and commonality with everyone else; that God sees you as an Other, and, at the same time, an integral component of the God-Self. It means you will likewise seek out relationships with people who will see you as an Other, yet at the same time as an integral part of their own Selfhood. Such an audience in your life is hard to come by, but the gift of their presence in your life is the nurturing not only of what you share collectively, but what you come away with individually. The more I honor your individual distinction from my own Self and from others, the more vivid does your sense of Self become to your own consciousness. And the more does my own sense of Self achieve

clarity for me, because I am loving you as my Self, and in my
relating to you, I am drawing from the richness of who I am
as separate from you and yet in relationship with you.

Teachings abound in the Babylonian Talmud which go
beyond merely honoring one another's individuality, but
which also discourage us from second-guessing the feelings
or sentiments of an Other. "Do not console your friend
in the moment of their bereavement," taught the second-
century Rabbi Shimon ben Elazar (Babylonian Talmud, *Avot*
4:18). In other words, no matter how close you are to a
mourner, or to someone who just lost their livelihood, nobody, not even you, can truly know their anguish. Ancient
Jewish law therefore instructs that when you visit a mourner,
you do not slap them on the back and engage them in conversation even so much as to say "I'm sorry." On the contrary, you are to sit down and be silent, and to speak only
when spoken to by the mourner (Babylonian Talmud, *Mo'ed
Katan* 28b). This protocol allows the mourner the space they
need to be with their grief and to not have to be yanked out
of wherever their Self place happens to be in the moment.
Otherwise, they would have to disrupt their processing of
their pain in order to respond socially to visitors. The last
thing a mourner needs, the ancient rabbis opined, is conso-
lation. Rather, what they need is the comfort of company and
the space to be with their mourning at their own pace of
healing. The third-century Rabbi Yochanan attributes the
teaching to the biblical story of Job (Babylonian Talmud,
Mo'ed Katan 28b). Job has lost everything—his family, his
property, his physical health, and is in deep mourning over
the lump-sum tragedy that succeeded in destroying everything but his faith. His friends come to console him, and they
do so by keeping Job company and being with their own pain
about the sufferings that have befallen their friend:

So they sat down with him upon the earth for seven days and seven
nights, and none of them said a word to him; for they realized that
his grief was very great. Then did Job open his mouth . . . and he
spoke . . . [and only thereafter did his friends begin to address him].
(Job 2:13–3:1, 4:1)

Likewise, if one hundred of the most competent physicians
diagnose a Jewish patient and conclude that fasting on Yom
Kippur will not in any way endanger the patient's health, yet
the patient feels the need to eat, the law holds that we listen
to the patient, for, again, nobody can truly assess the pain of
another (Babylonian Talmud, *Yoma* 83a). Jews are forbidden
to extinguish a fire on their Sabbath, yet if someone is ill and
cannot fall asleep because of the light, or is frightened that
the light might attract thieves, or suffers from delirium such
that the dancing flames might therefore evoke hallucinatory
terror, we are permitted to "violate the Sabbath" to alleviate
their discomfort (Babylonian Talmud, *Shabbat* 29b; *Yoma* 84b;
see also Rabbi Yechiel Michal Epstein's *Arukh HaShulchan*,
Orach Chaim, no. 278). The law does not instruct us to ignore
their pleas and dismiss them as paranoid, or to tell them that
their fears are unfounded and stupid, or that their illness
won't get any worse if they would hang in there until the end
of the Sabbath. It is not for us to judge someone else's standards of fright or illness. Rather, we are obliged to act immediately in terminating the source of their fear. Likewise, do
we "violate the Sabbath" by breaking down a door if there is
a frightened young child stuck on the other side, even though
the child's life is not in immediate danger, "and the more
expediently you [violate the Sabbath] on their behalf, the
more praised are you" (Babylonian Talmud, *Yoma* 84b).

The most clear portrayal of how Judaism values the
individual's Selfhood even above its own religious practice
is the teaching: "Great is the dignity of the human, that it even

supersedes a trespass of a religious commandment in the Torah" (Babylonian Talmud, *Berakhot* 19b). Plucking vegetation is forbidden on the Sabbath, for example, yet if your clothes became entangled in some thistles, you were not expected to leave your clothes behind and go home naked because it was the Sabbath and you might otherwise snap a few twigs. Or if you were defecating in the woods on the Sabbath and there was nothing available with which to wipe yourself, you were not expected to remain squatted until the conclusion of the Sabbath, but were permitted to pick leaves or grasses to clean yourself, because honoring your Self takes precedence over religious injunction (Babylonian Talmud, *Menachot* 38a; *Shabbat* 81b).

Contrary to common speculation, then, the laws of the Torah are violated not only for life-threatening situations, but also in situations where the emotional well-being of the individual is at stake, and—as illustrated—in cases where human dignity is concerned. Each case is dealt with in its particulars, in consideration of the unique experience of every individual Self. As Hillel taught: "Do not judge your fellow human until you yourself arrive at their very place of experience" (Babylonian Talmud, *Avot* 2:4).

> It happened that a man disheveled the hair of a woman in the middle of the marketplace and she came before Rabbi Akiva (second century) with her complaint. Rabbi Akiva ordered the assailant to pay her a fine of four hundred *zuz* (the equivalent then of the value of four plough-pulling oxen) for disgracing her in public. The man requested he be given time to gather the money, and Rabbi Akiva granted him some time. Afterwards, friends of the assailant said to him: "We have found a way to free you of this fine. Take a vessel filled with hair oil and drop it in front of the woman when she is again in the marketplace." This he did. And when the vessel shattered, the woman unbound her hair and applied to it the spilt oil. The man then appeared before Rabbi Akiva with witnesses to the scene, and he con-

tested her original claim of having been publicly disgraced. Said he: "Why should I pay a fine for shaming her in public, when she shamed herself in public for a few drops of spilt oil?" Replied Rabbi Akiva: "You must still pay her. For while a person may not harm themselves in any way, the Torah nevertheless exempts them from liability if they do. But if others harm them, then they are liable. She who has wronged herself is exempt. But you who have wronged her must go and pay her four hundred *zuz*." (Babylonian Talmud, *Avot D'Rabbi Natan* 3:3; *Baba Kamma* 90b)

Nor is Rabbi Akiva's ruling a one-size-fits-all standard of penalty for disgracing someone in public. Rather, "all is determined by [the individual's standard of] personal honor" (Babylonian Talmud, *Avot D'Rabbi Natan* 3:3; *Baba Kamma* 90b). An act which one person might experience as a major embarrassment might for another be experienced as inconsequential or as a minor incident. No individual or collective, Judaism teaches, can assume the standards for everyone. Judaism certainly has its basic, general creed and spiritual path guidelines, but the situation of every individual is assessed independent of the broader structure of the collective whenever the dictates of the religion contrast with the well-being and life-flow of the individual. Many of us assume, for example, that Judaism dictates a single and absolute standard of modesty in dress, especially for prayer; that we need to walk around in clothes all the time and that nudity outside the shower stall is immodest, if not outright immoral. But, again, a responsa on the issue by the late Rabbi Moshe Feinstein reflects the expansiveness of the Judaic tradition in its honoring of the individual and in its leaving ample space for varying personal standards:

The whole issue of wearing clothing is based solely on social dictates alone, which vary from place to place and from time to time, and so, barring the factor of social standards, there are no particularities in

Jewish law regarding the wearing of clothing. . . . If sitting totally in the nude in one's home is not felt as shameful, then it should not be considered as such and one may sit thus in the privacy of one's house even without any covering at all upon even those body parts whose exposure most people might consider shameful. . . . Therefore, the issue of modesty taught by our sages concerning the proper conduct in the bathroom, for example [to uncover only as little as needed (Babylonian Talmud, *Berakhot* 62a)], is only a matter of modesty for the individual, and perhaps to accustom the person to modest behavior in general. . . . These things are only pleasant customs and ways of piety.

. . .That people go around entirely dressed is not from among the prohibitions of our Torah, but it is rather a careful and exalted practice to be attired even in private. . . . However, if it is uncomfortable because of the heat, or for some other reason, then one may go about as such and there is not even an issue then of piety in such an instance. . . . The standard of modesty is dependent upon what it is that makes one ashamed when standing before people, each place according to its particular custom. . . . And in a pressing situation, it is even permitted to pray [in the nude]. . . . (*Iggrot Moshe, Yoreh De'ah*, vol. 3, nos. 47:3, 68:4)

The libraries of Judaism are stacked with centuries of halakhic responsa, records of the religious legal decisions of rabbis for personal inquiries by those whose life situations at some point brought them into conflict with the conventional directives of their tradition. Often, the law was either completely suspended or radically altered to accommodate these individuals in their extenuating circumstance, whether it was momentary or long term. The Jewish prophets who transmitted the biblical laws had, after all, implored the people to "live by these laws" (Leviticus 18:5; Ezekiel 20:11; Nehemiah 9:29), and—added the ancient rabbis—"not to die by them" (Babylonian Talmud, *Yoma* 85b; *Sanhedrin* 74a).

Similarly, the ancient Judaic laws about charity went beyond standard operational pity and strove instead for balance. A five dollar donation to a beggar may be a lot of money, but a five dollar donation to a beggar who was once accustomed to millions of dollars is an imbalance, an injustice. In Hebrew, then, what we call charity is known as *tzedakah*, from the word *tzedek*, or "justice." An authentic act of charity in Judaism requires balancing the scales in the life of an individual who has been thrown off balance. There are therefore as many standards of charity as there are individuals who need it. The Talmud recounts how a wealthy man, once accustomed to being led on his horse daily through the marketplace, lost his riches and was reduced to poverty. When Hillel the Elder heard about it he procured a horse for the impoverished tycoon and hired a servant to continue leading him on the horse daily. Once, however, the servant failed to show up for the daily walk, and so the rabbi himself replaced him and led the horse and its rider through the marketplace (Babylonian Talmud, *Ketuvot* 67b). The ancient Judaic concept of giving extends beyond general guidelines of welfare and aims not only at keeping the needy fed and clothed, but also at keeping their sense of personal dignity and their sense of Self as fully intact as possible. Each individual is to receive according to the standards to which they had been accustomed. Indeed, the biblical injunction is to "compensate what he or she lacks" (Deuteronomy 15:8), which goes beyond what he or she needs, but connotes rather that which the individual once had and now does not. Our obligation is then to try and bring back to that person what it is that they need for the fullest aliveness of their Self. We are not obliged to make them rich, but we are to try and help them recover their balance and provide them with what it is they need to restore as much of a semblance of their former sense of Self.

Hillel the Elder's injunction to "do not unto others as you would not want them to do unto you" (Babylonian Talmud, *Shabbat* 31a) reminds us that we should not determine the needs of others by our own needs; that what we might prefer, or tolerate, is not necessarily preferred or tolerated by others. Rather, each of us is a Self all its own, completely unique from any other, and for which—alone—the universe would have been worth creating (Babylonian Talmud, *Sanhedrin* 31a).

The Covenant with Self states that each of us counts no more and no less than another. Hillel's "Do not isolate yourself from the community" (Babylonian Talmud, *Avot* 2:4) is not a teaching about self-negation, or about supplanting your sense of individuality with a more collective sense of community. Rather, it means that we ought not to get caught up with the nurturance of our Selfhood to the neglect of the life of the community, or of other Creations. Otherwise, left exclusively to our Selfhood, we lack the reflective and interactive component of our Selfhood, which is Other. As Hillel put it: "If I am *only* for myself, then *what* am I?" Without a Thou, there cannot be an I, taught Martin Buber, because "through the Thou a man becomes I" (*I and Thou*, p. 28).

On the other hand, neither does "Do not isolate yourself from the community" mean a total subjugation of Self on behalf of the welfare of the collective to the extent that there is little Self left. Rather, it means, again: "Give at least a tenth, but not more than a fifth." How common it is among those of us who are obsessed with community service to end up neglecting our families and our friends and ourselves, coming home to a place void of any semblance of "I Am," and with only enough space remaining for an I-It quality of relationship. Is this what the ancient teachers wanted? Certainly not. Reading about them one reads about teachers who indeed worked diligently on behalf of the community, asking nothing in return. But we also read about how they exercised just as much love, caring, and attention to their Selves, and to their families. They were teachers and spiritual leaders, but they were also artisans and craftsmen, physicians and shepherds, cobblers and silversmiths, bakers and laborers.

One year there was a drought in the Land of Israel and the High Court in Jerusalem sent a delegation of rabbis to ask Abba Helkiah [first century B.C.E.] to pray for rain.

When the delegation arrived, they found Abba Helkiah laboring in the fields. They greeted him with greetings of peace, but he ignored them and did not reply. The rabbis were puzzled at his silence and waited. When he had finished his labor, the rabbis observed in amazement as he removed his work cloak and draped it over one shoulder and then carried his tools upon his bare shoulder. They followed him. When they came to a stream, the rabbis removed their sandals but Abba Helkiah, who had been walking barefoot, now put his on. Reaching the other side, they walked through thorny bushes. The rabbis lowered their cloaks to protect their legs but Abba Helkiah lifted his. When they arrived at his home, his wife was waiting at the door to greet him. The rabbis prepared to enter first—as was customary—but Abba Helkiah blocked their way and entered first instead, together with his wife. Seated around the table, Abba Helkiah did not invite the rabbis to eat, and they observed in puzzlement how he gave double servings to his youngest son, and but a single serving to his eldest. He then whispered to his wife: "These have come to ask us to pray for rain," and the two ascended into the attic. The rabbis watched how the two took up separate stations in the loft and began to pray for rain. To their amazement, clouds began to appear, but they first appeared from the direction his wife was praying, and only after that cloud had burst did other clouds appear in the direction he was praying. The couple then rejoined the others and Abba Helkiah finally greeted the rabbis with words of peace and bid them to eat.

But the rabbis, overcome with curiosity about his strange behavior, asked him to explain. He explained thus: "When you greeted me, I did not feel it right to respond because I am a laborer, and I am paid my wages for the time I work and did not wish to waste any of my employer's money socializing. I removed my work cloak rather than place the tools upon it over my shoulder because the cloak is borrowed, and the lender let me have it for the expressed purpose of wearing, not for laying tools upon it. I put on my sandals when we crossed the creek for I know not what lies at the bottom of the creek, but I can see what lies in the grass on dry land. I lifted my robes in the thorny bramble for it is well known that while scratched flesh heals, ripped garments do not. When we arrived at my home I entered first and with my wife, for I do not know you, and though one must welcome strangers, one need not, however, risk leaving strangers alone in the house with one's family. I did not invite you to eat right away because I wanted to make sure there was enough food for my family first. I fed the younger one more than I did the elder for the elder is home most of the day and has access to the kitchen, whereas the younger is away at school and does not have access to food whenever he wants. Now that I have answered your questions, what, pray, tell, is the purpose of your visit?"

The rabbis replied that they had come to ask him to pray for rain. Abba Helkiah smiled and pointed at the rain that was falling outside the window. "There is obviously no need for that, now, is there?" he said. Said they: "But we know that it is raining in the merit of your prayer and your wife's prayer, yet we are curious why the prayer of your wife was answered before yours." Said he to them: "For she provides for the needy." Said they: "And the master does not?" Said he: "I give indirectly and she gives directly. I give coins, which the needy then must take to the market and exchange for flour which they must then bring home and toil over for hours before they can finally have bread from it with which to satisfy their hunger. My wife, however, bakes extra loaves each day and has always bread prepared for the hungry so they could eat of it immediately, and thus, in turn, are her prayers answered more immediately than are mine." (Babylonian Talmud, *Taanit* 23a)

The story illustrates a fine balance between one's responsibility for the welfare of the community, whether the concern is a drought or a visiting delegation of community representatives, and for the welfare of one's own personal Aliveness, such as one's partner, one's children, one's Self—including seemingly eccentric behavior that others might deem trivial, unconventional or even neurotic. Everyone, Abba Helkiah's story teaches, is entitled fully to their *meshugaas*, their eccentricity, for their *meshugaas* is their private badge of Selfhood and of the distinctive quality of their particular individuality. With no apologies owed. Abba Helkiah did not compromise his personal space but went about the business of living, the business, that is, of how Abba Helkiah the man lived. Nor did he shirk his responsibilities toward his community. He saw to the immediate emotional and material needs of his family members first, and then, even before tasting a crumb of pita, he wasted no further time praying for the rain that the people of nearby Jerusalem were waiting for. He taught in the way he lived the art of drawing the fine line between compromise and Self-compromise. I will give, but my giving stops at the point I begin to feel chipped away at so that my own aliveness and rightness, rather than being shared, is being taken. Back in the Garden of Eden, the sin was not so much against God as against the integrity of personal Self, which, thereby, is sin against God Who desires we each preserve and nourish our integrity, our Self.

The sin of the proverbial Adam and Eve, for example, was not so much their consumption of the forbidden fruit as their abuse of their personal free will: that Eve's decision to partake of the fruit came not of her own conviction or will but of the external influence of the serpent; that Adam's decision to eat the fruit was not reflective of his own wishes but of the external suggestion of Eve. Sure enough, in their responses to God's inquiry they attribute their actions exclusively to the influence of *others*, Adam to that of Eve, Eve to that of the serpent (Genesis 3:12–13). Adam and Eve did not betray God; they betrayed themselves, their gift of free will, their individuality. They compromised their personal convictions, their right to say no, in order to placate an Other.

Even the consequences that follow in the biblical account address the so-called original sin as one of self-compromise. Since Adam and Eve compromised their own will and power for an Other, they would be subject to an increasingly intensifying sense of powerlessness—Adam to the forces of nature over which he intrinsically holds power, Eve to the bringing forth of new life that is part of her essential self, and both of them to the power dynamics between the sexes, which are intrinsically equal. Again, as discussed at length in the earlier chapters, the consequence of a sin is in the sin itself, not in any divinely judged sentence.

Only when Adam and Eve have lost their Selves to the influence of an Other does God call out to them: "Where are you?" It was indeed an appropriate question because neither of them was there. Adam and Eve were not home. They were absent from themselves, lost and confused in a void where once dwelt a Self. Had they eaten of the forbidden fruit because they were hungry, wrote Rabbi Yossel Horowitz of Novoredok, or because they burned with desire for it, then it would not have been so severe a trespass. The severity was in the fact that they ate not by their own choice but by the influence of an Other (*Madregat Adam*). I lay the foundations for sin, then, when I compromise what and who I am for what and whom others wish me to be; when I allow my "I Am" to be overtaken, overridden, by choices and inner voices that are not my own. Then is the stage set for wrongness, for bringing harm to myself and perhaps to others as well. Then does God ask me, too: "Where are you?"

> "Cursed is the one who does not uphold the words of this Torah" [Deuteronomy 27:26]—one who trespasses the Torah by eating pork or other forbidden foods but does so out of their craving for these, or one who fails to perform [the prescribed religious rites of the Torah] but out of laziness or procrastination, are not included in this curse. (thirteen-century Rabbi Moshe ben Nachman [Nachmanides] in his commentary on the Torah, Deuteronomy 27:26)

It needs to be said here that Nachmanides is clearly referring to religious rite, to the prescribed practices and observances in the Torah that constitute the particular creed that is Judaism. His examples do not therefore include acts of universal morality or immorality, for that realm of the Torah is applicable to all peoples (Babylonian Talmud, *Sanhedrin* 56a), not only the Jews. If I trespass the teaching of the Torah that forbids me to steal or murder or rape, then whether I do so out of personal craving or outside influence is of no consequence; likewise, inexcusable is my failure to save someone from drowning out of laziness. As the second-century Rabbi Akiva put it, "Concerning trespasses between you and God, is God lenient; but concerning trespasses between you and your neighbor is God strict" (*Numbers Rabbah* 11:15).

But in the religious observances of Judaism, says Nachmanides, the Torah differentiates between transgressing out of sheer lust or laziness—out of our own personal choices, whether out of our weaknesses or out of our yearnings—and transgressing out of spite (see Karo's *Shulchan Arukh, Choshen Mishpat* 425:5). A craving at least comes from within our Self place. It is a choice, a want, that is distinctly ours. But in the case of spite, while it does come from us, it does not come from the *core* of our Self, which is also the dwelling place for God. Rather, it comes from a Self that has been invaded, violated, by occurrences or influences outside our core Self, and these are the forces driving our animosity.

The same applies to some cravings when they translate into harm of Self or others, such as in the case of an addiction or an act of abuse. Such cravings do not emanate from the core Self but from the confusion that has filled some void within us, a void that has been created by our surrender of Self to the choices and influences of others or by experiences that have perhaps embittered us, and which we have allowed to overtake us nonetheless and supplant the Self. However, there are times we have no choice but to feel bitter, angry, hurt, and shaken or damaged—especially if we were abused as children or as adults by someone we depended upon heavily, someone we trusted. Yet, even when our Self has been compromised severely, we are still confronted with a choice, however difficult: to start pacing our painful way back toward full Selfhood again or to not try to reclaim our Self place from violation, and remain stuck in a place of augmenting bitterness and increasing resentment. We should certainly not negate the bitterness of the experience, but neither should we allow the pain of it to reformat us into abusers ourselves. Maybe we cannot always bring ourselves to forgive. Indeed forgiveness is something that arises of its own in a climate of welcome and should not be forced upon any wound. But we can at least let ourselves long for and aim for cleansing ourselves of the experience of rubble and debris, envisioning our own lives no longer poisoned by fear, pain, and hate. Even if we have become abusers ourselves, there is a level of healing that we need to reach for after acknowledging the wrongness that we have done. We must realize that it was something in our own woundedness that compelled us to act out our own unresolved Self hurt so that from now on the taking out of pain upon an Other can stop. For the Self is indestructible, and it is never too late to start toward wholeness. Never.

Forty-eight times does the Torah warn the newly freed Israelites—victims of two centuries of abuse by Egyptian slavemasters—to behave sensitively toward "the stranger, for you were once strangers" (Leviticus 19:34; see *Midrash Tanchuma, Vayikra* 2). The wisdom of the Torah did not assume that the redeemed would now certainly be kind to other strangers because they themselves had known suffering and abuse as strangers in Egypt. Rather, the Torah assumes that victims can just as easily become abusers, can just as easily turn unhealed bitterness and woundedness into aggression against an Other. To take our own hurts out on someone else is more the rule than the exception. And therefore is no other injunction in the Torah repeated as many times as this one.

"A person does not sin unless a spirit of foolishness has overtaken them," taught the third-century Rabbi Shimon ben Lakish (Babylonian Talmud, *Sotah* 3a), meaning that when we commit a wrong that does not correspond with who we are, but out of a momentary or perhaps chronic surrender of consciousness of Self, then we need to explore the possibility that we have become displaced, and that we need to come home. "If your heart runs off, return to the Place," advises the ancient mystical *Sefer Yetzirah*, or *Book of Formation* (chap. 1, *mishnah* 8). The Place, or *HaMakom*, is also one of the God-Names in the Judaic tradition: "For God is the place of the universe" (*Genesis Rabbah* 68:10) and therefore is God also the place of every person, the innermost sanctuary of our deepest Self: "O God, you have been a habitation for us" (Psalms 90:1). When God asked Adam and Eve, "Where are you?" taught the third-century Rabbi Abba Arecha, God was in essence asking, "Where has your heart gone?" (Babylonian Talmud, *Sanhedrin* 38b). When we become distant from our Selves by negating our Self-Will, we also become distant from God by neglecting the God-Will that we be present in our Selves. Therefore, if we wish to bridge the gap, to return to God, we can begin by returning to our Selves, to our own "I Am," and thereby to The Place.

The mystical Judaic concept of *bittul hayesh* (the negation of that which is) is sorely misunderstood by many to imply a meditation in which you would negate your Self. Actually, the meditation is an exercise of mental and spiritual cleansing, in which you would delete piecemeal all thoughts and awarenesses from your supraconsciousness so that when you emerge from the meditative state you emerge into the place of your very own Self as opposed to the clutter that had been there before and that had so muddled your inner senses that you could barely distinguish Self from Other. Rather than an exercise in self-negation, as some well-meaning ascetics would want us to believe, it is an exercise in self-restoration through the negation of the very stuff that often does negate our Selves, such as the voices, influences, aspirations, and perspectives that are not ours but which have been picked up like lint from Others as we weave in and out of the social and environmental fabrics of daily life.

On the contrary, self-negation is frowned upon by Judaism. If a man or woman wished to emulate the ascetics and take vows of physical abstention, not only were they severely limited in how much abstention they were permitted—no wine or haircut (Numbers 6:2-5)—but when the Holy Temple stood they even had to bring a "separation (sin) offering" at the completion of their period of abstention (Numbers 6:14) "because [according to second-century Rabbi Elazar HaKapar] they painfully withheld themselves from wine. And if the Torah considers it sinful to painfully abstain from wine alone, how much more wrong is it to painfully abstain from everything!" (Babylonian Talmud, *Taanit* 11a). Of course, the term *wine* is not to be taken literally, but implies any sort of pleasurable and wholesome experience of the senses. A recovering alcoholic who abstains from wine, for example, however painful the abstention, is certainly not wronging his or her Self but, on the contrary, is removing the very impediment that has stood in the way of the Self. There are times, then, when abstention from an otherwise acceptable pleasure is a positive step, when, for instance, that particular indulgence has become a detrimental addiction rather than wholesome nourishment for the well-being of both body and soul. In such instances, writes the twelfth-century teacher and physician Rabbi Moshe ben Maimon (Maimonides), it is certainly alright and often necessary "to go to the other extreme in order to bring oneself eventually to the preferred way which is the middle between both extremes" (*Mishneh Torah, Madda, Hilkhot De'ot* 2:2). The second-century Rabbi Akiva further warned that one who consumes foods that are harmful to them commits three wrongs: self-abuse, wasting food, and saying grace in vain by thanking God for some food or drink that they either dislike or endangers their health (Babylonian Talmud, *Avot D'Rabbi Natan* 26:5).

Nevertheless, cautions Rabbi Moshe ben Maimon, neither extreme is wholesome in the long run. He admonishes those who, fearing the negative effects of preoccupation with the physical senses, will deem it wise to practice its opposite extreme of total abstention from good food, clothes, sex, and luxurious housing. "This, too, is an evil way, and it is forbidden to go in that direction. And one who does is called a sinner" (*Mishneh Torah, Madda, Hilkhot De'ot* 3:1). As the third-century Rabbi Yitzhak put it: "Is it not enough what the Torah has forbidden you? Must you add unto yourself further prohibitions?" (Jerusalem Talmud, *Nedarim* 25a). "Do not be so overly righteous," wrote King Solomon (Ecclesiastes 7:9).

Rabbi Elazar HaKapar's use above of the term "painful abstention" rather than simply "abstention" is probably derived from the fact that the Torah appears to address only those ascetics who have taken a vow (Numbers 6:2), which can only mean that they are not ascetics in their Self place, by their nature, but are rather obligating themselves to abstain, for whatever personal or spiritual reason. Were they ascetics because of some true inner dictate of their Selves, they would have no need for oaths, for why would anyone need to take a vow of abstinence from parachuting out of an airplane if they had no interest in parachuting to begin with? In fact, the ancient teachers discuss a seeming discrepancy in the Judaic view on fasting as a spiritual discipline. According to the third-century Rabbi Shmuel, "One who fasts is called a sinner," although according to his contemporary, Rabbi Elazar, "One who fasts is called holy." The seeming contradiction in the teachings is then reconciled by the age-old Judaic lesson of context. One who will by fasting be abstaining, negating their Self-Will, holding back from what their Self truly desires, is called a *khotte*, "a sinner," or, more literally, "one who is missing the point." However, one who will by fasting be nurturing their Self-Will—and who will be getting personal pleasure thereby, who has reached a plane of spirit consciousness where fasting is not experienced as abstention or withholding, but as nourishment for the soul—is called *kadosh*, "holy" (Babylonian Talmud, *Taanit* 11a).

> Once Rabbi Pinchus of Koretz (eighteenth century) heard that one of his disciples was engaged in excessive fasting and meditation deep in the Carpathian mountains. Concerned, the rabbi saddled his horse and rode up into the hills to visit him. He found him huddled in the corner of a cave, trembling and emaciated. "Yankel," the rabbi called, "why are you doing this to yourself?" The disciple replied in a weak, hoarse voice: "But Master, you yourself told us of how your teacher Rabbi Yisroel Baal Shem Tov would go often into the mountains to meditate and that he would fast for days!" The rabbi pondered the response and then, drawing a deep breath, he said: "True, Yankel, but there is an important difference. When Rabbi Yisroel would go into the mountains to meditate he would always bring food along, except he would forget to eat! Because he was experiencing spiritual bliss! But you—you take no food with you at all when you come up here, and all you're experiencing is physical pain!" (Heard from Rabbi Shlomo Carlebach)

There are, however, times when a great teacher or a powerful spiritual experience can catalyze in you the *kavvanah*—"authentic intention"—necessary to experience the nourishing fast alluded to in the story, even while the unaccustomed body is experiencing hunger pangs. Yet, the story's lesson cautions you to keep a careful eye on when your motivation to continue the ascetic practice fades away from soul-nourishment to mere intellectual determination. When you begin to feel that you are shifting away from the initial mode of inspiration and *kavvanah*, you need to then listen to your senses, to find out whether you are still in a place of blissful nourishment, or of painful starvation. The essential truth is that physical matter and our bodies were given to us for our growth and enlightenment—and this includes sex, affection, food, play, and much much more.

According to a teaching found in the Jerusalem Talmud at the end of the fourth chapter of the tractate of *Kiddushin*, when we meet our Maker we will have to account for all the pleasures of life that we wanted to enjoy, were permitted to enjoy, and had the opportunity to enjoy—but of which we nevertheless chose not to avail ourselves. As with the gift of Self, life, too, is a gift to be celebrated and not negated. The fullness of our being is determined by the fullness of our living, by how honoring and appreciative we are of the sanctity of our very distinct Selves, and by how conscious we allow ourselves to be about the God-Presence within us and therefore about how precious we each are to the Creator—how everything about us counts, matters. Taught the third-century Rabbi Elazar: "You should always consider as if the Holy One were within you, as it is written (Hosea 11:9), 'For I am God . . . the Holy One Who is in the midst of you'" (Babylonian Talmud, *Taanit* 11a).

The preciousness of individuality and the right, even the obligation, to honor your personal aliveness, your Selfhood, is illustrated again and again in the Judaic tradition throughout the Bible and the Talmud.

In the Bible, when Abraham invites the three wayfarers, he promises them bread and assigns Ishmael to prepare some meat and Sarah to bake the bread. The narrative then reports that Ishmael prepared the meat as instructed, but there is no mention of any of the promised bread ever getting there (Genesis 18:6-8). One could infer that Sarah simply did not do Abraham's bidding. One could infer that as meritorious as it might be to carry out the request of someone you are in relationship with, it is sometimes just as meritorious not to; that there are times when the Other's request of you clashes with the then particular needs of your selfhood; that as there are times when stepping out of your personal flow to meet the needs of an Other is positive and wholesome, there are also times when it is not. Perhaps Sarah was at that moment involved with the needs of her own Self space. In fact, when the ancient rabbis noticed the lack of mention of the bread getting made, they speculated that perhaps Sarah had begun to menstruate just then (Babylonian Talmud, *Baba Metzia* 87a), symbolic of her need to go within and attend to her Self. Nor is there a verse that follows where Abraham gets upset about it. Rather, he goes about his business of dealing with his guests without Sarah's bread, in complete honoring of her right not to join her itinerary to his at that moment. And when the guests inquire about her whereabouts, he replies simply: "She is in the tent" (Genesis 18:6-9).

In the same story, as the wicked cities of Sodom and Gomorrah are being destroyed, Abraham's nephew Lot, who had lived there with his family, is rescued by angels of God and ushered to a safer place. One would think that Lot would be satisfied with being rescued—period. But Lot is a former disciple of Abraham and was taught about a God with whom one can negotiate, and who honors each Creation with its very particular needs. And so, in the midst of his dramatic and miraculous rescue, he requests that the angels take him to a destination he preferred over the one God had chosen for him. His wishes are accepted and fulfilled:

And it came to pass, when they had brought him forth and set him outside of the city, that [one of the angels] said unto him: "Flee for your life; look not behind you, nor remain in this valley. Escape to the mountains, or you will be swept away." And Lot said to them: ". . . You have shown me great mercy in saving my life, but I cannot escape to the mountains for harm might come to me there and I will die. Behold, there is this city I prefer to flee to that is nearby, and it is a little one, so please let me escape there . . . for then shall my soul live." And [God replied]: "See, I have accepted you concerning this request of yours and I will not overthrow the city of which you have spoken. Go quickly, then, and escape there, for I cannot do anything until you have arrived there." (Genesis 19:17-22)

Eventually, Lot ends up heading for the mountains anyhow (Genesis 19:30), since he experiences fear also in the "little city" he had chosen nearby—perhaps, posits the eleventh-century Rabbi Shlomo ben Yitzchak (Rashi), because it was too close to the fire storms that struck neighboring Sodom and Gomorrah (Rashi, Ibid.). But in the moment, God honored his feelings, his confusion, the vulnerability he was experiencing in his sense of personal Aliveness ("then shall my soul live"), and even held up the entire divine plan to overthrow the doomed cities of the region ("Go quickly . . . for I cannot do anything until you have arrived there"). As an urban dweller, Lot might have felt uneasy at first about suddenly heading for the hills. Yet, through every phase of his confusion, of his needing to make varying, even contradicting, choices, God sticks with him.

The biblical account of the fledgling Jewish nation oozing out of the constrictions of Egyptian bondage is a story of how unity is achieved only by the honoring of diversity; how the collective is nurtured only through its respect for individuality. The Torah takes great pains to describe the very distinct characteristics of the diverse tribes that comprised this

One People, the Israelites. Each tribe had its own customs and ways of spiritual practice (*Sefer HaBahir, Mishnah* 112; see *Likutei MaHaRan*, chap. 9, para. 2, *shaarei tefillah*); its own leader, flag, and particular station alongside the portable tabernacle as it was carried through their desert journey toward their homeland (Numbers 2:2-31); and its own unique birthstone sewn into the single breastplate of the one High Priest the people commonly shared in collective worship three times a year (Exodus 28:15-22, 29). There was no attempt to strip the people of their selfhood or the tribes of their peculiarities and instead to lump everyone into one single robotic glob under a single one-size-fits-all banner. On the contrary, the very personal characteristics of each group within the collective were honored and nurtured by the fact that Judaism's sense of one-ness was based, from its inception, on the respect for diversity. Even though this mass of people pushed forward with a collective dream of reaching the home of their ancestors, with the collective vision of creating a homeland for the entire people as one, they nevertheless also left each tribe the option to choose to live elsewhere. Indeed, the tribes of Reuven and Gad were more attracted to the land they were passing through enroute to the Promised Land and boldly informed Moses that they were going to settle there instead of the land of their ancestors. At the same time, however, they also demonstrated that their choice was not coming from a place of Self to the neglect of Other, but that they would first fulfill their responsibilities to the collective by assisting in the settling of the Promised Land, and that then—and only then—would they establish their alternate choice of a homeland (Numbers, chap. 32; Joshua 22:1-4, 9-10). Had they not preserved their Self place all along, there would have been no sense of what was most beneficial for them, and they might have lost track of their aspirations and aliveness, letting them be swallowed up by the dreams of the larger collective. Likewise, had the ancient Judaic sense of peoplehood not been honoring of individualism, there would have been no tolerance for such dissension; it would have been seen as a threat to the ideals of the collective, threatening to arouse alternative notions in others among the people. But Moses was not afraid of this, nor were the people. Judaism in its original Abrahamic spirit had room for divergence, for individual notions, and for Self-ing.

The biblical teaching about the importance and sacredness of individuality is not confined to its particular teachings for and about the Jewish people. Before telling of the advent of the first Jews, the Torah recounts the universal story of the Tower of Babel, a story about how God personally sabotaged a world plan to unite all humanity into one peoplehood. Now, it would seem that the highest and most noble human ideal is that every Self be thrown into the kiln of collective cause to forge a united world community where everyone shares a single society, culture, language and religion. Yet the biblical story of the Tower of Babel (Genesis 11:1-9) demonstrates the discrepancy between the human definition of unity and the divine definition of unity. The human seeks to unite by folding up and contracting. God seeks to unite by unfolding and expanding.

> And the whole earth was of one language and of the same speech. And it happened that as they journeyed eastward, that they found a plain in the Land of Shin'ar; and they settled there. And they said to one another: "Come . . . let us build a single city, and a tower, with its top reaching to the heavens . . . lest we get scattered abroad across the face of the earth." . . . And God said: "Behold, they are one people, and they all share a single language. . . . Come, let us go down there and confuse their languages so that they may not understand one another's speech." So God scattered them abroad from there across the face of the earth. . . . (Genesis 11:1-8)

The human envisions a single world order where everyone will be molded into a single mindset. God, too, envisions a single world order, but one in which there is ample room for variety: "For My house shall be called a house of prayer for *all* peoples" (Isaiah 56:7). In fact, it was in that spirit that Solomon built the first Holy Temple of the Jewish people, as clearly stated in his inauguration prayer:

> Moreover, concerning the stranger, that is not of Your people Israel, when they shall come out of a far country for Your great name's sake, and Your mighty hand, and Your outstretched arm; when they shall come and pray toward this house; then hear You from heaven, even from Your dwelling place, and do according to all that the stranger calls to You for; that all the peoples of the earth may know Your name, and be in awe of You. (1 Kings 8:41–43; 2 Chronicles 6:32-33)

While Judaism's ultimate ideal is unity, it recognizes that unity can only thrive when there is an honoring of diversity. There can be no semblance of the One-ness of God, for example, if there is no room for diverse ways of acknowledging the One God. It does not teach that you have to be Jewish to go to Heaven (Babylonian Talmud, *Tosefta Sanhedrin* 13:1), but that paths other than the Judaic have their truths, too: their wisdoms, their prophets, and their revelations (Babylonian Talmud, *Baba Batra* 15b; *Eliyahu Rabbah* 9:1, 22:2; *Eliyahu Zuta* 20:3). Likewise, there can hardly be any unity of the human race if there is no room for as many diverse ways of being human as there are people on the planet.

As Judaism grew inceasingly institutionalized over the centuries, it appears to have joined the ranks of organized religion's campaign to obliterate the haplessly tabooed Self for the alleged higher good of its own perpetuation or its own version of how to be OK with God. Yet one can still discover in the ancient writings remnants of stories and teachings that celebrate the individual:

Once, during a year of drought in the Land of Israel, the people came to Honi the Circle Drawer (first-century B.C.E. grandfather of Abba Helkiah) to request that he pray for rain. He prayed but no rain fell. He then drew a circle and stood in the middle of it and cried: "Creator of the Universe! . . . I swear by Your Great Name that I will not move from this circle until You show mercy to Your children!" Rain began to trickle and the people said: "Master, we witness your greatness and have become assured that we will not die, but it seems to us that the rain comes only to free you of your oath!" . . . Honi then turned his eyes toward the heavens and prayed again, saying: "Not for such rain did I pray, but for rain that will fill the cisterns, ditches and caves!" The rain then poured in torrents, each drop as big as the opening of a barrel. . . . The people again said to him: "Master, we have witnessed your greatness, and we are assured that we will not die. But it seems to us that this kind of rain comes to destroy the world!" . . . He prayed once more, saying: "Not for this kind of rain did I pray, but for rain of benevolence, blessing and graciousness!" The rain then continued pouring but with gentleness and in proper measures. But it rained continuously so that the people of Jerusalem had to leave the streets and ascend the Temple Mount on account of the rain. Then said they to him: "Master, just as you have prayed for the rain to come, pray now for the rain to cease!" Said he to them: "I have a tradition that it is improper to pray for the cessation of too much good." . . . He then prayed again, saying: "Master of the Universe! Your people, the children of Israel, whom You have brought out of Egypt, can stand neither too much good nor too much harshness. When You appeared angry [by withholding rain] they could not bear it, and when You graced them with too much good, they could not bear it. Let it be Your Will that the rain cease and that there be ease in the world!" Instantly, the wind blew, the clouds scattered, and the sun began to shine, and the people went out into the fields and picked flowers and mushrooms. (Babylonian Talmud, *Taanit* 23a)

This story, too, illustrates the Judaic focus on the right of the individual, whether before his or her peers, or before the Supreme Power of the universe. Honi did not dismiss himself as an insignificant small fry in relationship to God, but as a being who counted. In his understanding of God, in the spirit of his ancestors, he knew that there was ample space and allowance for him to ask not just generally for what he needed, but for precisely what he needed; not a vague ballpark figure but what would be just right and on the mark. One may not always be answered the way Honi was, but one certainly has the right to put forth the request. Honi's message is clear: the individual counts, every one of us is precious, and as small as we are compared to the infinite cosmos, we are never too short to reach out and touch God. To be in such a vivid place of understanding God, to be capable of standing so firmly in the center of a circle as did Honi, we need to be honoring of our Selfhood and to experience our Self as so important and valuable a gift of God that in our own honoring of our Self we might be able also to experience God's honoring of our Self just as intimately and as clearly.

Of course, there are those who might find the idea of giving ultimatums to God as going too far. Indeed, one of Honi's colleagues, Rabbi Shimon ben Shettach, found Honi's seeming arm-twisting technique of prayer as bordering on the sacrilegious. But ultimately he conceded that it was kosher when carried out with the consciousness of a Honi, in a way that is void of arrogance and yet self-affirming; in a way that demonstrates a real-time relationship with God as parent, and as caring and loving of every individual personally:

> Were you not Honi, I would have had you excommunicated. But what can I do, since you entreat before The Place and [God] fulfills your desire as a son who entreats his father who then grants the son's desires. And if the son says to him, Father, bathe me in warm water, the father bathes him in warm water; if he says to him, Bathe me in cold water, he bathes him in cold water; if he says, Give me nuts, peaches, almonds and pomegrantes, he gives him nuts, peaches, al-

monds and pomegrantes. About you was it written: "Let your father and your mother be glad, and let her that gave birth to you rejoice" [Proverbs 23:25]. (Babylonian Talmud, *Taanit* 23a)

It is important to focus on the Hebrew-Aramaic term that Rabbi Shimon ben Shettach employs to describe Honi's way of entreating God: *mit'chatteh*, as in "You *mit'chatteh* before The Place and [God] fulfills your desires, like a son who is *mit'chatteh* before his father. . . ." The term is rooted in the word *chet*, which can mean "to miss the mark" or "to fail"— most commonly translated as "sin"—or "to lord over" or "to act irritably," and also, ironically, "to delight" (Babylonian Talmud, *Menachot* 66b. See Rashi's interpretation, too). Most commentators interpret *mit'chatteh* in Rabbi Shimon's remarks to connote the more negative act of "missing the mark," committing a wrong by approaching God like a nagging, insistent child. Such an interpretation beckons for qualification since it does not fit into the context of Rabbi Shimon's statement. Had it been intended as a negative, Rabbi Shimon would not have tempered his admonishment by saying, "But what can I do when you *mit'chatteh* before God and are answered. . . ." Nor would he have concluded his epistle to Honi by saying, "About you was it written, 'Let your father and your mother be glad, and let her that gave birth to you rejoice.'" Clearly, then, Rabbi Shimon's use of the term *mit'chatteh* needs to be reexamined.

Even if Rabbi Shimon did indeed mean "insistent" or "demanding" by the word *mit'chatteh*, it does not necessarily have to be interpreted as a criticism. When an adult behaves this way it could be inappropriate. But when a young child behaves this way, it is more likely to be an expression of the child's sense of Self. Children are innately too small and too unskilled to do for themselves even that which may be essential to the preservation of an intact Self. They are drastically dependent on the whims, abilities, and intentions of Others—the adults. Therefore, when a small child is demanding, adults too often hear this: "I wield power over you to force you to do as I please." But actually the child is saying "I am stating my Right to Self. And my Self needs such and such and I can't do it and *you can!*" And God responded to Honi like a parent who heard what was coming from Honi's "child place," as if his prayer was a plea, strongly put, and not as an attempt at coercion.

Therefore, Rabbi Shimon's use of *mit'chatteh* as petulant does not contradict the tone of praise he uses with the quote from Proverbs, or with his intimation of the rightness of Honi's behavior in the words, "But what can I do when you *mit'chatteh* before God and are answered. . . ." For throughout his epistle he consistently compares Honi's consciousness in that controversial mode of entreating God to the consciousness of a young child rightfully entreating a parent. This is borne out not only in the analogy Rabbi Shimon offers of the child who is asking for this and that and the other, but also in his choice of scriptural passage from Proverbs, which speaks of parental joy, not irritation, at the child. In prayer, then—and when all else has failed—we stand before God in the very fragile, powerless, and dependent child place, where it becomes all right to be petulant sometimes, to draw circles around ourselves and declare ultimatums, to stand before God in the manner—however petulant—of the young child who is not feeling heard by the parent and who is left with little recourse for the preservation and perpetuation of their sense of self-worth but to pull and tug at the parent's shirtsleeve and stomp their feet. There is no doubt that Honi's brazen stand followed the more standard procedural attempts of normative public prayer and fasting by the people. By drawing the circle, then, he was also drawing the line: "Mother, I need. And I need now." He was speaking

the simple, arrogant-sounding expression of the helpless, vulnerable child that is in each of us, before Our Parent Who
Art in Heaven. More than the nature of the expression, it is
the act of expressing, the sense of license to freely communicate in this manner, that reminds us that we are not insignificant nothings before the Almighty One like lowly peas-
ants before the monarch, but that we are beloved babes of
our Heavenly Parent who not only brought us into being but
celebrates our right to be and rejoices in us: "Let your father
and mother rejoice, and let her that gave birth to you rejoice!"

This is a fundamental Judaic teaching: you draw near to
God when you realize that God is your parent, and you are
God's child. And therefore you count, you the individual,
because you and your Cosmic Parent are one. Furthermore,
Judaism teaches that there is space for the individual to be
with their personal experience no matter how arrogant or
seemingly "sinful"—to be *mit'chatteh* in moments and situations that call out for the resurrection of a demolished sense
of Self, and for the rescue of the vulnerable child within.
While Jewish law forbids breaking down a door on the Sabbath, for example, it mandates it if there is a frightened young
child trapped behind it (Babylonian Talmud, *Yoma* 84b).
When there is a reclaiming of our God-given gift to be fully
alive, to be fully in the experience of our personal rightness
of being, *mit'chatteh* then transforms from its connotation
of "sin" or "missing the mark" or "petulance," to its alternate
connotation of "delight":

> A young child may jump and bounce atop the holy Name of God again
> and again, without consequence. On the contrary! For God says, "[The
> child's] very jumping I love." (*Song of Songs Rabbah* 2:13)

Whether *chet* means missing the mark of the God-Will in
a negative way—what we call sin—or missing it in a way that

is positive, depends then upon the context of the situation. Stomping upon God's Name appears to be an act that creates distance from the Creator, an act that misses the mark and is sinful. Yet, when a toddler does it in play, while the act in itself is not the preferred way, the child's experience in the moment is delight, not only from the perspective of the child but from that of God as well. It is sort of like a young child jumping playfully on its parent's back or belly. The act of jumping on someone is missing the mark of how to be with people; but there is a difference in context between who does it, with what intention, and when. *Chet*, then, even in a context of "error," can simultaneously also be "rightness" in the eyes of God who "looks upon the heart" (1 Samuel 16:7), and who delights in our reaching into our Selves to discover our sense of rightness—the internal sensing of the "still small voice within." External definitions of right and wrong can be extremely helpful in guiding us to find that still small voice within, but it is each person's listening for their own *heart/gut sensing* of rightness or sense of wrongness that leads to a knowing of Self, and of the God-Will for the individual.

As the twelfth-century Rabbi Moshe ben Nachman of Spain wrote about his disagreements with some of the decisions of his "superior" predecessors:

> I will not be for them like a donkey, eternally hauling their books. I will explain their teachings and study their ways, but when my vision does not complement theirs . . . I will then decide according to what my own eyes are seeing, and with legal certainty. For God grants wisdom in every generation and in every period, and will not deny goodness to those who are sincere. (From his introduction to *Sefer HaMitzvot L'HaRambam*, quoted in Rabbi Abraham Joshua Heschel's *Torah Min HaShamayim*, vol. 2, intro., p. vi)

Similarly, the sixteenth century mystic Rabbi Judah Loew of Prague writes how important it is for a rabbi to render reli-

gious legal decisions through the process of study and reasoning, and for the ruling to emanate from the rabbi's Self
place rather than from what has already been codified in the
texts by others. "And even if by his own understanding and
knowledge he arrives at an erroneous decision," he writes,
"he is yet beloved by God because he developed his decision from his own mind" (*Sifrei Maharal, Netivot Olam*, vol.
1, *Netiv HaTorah*, end of chap. 15).

Wisely used, then, is the Hebraic word for what we call
sin—*chet*—that it can in the same instant mean "missing the
mark" *and* "hitting the target," for there are also times when
missing the mark can be delightful all around.

There are also times when *chet* is more than a delightful
experience in the moment, but even a necessary experience
toward personal healing of woundedness, toward regaining
one's sense of self-worth and dignity after it has been shattered. For example, in the biblical account of the ancient
Israelites' flight from Egypt after two centuries of enslave-
ment, the waters of the Sea of Reeds are miraculously separated for them just when the Egyptian army is approaching
from behind in full force to recapture them. The pursuers
are then caught in the engulfing waters as the sea resumes
its natural state. Relieved, the Israelites sing and dance in
celebration of their safety and of the fall of their pursuers
(Exodus 14:21–15:21). Yet Judaism teaches that we ought
not to rejoice over the fall of our enemy (Proverbs 24:17).
The seeming contradiction is clarified, however, in an ancient
rabbinic teaching about how God silenced the heavenly
angels when they, too, rejoiced and began to sing praises:
"The works of My hands are drowning and you wish to
sing?!" (Babylonian Talmud, *Megillah* 10b). Sympathizers are
not to celebrate, but victims are allowed their full time of
rejoicing over their safety, over the recovery of their nearly

extinguished aliveness and sense of rightness of being, even if part of that celebration includes the tragic loss of life. But when Jews commemorate the exodus of their ancestors at the Passover Seder today, while they celebrate the miracle of the Ten Plagues that gave their ancestors respite from slavery and showed the Egyptians a thing or two, they also spill wine from their cups to reflect momentarily over the tragedy that befell the Egyptians. And while they commemorate the miracle of the Sea of Reeds, they also memorialize the tragedy of the fallen Egyptian soldiers by not reciting the complete Prayer of Praise on that day: "At the mention of every festival, scripture states 'And you shall rejoice'—except for the festival of Passover, because of the deaths of the Egyptians during that time. At every festival we recite the Prayer of Praises, but on the festival of Passover we recite it only during the first day and evening, for it is written in Proverbs, 'When your enemy falls, do not rejoice'" (*Pesiktei D'Rav Kahana* 189a). Those who were victimized and had their Selves shattered are allowed their time of celebration, of recapitulating their shattered sense of being. Those who are merely commemorating it are not. As King Solomon taught: "There is a time for everything" (Ecclesiastes 3:1-8)—off the mark or right on.

Ideally, the ancient rabbis taught, one should love one's enemy, and not hit back (e.g., Lamentations 3:30; Babylonian Talmud, *Shabbat* 88b; *Derekh Eretz Zuta* 6:3; *Shochar Tov* on Psalms 86:1). But ideally, too, one should be so solid in one's sense of Self that someone else's assaults or epithets could have no effect. If we are not that solid that we can act according to the ideal and still keep our Selves intact, then we owe it to our personal preciousness to reaffirm whatever parts of our Selves have been shattered—then we need to have it out with the one who has hurt us. Otherwise, we end up hating ourselves, and, in kind, hating the Other. "Do not hate your brother in your heart," the Torah instructs us. Rather, "rebuke rebuke your friend" (Leviticus 19:17)—in other words, wrestle it through with them, express your discomfort with what has happened or is happening. In the original Hebraic text, the word "rebuke" is written twice, perhaps to teach us that there are times when we are accomplices to the wrong we experience from an Other. In such instances, we need to rebuke the Other for their part, but we need also then to be open to hearing their side of the story, for there are times when we are accomplices in some way to the wrong we experience from an Other. The way best to do that, and how to deal with situations in which the Other refuses to enter into a dialogue or is deceased and so on, will be treated in the chapter Covenanting with Other.

It is ideal, for example, if we can respond to tragedy like the second-century Rabbi Akiva, who said about everything wrong that happened to him that it was "for the good" (Babylonian Talmud, *Berakhot* 60b; see also 54a). At the same time, the teachers of the Ideal also remind us that while we should aspire toward the Ideal, we should not blindly presume we know what it is, not about ourselves—"Do not be so sure of yourself until the day you die" (Babylonian Talmud, *Avot* 2:4)—and not about others—"Do not judge your friend until you have actually been in their place"(Babylonian Talmud, *Avot* 2:4). So if your friend is grieving over a tragic loss of life or property that had been an essential component of their Self, "do not try to appease them in the moment of their anger" (Babylonian Talmud, *Avot* 4:18). They might need to express that anger unimpeded in order to reassemble whatever parts of Self-ness have gotten disconnected by the unwelcome intrusion of loss into their life-flow. So, allow them their expression of Self, of being here on the planet and in life, and of not being happy with what has happened. Likewise, if you yourself have experienced an "earthquake" in your Self place, allow yourself your reactions, your personal time to be fully in your woundedness, so that you can pick up the pieces and begin your journey toward healing and growth.

Rabbis like the third-century Rabbi Hanina would espouse Ideal teachings like not taking suffering too hard, and seeing bad things that happen to you as ways of bringing you greater spiritual reward in the World-to-Come. Yet, when he once suffered from a severe ailment and was presented with this very same teaching, his reaction was, "I do not want this [the suffering], nor its reward" (*Song of Songs Rabbah* 2:35):

> Rabbi Yochanan suffered for three years and a half from a fever. Rabbi Hanina came to visit him and said: "How are you feeling?" Replied Rabbi Yochanan: "It is more than I can stand." Said Rabbi Hanina: "Do not talk that way, for God will compensate you." . . . After a time, Rabbi Hanina himself became ill and Rabbi Yochanan paid him a visit and said: "How are you feeling?" Replied Rabbi Hanina: "My suffering is too hard to bear!" Said Rabbi Yochanan: "But how great is its compensation!" Said Rabbi Hanina: "I prefer neither the suffering nor its reward." Asked Rabbi Yochanan: "But why do you not take to heart the very words you offered me when I was sick?" Replied Rabbi Hanina: "When I was free of pain, I was able to comfort others. But now that I, too, am in pain, I need others to comfort me." (*Song of Songs Rabbah* 2:35; Babylonian Talmud, *Berakhot* 5a)

The ancient teachers fared well in contradictions only because they did not live in absolutes. As Covenantors, their teachings and personal behaviors reflected a way of being that was honoring of the space to be real with yourself, with God, with others; to be organic, not static; to be everunfolding and to honor each moment and its particular experience as separate from what was before or what would be afterwards. The Talmud recounts a powerful teaching about this in its story of the third-century Rabbi Yehudah HaNasi's toothache:

> Once, when Rabbi Yehudah HaNasi was teaching Torah to an assembly of Babylonian Jews in Sepphoris, a calf escaped from the slaughterhouse and sought refuge behind him. When it communicated to the rabbi that he should rescue it, the rabbi said: "What can I do? It is for this that you were created." Thereafter, the rabbi began to suffer a toothache that lasted for thirteen years . . . until, once, a lizard ran past his daughter, and she went after it to kill it. He then said to her: "Let it be, for it is written, 'God's mercies are over all creations' (Psalms 145:9)." A Heavenly Voice then proclaimed: "Because he showed pity, so shall pity be shown to him." And his toothache ceased. (Babylonian Talmud, *Baba Metzia* 85a; *Genesis Rabbah* 33:3)

While we might attribute the rabbi's toothache to decay, he himself attributed it to the fact that he sent the fleeing calf back to the slaughterhouse. The ideal of vegetarianism aside, what possible wrong could the teacher have later felt about sending the calf back? In the mindset of his religious practice it was certainly not immoral to eat it, or to raise cattle for that purpose. What, then, was the wrong in telling the animal to "return to the slaughterhouse, for it is ultimately for that purpose that you were created"? But the answer to the question lies in the remedy to his toothache. It was not the act of going to an orthodontist that cured him in the end, but the act of recovering the consciousness that had gotten lost in the act of turning the fleeing calf away. Yes, slaughtering an animal for food is permissible by Jewish law, is, in every sense of the word, kosher. However, it was only kosher until that moment, and would remain kosher after that moment. But it was *not* kosher *in* that moment. When the calf had stepped out of the droning flow of time and protocol to seek refuge because it had figured out what was going to happen in the slaughterhouse, it was left to Rabbi Judah

to do the same, to step outside the framework of ongoing
time and standards and all that is acceptable, and to home
in on the experience of the moment; to unbind that situation from the rote of time and custom and to act compas-
sionately. Maybe it would not have been expected that there
be that kind of feeling of compassion in the course of preparing an animal for consumption in the atmosphere of a
kitchen or slaughterhouse—though there are many stories of
rabbis who wept during the act of ritual slaughter for each
and every animal, and thanked them, as well. But the teaching is that it is wrong to withhold oneself from feelings of
compassion that may be gradually swelling to the surface and
to replace them instead with feelings and rationale that are
not from the Self place. The Bible is even more clear on this
regarding people. Ancient, and even some modern, nations
treated their slaves worse than their livestock, and slaves who
fled from their owners were hunted down and returned, if
not tortured or killed. In ancient Judaic law, however, if you
came upon an escaped slave you were forbidden to return
him or her, but were obligated to take care of them for it was
assumed their master had mistreated them (Deuteronomy
23:16). You were supposed to step out of the societal norms
and standards of the time and see the refugee not as a fugi-
tive, not as someone who owed a debt in labor to someone
else, or someone who had sold themself to servitude for eco-
nomic reasons, but as a fellow creation of the One God. You
were not to harden your heart against the deep-down feelings your Self harbored about the equality of all humans, but
you were, as Rabbi Yehudah HaNasi's story teaches, to call
forth the best feelings in your Self, whether calves belonged
to the slaughterhouse or not, and whether the escaped slave
still owed a debt of servitude to someone or not. You were
to be conscious of the heart of the moment and its distinct
qualities, and of the heart of your Self and your feelings of

rightness. "When an opportunity for doing a positive deed comes into your hands," taught the second-century Rabbi Shimon bar Yochai, "you are duty-bound to seize it" (*Leviticus Rabbah* 9:9). You are not obligated to run about freeing calves from slaughterhouses, for example (*Leviticus Rabbah* 9:9), unless that is truly a call out of your Self place, but if one of them happens upon you and calls forth from within you so much as a sprouting seed of compassionate sentiment, listen to it, honor it, and be prepared also to pay the price:

> Once, while lodging at an inn, Reb Zusia of Hanipol noticed how the innkeeper kept numerous cages of exotic birds in the lobby. Feeling compassion for the trapped winged-beings, he opened the doors to all the cages and set the expensive birds free. The innkeeper leaped upon the rabbi, beat him senseless and threw him into the street. Reb Zusia staggered onto his feet and went on his way, exhilarated over having brought joy and freedom to the birds. (Heard from Rabbi Shlomo Carlebach)

The very individual process of the Self's being and unfolding therefore holds immense priority in Judaism. If you are confronted with an opportunity for exercising your best traits, for bringing forth more and more of the rightness and aliveness of your Self, then that experience takes precedence over whatever might be important in the broader, external realms of standard procedure, social protocol, and even religious principle.

It is good social conduct, for example, to help your best friend who is overladen with grocery bags. However, if at the same time you also spot your worst enemy in a similar situation, the Torah implores you to run first to the aid of the person you dislike (Exodus 23:4-5; Babylonian Talmud, *Baba Metzia* 32b). Because, all "right thing to do" aside, there is a segment of your Self that beckons for restoration of that part of you that holds a void, an abyss, from the feeling of hate you have been carrying inside of you toward your enemy. And here is an opportunity to fill that void, to recover a part of your Self that had gotten lost in the dis-ease of being at odds with someone. The Torah then bids you to choose between the two opportunities the one that would foster the most badly needed repairs for the world, in your individual Self and, simultaneously, in the collective consciousness. This act is known as *tikkun olam*—"the repairing of the world." Helping your enemy will eradicate the scar that has existed in the universe because of this enmity; it will forge a healing, and restore wholeness where there was brokenness, in both the arena of I Am and in the relationship of I-Thou. Therefore, says the Torah about this opportunity, "seize it." (Of course, common sense is in order here: so you might want to tend to the needs of your friend first if their bag is tearing or their hernia is bursting.) Indeed, how overwhelming is the feeling we experience when we make peace with those with whom we are in conflict. Do we not in such moments experience a sensation of swelling inside? Nothing is swelling, however; what we are experiencing is restoration, recovery; and more than a feeling, we are experiencing a *filling*, a filling in of the void that gets created in those places of our Self that are in conflict and unresolved about an Other.

Similarly, it is a religious principle to wait your head off for the Coming of the Messiah. But, taught the first-century Rabbi Yochanan ben Zakkai: "If you are holding a seedling in your hand, and you are informed that the Messiah has come, first complete your planting, and then greet the Messiah" (Babylonian Talmud, *Avot D'Rabbi Natan* [version 2] 31:2). In other words, if you were in the middle of a personal life process that is in your grasp, unfolding by your own hand, your own doing, then that experience of Self aliveness and unfolding needs to have the space in which you can feel it as yours and yours alone, not something some savior would make happen for you, but the fruits of your very own effort and accomplishment. Free Will, as discussed earlier, is costly, but its gift lies in the fact that it enables us to live Life according to our own volition and by our own choices. Thanks to free will, whatever we accomplish, wherever we persevere, and whatever spiritual heights and God-consciousness we attain, we will have thereby attained it on our own, by our Selves. So if you have got life by the throat, if there is "a seedling in your hand"—if you are engaged in the unfolding of your Self—and you are told that the long-awaited Messiah is here to save the world and set everything aright, to fix everything for you that you are in that very moment fixing by yourself: "first complete your planting, and then greet the Messiah."

This seemingly brazen principle of Self-ness does not originate in the teachings of a handful of postbiblical rebel rabbis, but blossoms forth from down-home biblical writ itself. For example, according to the law of the Torah, the following were exempt from going to war: one who had just built a house and had not had a chance to live in it; one who had just planted a vineyard and had not yet tasted its produce; one who just got married but had not lived with their partner for at least a year; and, finally, one who was simply afraid (Deuteronomy 20:5-8). It is simple to understand the exemption of those who are fearful of the front because not only would they further endanger themselves, they would also endanger other soldiers. But what is the meaning behind the other exemptions? Yet even a casual review of them reveals their common characteristic, and the exemption granted them in turn reflects the Torah's profound sensitivity toward the individual Self's unfolding through the experiential gift of Life, even in the face of Death, as in a time of war. Those who have labored to build something, to create something, whether it be a house or a garden or a relationship with someone special, share the experience of bringing potential to fruition, and of nurturing within their Self their sense of Love, whether it is for the works of their hands or of their hearts. In that moment, a precious moment of accomplishment, of attainment, of fulfillment, the Torah draws the line between the honor of the individual and that of the collective. There is a war raging on the outskirts of the Judean hills, but the Torah finds it more important for the individual Self to experience the realization of its personal aspirations than those of the communal aspirations. As Rabbi Shimon bar Yokhai, quoted above, said: If an opportunity to raise your Self happens into your hands, seize it. It is a gift in the moment for you to perhaps shift your Self from a place of being to a place of happening, from sedentary to movement. And the Torah will then step in to sift you out of the crowd of warriors preparing themselves for possible death, so that you might instead avail yourself of the gift of Self aliveness that has been accorded you in the moment. It is not then an exclusive teaching of one particular rabbi named Yokhanan ben Zakkai that when the opportunity for personal "gardening" is in your grasp in the moment it is more precious than any messianic redemption. The Torah is clear and consistent in its position that your individuality, the freshness of your moment-by-moment unfoldings, is an important priority that should not be allowed to get lost in the collective glob of peoplehood, regardless of how noble its ideals and aspirations. "More beautiful," taught the third-century Rabbi Yaakov, "is a single moment of personal improvement and deeds of loving-kindness in this lifetime, than an eternity in the World To Come" (Babylonian Talmud, *Avot* 4:17).

4

COVENANTING WITH OTHER

One who deals responsibly and truthfully with Others
and with whom the souls of others are at ease, it is as
if they have fulfilled the entire Torah.
—*Mekhilta* on Exodus 15:26

Judaism views Life as relationship-ing. It is about reflecting
and projecting, interacting and reacting, expressing and
impressing. It is not about a bunch of souls scurrying about
on their way to the hereafter in lemminglike swarms of collective consciousness, but about a bunch of individually
cocooned souls dancing their way to fruition by weaving in
and out of their experiences with one another. Virtually all
of the physical senses are designed for Other-ing. With our
eyes we see Other, whether a mountain, a horizon, or another human being. With our ears we hear Other. With our
nostrils we smell Other. Many of our physical faculties and
senses are necessary for survival of Self, but many more of
them are necessary for reacting to or interacting with Other,
for being in relationship with Other.
   Likewise, as many commandments as there are in the

113

Torah concerning humans and God, there are many more that address humans and Other, whether that Other be a person, an animal, or a tree. Other-ing, then, is perhaps the most difficult challenge in the subjective human experience, even more difficult than God stuff. It is far easier to relate with an unseen, physically absent, and often experientially nonreactive and silent God than it is to relate with the corporeal, reactive, and physical presence of another person. As the first-century Rabbi Eliezer blessed his disciples: "May your awe of God be at least as real as your awe of other humans" (Babylonian Talmud, Berakhot 28b). So great is harmony with others, taught the second-century Rabbi Elazar HaKappar, "that even if we worship idols, God will not judge us for it when there is at least peace between us" (Babylonian Talmud, Derekh Eretz Zuta, chap. 9). According to a presecond-century mishnaic teaching (Babylonian Talmud, Berakhot 54a; Makkot 23b), one is permitted to pronounce the sacred God-Name of the tetragrammaton (YHVH) in the course of a social greeting in spite of the commandment: "You shall not take the Name of the Lord your God casually" (Exodus 20:7):

> At times one abrogates dictates of the Torah to act for God. So in this case, too. One whose intention is to inquire about the well-being of another person is doing the Will of God, for it is written: "Seek peace and pursue it" [Proverbs 34:15]. (Eleventh-century Rabbi Shlomo ben Yitzchak [on Babylonian Talmud, Berakhot 54a–et laasot])

More personal, inside, Self stuff gets churned, gets stirred, and empowers our being in the dynamics between Self and Other than between Self and God. More of what the Judaic mystics call partzuf—a dance of projective and reflective interaction, which weaves the fabric of our Soul-Being—can happen between two or more people than with one person alone.

Partzuf connotes a mirroring back and forth between one persona and another, between Creation and itself. It is as if we were living in a universe of mirrors, in which all natural beings, as diverse as each might be from the others, mirror back to us something about their essence thereby invoking in us consciousness of something about *our* essence that we could not otherwise experience. Every time we tune in to this mirroring, our consciousness of Being spirals, our experience of Self gains dimension, and our sense of Aliveness becomes that much more vivid. There is a quality of self-knowledge that comes into play when we relationship with a tree or a mountain or a person that is unavailable when we are aware of them only peripherally, or not at all. When we deprive ourselves of Other, in whatever form, then we also deprive ourselves of Self. Peoples we often call pagans, or primitives, are probably more keenly in tune with *partzuf* than most "civilized" devotees of the very science of *partzuf* as delineated in the more sanctioned realms of "legitimate" paganism we call Judeo-Christian mysticism. Aboriginal religions across the globe integrate consciousness of Nature with consciousness of Self. Every individual, they teach, is in *partzuf* relationship with an animal, whether an eagle or a panther, corresponding to his or her personal power place. Devotees of the Bible who are moved to dismiss such ideas as idolatrous or animism might first want to reopen their Bibles to the account of the patriarch Jacob blessing his twelve sons with the elements of Nature, such as oceans, animals, and plants (Genesis, chap. 49). They might also want to read in the Bible about how celestial beings were described with various animal features, such as the face of an eagle, a human, a bull, and a lion (Ezekiel 1:5-10). Elsewhere, the Bible also describes God in the metaphor of animals (Exodus 19:4 [eagle]; Deuteronomy 32:11 [eagle]; Isaiah 31:4-5 [lion and bird]; Hosea 5:14, 11:10 [lion], and 13:7 [lion and leopard];

Lamentations 3:10 [bear and lion]). Clearly, then, all of Nature can teach us about ourselves and *partzuf* with us. In them all we can find a reflection of parts of our Selves we would otherwise never realize. As the Book of Job puts it: "Ask the beasts and they shall teach you; and the birds in the air, and they shall tell you; or speak to the earth and it shall teach you; and the fishes of the sea shall declare unto you" (Job 12:7–8).

Partzuf, then, is more than a kabbalistic term for an abstract concept that only seasoned mystics can fathom. It is both a spiritual and down-to-earth psychological reality. The proverbial wisdom that "you are affected by your environment" is an understatement, and it is a universal truth whose mysteries are locked in the spiritual dynamics of *partzuf*, of the soul-deep yearning in all created matter toward its shared matter-essence and toward its mutual Spirit Source.

Partzuf, therefore, extends also to the sphere of our relationship with the Great Spirit and with the cosmic universe. How we choose to be in the world will in turn be mirrored back to us in the kind of world we end up with. What we choose, in other words, for ourselves or for the planet, becomes a sort of request, and whatever happens as a result, for better or for worse, becomes a sort of response. If I look at a rose to be inspired by it, to be moved by it, I put out my request thereby for beauty, for the gifts of Nature, and that is what I, in turn, experience. If, on the other hand, I find the rosebush an impediment to my plans for paving my front yard, then I *partzuf* with the rose in a whole other way, and my message to the universe is that I prefer cement to rosebushes, and the answer I might get one day is a marred countryside ravaged by strip-mining or a stuffed nose that keeps me from enjoying the aroma of Spring.

Partzuf is then more about what we want than what we need, and is therefore not always good for us. It is sort of akin to the proverbial adage: "Be careful of what you ask for. You might get it." Not that the Creator is a mechanical deity who responds indiscriminately every time someone throws a quarter into the quest machine. Rather, it is about the human power of invocation, of calling forth a response to a *want* in the moment, which may or may not correspond to a *need*, or to what is best in the long run. It is also about our perhaps not being ready in the moment of the quest for its fulfillment, or not being ready to have what is better for us happen instead. There are times, then, when the absence of response to a prayer may be its very answer. And then there are also times when fulfilling a quest may not be the most wholesome response but addresses the petitioner where they are in the moment—anything more appropriate would probably go right over their head.

The eighteenth-century mystic Rabbi Yisrael Baal Shem Tov taught that sometimes God will answer your prayer-quest though it is detrimental to you, and will then answer you a second time when you pray once more for the withdrawal of the first request. He derives this from the passage in Psalms (145:19): "God will perform the will of those who are conscious of God, and upon hearing their cries shall come to their aid." Asked Rabbi Yisrael: "If God will perform their will, what need is there to mention that God will also hear their cries? It means, then, that . . . if the answered prayer is not what is best for the individual, God will hear the subsequent complaint, the cry for rescue from the discomforting experiences brought on by the initial prayer, and withdraw it" (*Keter Shem Tov HaShalem* 16a–b).

Partzuf also implies that how we perceive God is very much determined by how we *choose* to perceive God, by what form of relationship we are prepared to engage in with God. Calling God "Lord" or "Master" or "King" may perpetuate subservience to those "above" us and, in turn, our own expecta-

tions of obeisance from those "beneath" us. Rabbi Zalman
Schachter-Shalomi calls this form of relating "hydraulic," in
which the ascension of one happens by the descent of another. Hydraulic forms of relationship are inherited from
earlier paradigms of hierarchical power structures and societal caste systems. If, indeed, we feel we have outgrown this
way of being with one another and have seen enough of the
tragedy it has wrought throughout history even to this day,
we might prefer to address God as "Friend" rather than "Master." We might want to perceive God as "Our Life Source who
is right here beside us" rather than "Our Father who is in
Heaven."

Various metaphors for God emerged out of personal
human experiences of God, but may not resonate the same
way for everyone in every era. For someone who was abused
by their father, for example, referring to God as "Father"
would create a perception of God as uncaring and cruel.
People who have had great luck with monarchical rule may
find "King" a pleasant metaphor for God; while those who
have suffered under royal tyranny would not. What we call
God, then, needs to correspond with how we want to experience God. Regardless of how loving God is, for example,
we cannot experience that quality if we are shut up to it
because of negative experiences or perceptions attached to
a particular metaphor. As long as we remain stuck in the old
ways of God-ing that were fine for past paradigms, we will
invoke the same old karma, and our experience of God may
remain clouded by cosmic dust and mildew.

> Way back when I was a *yeshivah* student, I would often pray with such
> intensity that I would grimace, kvetching out my supplications with
> an "Oy-oy-oy!" At one point, the *mashgiach* (supervising rabbi) no-
> ticed my facial contortions and jolted me out of my stupor with a
> sudden jab to the rib cage. "So tell me, Zalman," he said, "have you
> already tried it with a smile, and it didn't work?" . . .

I believe that God wants us to communicate how we need to experience God today. The eternal question God asks us for homework is still, "Where are you at?" (Genesis 3:9) ... For example, the world sorely needs God to make us sane. A contemporary prayer would then go something like this: "I call upon You, O thou Sane-Maker, to become permeable and allow the smooth transfer of the kinds of energy we need to be sane. Hear our prayers and send down Your Light and Your Truth. Make us sane before we commit the Big Oops!"

The words "civil rights," "Greenpeace," and "Amnesty International" are more alive today than the word "God." It is my sense that this is because the old *name* of God has died, not God. Call God "Universe," rather than "King" or "Lord," and we are more likely to dialogue together; more likely to save the planet. (Rabbi Dr. Zalman Schachter-Shalomi in conversation with the author [1987]).

Likewise does *partzuf* operate in down-home mortal relationship-ing. How we perceive an Other is determined largely by how we *choose* to perceive them, and by how we define relationship altogether. If a woman, for example, inherits an image of husband as a demanding authority figure, she might indeed end up with just that sort of experience of her husband, even if she marries a sweet feminist man. Her assumptions about his expectations will inevitably create phantom relationship dynamics, feelings, and perceptions from and about him that may not even be there. Or, her interaction with him may trigger reactions from him that come from the residual dust stirred up by being related to as a husband in the old-paradigm way. And so did God warn Eve after the forbidden fruit was consumed: "If you give in to what you perceive as a larger, more powerful Adam, then your willful submission to him will cue him to lord over you" (Genesis 3:16).

Similarly, if we continue to raise children and have marriages, for example, following the same routes on maps drawn by earlier explorers, we may just go on making the same old wrong turns. If we enter such relationships with the same old expectations and assumptions people of yesteryear had of marriage, of children, of parents, of spouses—assumptions and expectations that do not resonate with all of us today except as intimidating—we will never arrive at relationships that foster aliveness *now.*

> The problem with relationships in this archaic but otherwise work-able system is the hydraulic nature of it, not the role game but the power game which comes into play. Each time the hydraulic num-ber is used there is some degree of pecking. When one party decides to call the shots, the other party feels abruptly and brutally hurled from the I–Thou level down to the I–It. Next, communications break down, often followed by the relationship regressing rapidly to the level of Primal Screaming. (Rabbi Dr. Zalman Schachter-Shalomi in con-versation with the author [1987])

A man needs to be careful not to fall back on archaic as-sumptions about women so that in a relationship he will not come to dishonor her by talking down to her, second-guess-ing her needs without communication, or smugly shrugging off her behavior or needs when they do not correspond to his. How many of us so-called liberal male feminists, for in-stance, actually end up having nonsexist relationships with the women in our lives? How much of the old stuff men and women assume about each other still lingers in each gender group about the other, notwithstanding all the contempo-rary preachings against sexism? Change does not happen overnight, nor does it happen by the flick of a paradigm switch. It happens, rather, by our conscious choice of how we truly want to *partzuf* not only with God but with each other, with our lovers, our parents, our children, our gov-ernment, our employers and employees. It is not God who ordained that there be a hierarchy of: men first, then women, and then children. It is men who ordained it. It was our mortal choice of interface with each other, which in turn determined the nature of our interface with the divine, and vice versa. In the eyes of God, the ancient rabbis taught, men are not held in any special status in relationship to women. Such teachings in religion are purely mortal, not divine. "Men are more compassionate toward other men than toward women, but God's compassion extends equally to both men and women" (*Midrash Tanchuma, Netzavim*, no. 2; *Sifri* on Numbers 27:1). The way to achieve a nonhydraulic relationship is by honoring the Self at the same moment you honor the Other. Mostly it is when the Self feels vulnerable or unsure of its meaningfulness that it makes artificial attempts at its own reaffirmation by negating Other, by relating hydraulically.

The hydraulic pump of uplifting myself by putting you down was strongly reinforced by institutionalized religion. Yet the ancient rabbis constantly reminded the people of the often gaping discrepancy between religion and God (see earlier chapter Covenanting with God). And though many of their teachings reflect their complicity in feeding the monster of hydraulic *partzuf*-ing, a great many more reflect their tenacious grasp of the spirit behind the dogma. The third-century Rabbi Hisda, for instance, held that teachers may not relinquish the honors due them from their disciples (Babylonian Talmud, *Kiddushin* 32a). At first this sounds like a typical patriarchal dictum designed to preserve and perpetuate the perniciousness of authority and superiority. But as the lesson is allowed to gel, the form it takes bespeaks the complete opposite: Honor is not yours to relinquish, the teacher is admonished. It belongs rather to your disciple to use toward his or her learning process and openness to you as a teacher. Likewise, does the lesson admonish the parent: Honor is not yours, but belongs rather to your children to employ as their lens for perceiving you as their guide and mentor. On the contrary, if honor was indeed yours to relinquish, it would then also be yours to demand. By teaching that honor is not ours to relinquish, the sages taught that neither is it ours to expect to begin with.

> Rabbi Eliezer, Rabbi Yehoshua, and Rabbi Tzadok (first century) were visiting their teacher Rabbi Gamliel. Rabbi Gamliel began to serve them wine but Rabbi Eliezer declined. And when he saw Rabbi Yehoshua accept the wine, he admonished him, saying: "How could you accept the wine and thereby make it so our teacher serves *us?*" Replied Rabbi Yehoshua: "Greater ones than Rabbi Gamliel were known to have served lesser ones than they. Such as Abraham our ancestor who served the three angels whom he thought were idolatrous wayfarers [Genesis 18:2–3]." Rabbi Tzadok, overhearing the conversation, interrupted the two and declared: "How many more times will we keep bringing examples only of human kindness for our analogies, when we could just as easily bring examples of God's loving-kindness? For the One Who Created All and is greatest of all is preoccupied day and night with caring for the world, feeding us, clothing us, healing us and comforting us; providing the planet with rain and seasons, with vegetation and sustenance!" (Babylonian Talmud, *Kiddushin* 32b)

As the second-century Rabbi Elazar ben Shamua put it: "The honor of your disciple shall be as dear to you as your own" (Babylonian Talmud, *Avot* 4:12). Indeed, when high spiritual teachers enter a room, those present rise in respect, but the revered teachers will expend just as much energy gesturing to them to remain seated as it took for the disciples to rise. This is a common scene not confined to *yeshivot*, religious academies of Jewish studies, occurring equally at the Hindu *ashram* of Sri Swami Satchidananda, for example, or at a Sufi retreat with Pir Valayat Kahn. High beings know that honor belongs to no one; that it is an invisible yet experiential *partzuf* zone between people in which they might be able to encounter one another in ways that would benefit them both.

The *partzuf* zone, however, need not be enshrined in a *yeshivah* study hall or an *ashram*. It ought to get developed and enshrined right at home with our Selves and those we love. A smiling face will set off other smiling faces, and a gesture of honoring will beget a sense of honor and create a Sacred Space between the Self and the Other. Conversely, because of the potency of *partzuf*, we need to be that much more cautious in our dance of relationship. Our effect, our impression upon an Other, can just as easily strip an Other of their dignity as it can empower them. Therefore, taught the first-century Rabbi Akiva, God deals more stringently with wrongs against people than with wrongs against God (*Numbers Rabbah* 11:15). God's Covenant with us is then founded on our relationship with each other. "Have we not all one father? Did not one God create us? Why do we break faith with one another, profaning the Covenant of our ancestors?" (Malachi 2:10).

The Talmud is therefore replete with teachings about behaving with cautious sensitivity toward an Other. The laws about hurting someone monetarily, for example—known as *onaah* (Leviticus 25:14, 17)—were equally applied by the ancient teachers to hurting someone's feelings, saying hurtful things to someone, or insulting them (Babylonian Talmud, *Baba Metzia* 58b). The path of the Torah, then, is one that stretches across all that is life, spilling into every facet of the human experience. Laws about usury can just as easily find their application for laws about slander or mockery. *Onaah* is *onaah*, whether it is shortchanging a customer or hurting a friend's feelings. In both instances, Judaism teaches, you are selling them short.

The gravity of *onaah* intensifies the more intimate the relationship. We are taught to love our relationship partners like our own persons, but to honor them beyond our own standards (Babylonian Talmud, *Yevamot* 62b). The wisdom of this teaching is that we cannot love someone more than ourselves, but we are capable of honoring them more than ourselves. And honoring someone more than by your own standards for yourself would avoid the assuming we often do when it comes to figuring out what is OK for someone else. If, on the other hand, we were to honor the Other as we do ourselves, we might behave toward them with sarcasm or play practical jokes on them because we find it personally OK and far from dishonoring, while our partners might find it insulting and hurtful. "Why are you taking it so seriously? I was only kidding!" is an often-heard defensive reaction when we assume that someone else's standards of personal honor are no different from our own. Another common declaration of assumption about an Other is: "Oh, they won't mind. Go ahead."

The above teaching is also a reminder to us that each of our perceptions of reality is unique. In our interaction with Other, then, we are challenged with looking beyond Self to see Other; to engage in I-Thou. In no way, however, does this imply so much as a momentary dropping away of Self, or a transcending of Self. On the contrary, in order to honor an Other more than yourself you need to be very present in your own Self place, to the point that you are in that moment of relating with Other very conscious of the uniqueness of your Self and thus of the Other's Self.

How easy it is to hurt an Other, and therefore how important it is to be cautious when we interact with Other, is demonstrated by a number of rabbinic teachings about the severity of embarrassing someone or hurting their feelings. Not that we would be naïve about any of this without these teachings. After all, every one of us at some time or another has been hurt by an Other, verbally and physically, both intentionally and unintentionally. But the rabbis realized that most religious adherents were inclined to get lost in the dogma of

being OK with God, to the sore neglect of the more important creed of being OK with people. The third-century Rabbi
Abba bar Kahana taught, for example, that "the generation
of David was very religious, but since there were slanderers
among them, they would go to war and lose. The generation of Akhav, however, were worshipers of the stars, but
since there were no slanderers among them, they would go
to war and win" (Jerusalem Talmud, *Pe'ah* 4a). The third-
century Rabbi Rabbah bar bar Hannah quotes his contemporary Rabbi Yokhanan as teaching that to shame someone
publicly is more severe than to commit the cardinal sin of
adultery (Babylonian Talmud, *Baba Metzia* 59a). A fourth-
century teaching likens it to murder (Babylonian Talmud,
Baba Metzia 58b); that to shame someone is to momentarily
separate them from their aliveness.

Nor were teachings like these applied to the treatment of
adults alone, but apply to our treatment of children as well,
whose feelings we often take for granted or less seriously. In
fact, ancient Judaic law held an adult no less liable for publicly shaming a child than for shaming an adult (Babylonian
Talmud, *Baba Kamma* 86a), and in cases of physical injury
exacted the same punitive damages legislated for injury
caused to an adult, which included payment for embarrassment, loss of wages, pain suffered, and medical expenses
(Babylonian Talmud, *Baba Kamma* 83b). Punitive fines were
not enough, however. The Mishnah further required that the
perpetrator acknowledge to the victim the wrongness of what
was done to them, and that the victim be asked for forgiveness (Babylonian Talmud, *Baba Kamma* 92a).

The bottom line of these teachings implores us not to take
Other for granted, not to see Other as the property of our
own reality, and not to assume anything about an Other, nor
to judge them without at least granting them the benefit of a
doubt or two (Babylonian Talmud, *Avot* 1:6). It is a common

human inclination to assume knowledge about an Other, or about what is best for them. As parents, we do this quite a lot with our children; as lovers we do this quite a lot with our partners. The teachings about the sacredness of individual dignity and right to be can never be exhausted and can never be sufficiently promulgated. Indeed, the second-century Rabbi Eliezer HaGadol reminds us that the Torah spares little verbiage in emphasizing and reemphasizing beyond superfluity and redundancy the need for extra sensitivity in our relationship with people far from their homes, or not acquainted with our faiths, or who in any other way find themselves in a situation of vulnerability and awkwardness in our presence. No less than thirty-six times, taught Rabbi Eliezer, does the Torah caution us about proper behavior toward the stranger (Babylonian Talmud, *Baba Metzia* 59b). This could just as well apply to those with whom we are in relationship—who are strangers to our personal reality structure—and to our children—who are strangers to the planet.

Sensitivity to how we deal with the "stranger" is also an important discipline for what Rabbi Zalman Schachter-Shalomi calls Group Shadow Syndrome. In the company of others we can easily end up shunning those who "don't fit," and thus in the guise of honoring one set of Other, we dishonor a second set. In its more severe form this is known as scapegoating. Once the undesirable member of the group is ousted, yet another must be found. "The group needs to always have a 'shadow' person on duty," says Rabbi Schachter-Shalomi, "someone upon whom it can cast any of its own unacknowledged discrepancies and inadequacies" (conversation with the author). Conversely, if we ourselves are the subject of such group dynamics, we need to deflect the negative vibes of that kind of *partzuf*-ing and reaffirm our Self.

Lakme recalls an evening meal she spent with the late storyteller Reuven Gold at a spiritual-retreat gathering in the Midwest. Reuven then suffered from a severe asthmatic condition, and his intense emotional neediness often made those around him uncomfortable. Consequently, some of the retreatants at the table seemed to be deliberately avoiding him. And though Reuven felt snubbed by them, he took it in stride and, leaning over toward Lakme, wheezed and coughed the following story:

> At the height of synagogue services during one Yom Kippur, a peasant observed with curiosity how the rabbi and the cantor swayed with fervor and bawled aloud from a liturgical hymn about how God should forgive them their sins because they were as mere worms. Feeling left out, the peasant heaved in a deep breath and joined the weeping officiators and bellowed out the same reading, shaking with vigor and pleading before God to consider him, too, no greater than a worm. When the rabbi and the cantor heard the peasant's moaning, they ceased their cries and looked at one another in puzzlement. "Ho ho," the rabbi remarked to the cantor, "so look who thinks he's a worm!"

Like Reuven, we need to be present in our Self place while dancing in the dynamics of Other. Though we might sometimes feel hurt by what goes on in those dynamics, our Self place needs protection from reflections of who we are that are not welcome. For Other wields a power that often overwhelms us and numbs us momentarily from our own sense of Self and personal worth. As a result, we often have difficulty saying no to the requests, demands, and expectations that Others might bring to us, or yes to the gifts and offers that might come our way.

> Once, Shimon ben Antiphorus (first century) hosted some guests and implored them to eat and drink. They declined and swore they were not hungry or thirsty, but eventually they ate and drank anyway. At

the end of their visit, he seized a whip and flung it at them as they fled in terror. When the sages heard of the incident they asked: "Who will investigate and report to us on this matter?" Rabbi Yehoshua stepped forward and said: "I will go." Said they to him: "Go, then, in peace." When he came to the house of Shimon ben Antiphorus, the latter greeted him and he returned the greeting. Said Shimon: "Do you need anything?" Replied Rabbi Yehoshua: "I need a place to lodge." They sat together and studied the Torah.

. . . When the time came for Rabbi Yehoshua to depart, he became worried that perhaps his host was going to whip him. But he let him go in peace. Rabbi Yehoshua stopped midway and called to his host: "Who will escort me [to the road]?" Said Shimon: "I will," and he escorted him part of the way. Rabbi Yehoshua continued on his way in peace and thought to himself: "What will I report to the elders who sent me?" He turned around and went back. Said Shimon: "Rabbi, why did you return?" Said he: "I need to ask you something. It is said that you whip people who come to visit you. If this is so, why did you not whip me, too?" Replied he: "Rabbi, you are greatly wise and authentic in your manners. But these other people who visit me, when I urge them to eat and drink, they swear by the Torah [that they are not hungry or thirsty, and then they end up eating and drinking soon thereafter anyway]. And I have heard from the discourses of the sages that one who makes a vow without intent to keep it is deserving of lashings." Said Rabbi Yehosuha: "If that is the case, then lash out at them also on behalf of the sages who sent me here!" He then returned to the elders and reported what he had experienced at the home of Shimon ben Antiphorus. (Babylonian Talmud, *Derekh Eretz Rabbah* 6)

The story may seem a bit harsh, but the lesson is clear. If Other is reaching out to you, then, unless it is not what you want, do not presume it is an imposition on them. Otherwise, you rob them of their choice, of their personal power, by not allowing them the space to be fully their Self in the moment and in relationship to you. Further, if what is being offered to you is something you need, but you are, again, assuming it is an imposition, then you deprive your Self place, too, of what it needs in the moment. On the contrary, you may end up actually imposing upon an Other when you decline their gesture out of fear of imposing on them, and upon your own Self when their offer is something you need. Conversely, if what the Other is offering you is something that violates your Self place, then decline it. You do not owe anyone an affirmation of their Self power at the expense of your own.

There are those who teach the opposite of this and insist that we are to sacrifice our Self place in deference to Other, and thereby take the teachings of honoring Other to the extreme, far beyond the boundaries of self-worth and self-importance. The eighteenth-century Rabbi Abraham of Vilna writes of his father, Rabbi Eliyahu (known as the Vilna Gaon), that once when he was invited to dine with an Other, he found the meal harmful to his stomach but kept eating it at his host's prodding even though he felt increasingly ill with each bite. When one of his disciples asked him why he tortured himself like that, he replied: "Our sages taught that whatsoever your host commands, so shall you do (Babylonian Talmud, *Derekh Eretz Rabbah* 6). And even though this is a rabbinic injunction (versus a biblical one) we must follow their teachings even at the risk of our lives" (Rabbi Abraham's introduction to Karo's *Shulchan Arukh*, *Orach Chaim*).

But teachers far greater than Rabbi Eliyahu of Vilna remind us again and again about the dictates of the Torah that "you shall *live* by them" (Leviticus 18:5; Ezekiel 20:11, 13, 21; Nehemiah 9:29), to which the ancient rabbis logically added: "And not die by them" (Babylonian Talmud, *Yoma* 85b; *Sanhedrin* 74a). Teachers who recount the above and other such anecdotes to their students as examples of model piety are misleading them. These are not teachings but personal stories about individual people of transcendant spiritual greatness whose actions are reflective solely of what they experienced as rightness for their own personal choices of spiritual betterment. They are not, however, reflective of the Judaic regimen of spiritual discipline.

While it is noble to go all out for a friend even at our own expense, and to make compromises on behalf of others, the fine line is drawn where such action takes us too far outside our Self place and begins to hurt us or to seed resentment. Where is the greatness in keeping humbly silent in deference to an Other's honor when that person is hurting us? On the contrary, in such a situation, our silence, our compromise, is misleading the unwary Other into wrongness by continuing to cause us harm or create in us resentment. As the Torah puts it: "Do not place a stumbling block before the blind" (Leviticus 19:14).

The third-century rabbi Abba Arecha implored marriage-minded couples to make sure they were attracted to one another before tying the knot (Babylonian Talmud, *Kiddushin* 41a) because of the levitical injunction to "love your fellow human as yourself" (Leviticus 19:18). If I am in a relationship situation that is hurting me, and I bear with it nevertheless "for the sake of peace," I end up building resentment and hatred in myself toward the Other and violate the commandment "You shall not hate your brother [or your sister] in your heart" (Leviticus 19:17). "One who marries someone who is incompatible with them," said the first-century Rabbi Akiva, "will come to violate five biblical commandments: 'You shall not take revenge' (Leviticus 19:18), 'You shall not bear a grudge' (Leviticus 19:18), 'You shall not hate your brother in your heart' (Leviticus 19:17), 'You shall love your fellow human as yourself' (Leviticus 19:18), 'Your brother shall dwell with you' (Leviticus 25:36)" (Babylonian Talmud, *Avot D'Rabbi Natan* 26:4). Therefore, if a relationship is destroying you, the ancient rabbis taught, set aside all notions of martyrdom and get out (Babylonian Talmud,

Ketuvot 63b; *Yevamot* 63b. See also Maimonides' *Mishneh Torah, Hilkhot Ishut* 14:8), "for no one can be expected to share a den with a serpent" (Babylonian Talmud, *Yevamot* 112b). Not that the Other is necessarily like a snake, but if the relationship is to you like living in a snake den, it is obviously unsuitable for you.

It is important, then, to honor Other but not at the risk of violating the Self. It is important to compromise for the sake of harmony in a relationship, for example, but not if it means relinquishing our sense of personal Aliveness and Rightness. When what an Other demands of us in compromise begins to chip away at who we are and slowly begins to feel more like we are transforming our Selves into what the Other wishes us to be, then is it time to draw the line. There is a vast difference between honoring someone and paying blind obeisance to them. The fifth of the Ten Commandments wisely refrains from bidding us to *obey* our parents, for example, and instead implores us to *honor* them (Exodus 20:12). The ancient rabbis further qualified the wording of this precept with the following teaching:

> For one might otherwise assume that they must honor their parents' wishes even if they bid them to violate [God's Will]—but Scripture then reminds us, "Everyone shall be in awe of their mother and their father, and my Sabbaths shall they observe" [Leviticus 19:3], meaning that [it is as if God is saying:] "both you and your parents must honor Me." . . . And if your parents tell you to go against [that which is the Will of God], you must not obey them, for both you and they answer to God. (Babylonian Talmud, *Yevamot* 5b-6a)

As discussed in the two previous sections, "Will of God" here implies more than religious observances considered by organized religion to be the Will of God; it includes the God-Will that transcends religious ritual and dogma to address the dignity and well-being of the individual Self. "Do not think badly of yourself," admonished the first-century Rabbi Shimon (Babylonian Talmud, *Avot* 2:13), and certainly do not allow others to make you think badly of yourself. If a parent, then, orders a child to commit an act that would violate the child's Self place and wound their self-image, or sense of personal worth, or rob them of their Aliveness, going dead set against what feels right to them, the child must honor first and foremost the God-Will that a person not hurt like this: the child, that is, must honor first and foremost their precious, valuable Self. Parents are warned not to compel their children to marry, for example, though marriage was considered part of the God-Will (Babylonian Talmud, *Kiddushin* 41a, 81b). "Honor your father and your mother," the decalogue states, not "obey." There are times, Judaism recognizes, when honoring your elders might preclude obeying them. "If the master [God] tells you one thing and the disciple [parent] tells you another, the words of whom do you heed?" (Babylonian Talmud, *Kiddushin* 42b).

Distinctions need to be made, of course, between children at different stages of intellectual and emotional maturity. While a minor is not responsible for discerning between God's will and parental will, a parent should examine carefully if the source of defiance is spiteful disobedience or perhaps a reaction to inappropriate expectations.

It needs mentioning here that a number of Jewish educators have recklessly employed talmudic accounts of how some of the ancient teachers would go to all conceivable lengths to honor their parents even to the point of what would appear as self-compromise. One example is of the fourth-century Rabbi Dimmi, who, when his mother ripped his golden robe off during an important meeting with Roman royalty and whacked him across the face with her sandal and then spat on him, remained passive about it and even retrieved the fallen sandal for her (Babylonian Talmud,

Kiddushin 31a). Or of the first-century Rabbi Tarfon, who let his mother step on him to get into her bed, and who once placed his hands under his mother's feet so she could walk in comfort after the straps of her sandals had torn (Babylonian Talmud, *Kiddushin* 31b; Jerusalem Talmud, *Pe'ah* 2b). Accounts like these are noble and beautiful but ought not be taught without qualification. There is enough child abuse going on, as well as general disregard for the honor of the child, that we should be more careful about how we communicate these stories to our children. These rabbis were adult leaders and teachers, whose self-esteem was intact so that such saintly performances would not damage their sense of self-worth. Such above-and-beyond conduct, then, is not to be expected of the average adult, and certainly not of children. The ideals of the Torah, the fourth-century Rabbis Rava and Pappa remind us, were intended for us as mortals, not as celestial angels (Babylonian Talmud, *Berakhot* 25b; *Yoma* 30a; *Kiddushin* 54a; *Me'ilah* 14b).

To interrupt our involvement in a personal task to meet the needs or reaching-out gesture of an Other, or to extend ourselves beyond our personal comfort zone for someone else, is indeed an opportunity to stretch our spiritual muscles. After all, the way to God, taught the first-century Rabbi Hannina ben Dosa, is through our practice of loving-kindness toward others (Babylonian Talmud, *Avot* 3:10).

When Abraham encountered Malkitzedek, who was also Shem the son of Noah, he asked him: "Through what deed did you merit survival in the Ark during the flood?" Said he: "Through the deed of charity and loving-kindness." Asked Abraham: "How so? Were there beggars aboard that you could perform deeds of charity?" Said he: "No, but we were preoccupied constantly with the care and feeding of countless species of birds, beasts and other animals, each requiring very special attention, and this we did day and night with no sleep." Said Abraham: "If loving-kindness toward birds and beasts can save the world, so much more so can loving-kindness practiced toward other human beings, created in the Image of God!" (*Shochar Tov* on Psalm 37)

We become ennobled and refined each time we stretch our Selves to meet an Other. It is when our stretching goes so far as to start turning into a ripping that we need to draw the line. Be honoring of Other, in other words, but also be just as honoring of yourself. "Let the honor of your friend be as dear to you as your personal honor," taught the first-century Rabbi Eliezer ben Hurcanus (Babylonian Talmud, *Avot* 2:10). And while the Torah reminds us thirty-six times to honor the stranger, the ancient teachers remind us also to honor ourselves: "Honor the stranger like you would honor royalty, but suspect them like you would suspect a thief" (Babylonian Talmud, *Kallah Rabati*, chap. 9). The act of honoring Others, then, should not thereby render them lord and master over you.

> Once Rabbi Yehoshua (first century) invited a stranger to his home and honored him with food, drink and lodging in his loft. After his guest had gone to sleep, Rabbi Yehoshua removed the ladder to the loft. In the middle of the night, the guest removed his shawl, filled it with stolen goods and prepared to descend from the loft. As the ladder was missing, the guest fell to the ground along with his booty. When Rabbi Yehoshua came to investigate, the guest cried: "I did not know you would remove the ladder!" The rabbi replied: "We are entitled to suspect someone like you!" (Babylonian Talmud, *Kallah Rabati*, chap. 9)

But lest we assume that it is toward strangers that we need to conduct ourselves most cautiously and respectfully, the ancients warn us that those most easily hurt by us are those who are most familiar to us: "Humble yourself before others, but humble yourself even more before your [spouse] and children than anyone else" (Babylonian Talmud, *Derekh Eretz*

Zuta 3). Taught the third-century Rav: "Be ever so careful not to hurt the feelings of your [spouse], for their tears are brought on easier [than others], and they are more vulnerable to hurtful gestures from you" (Babylonian Talmud, *Baba Metzia* 59b).

> Rabbi Yisrael Salanter (nineteenth century) once accepted an invitation by a prominent member of the Jewish community to dine with him and his wife on the eve of the Sabbath. The rabbi accepted, and following the synagogue service joined his host at the dinner table and prepared for the blessing over the meal. Suddenly, the man threw an angry fit at his wife for her failure to cover the *challot* (ceremonial bread loaves which are kept covered during the predinner benediction over wine). The woman ran off to the kitchen and remained there, weeping in embarrassment from her husband's reprimand in front of the rabbi. Shocked by his host's behavior, Rabbi Yisrael leaned toward him and said: "I am getting on in years and I am getting more and more forgetful these days. Perhaps you can refresh my memory with the reason behind the custom of covering the *challot*." Proud to be of assistance to the aging sage, the man began a lengthy and eloquent explanation of the custom, delineating how it was in respect to the loaves that they be spared embarrassment from exposure during the ritual attention accorded the wine and its accompanying benediction. When his host had finished, Rabbi Yisrael rose and chastised him: "You are so meticulous about a mere custom of showing respect to a loaf of bread and making sure you don't embarrass it?! And yet you are so quick and light about dishonoring your wife and hurting her feelings?! I cannot eat with you. This home is not kosher!" He put on his coat and started to leave, when the man hurried into the kitchen and pleaded with his wife to forgive him. (Heard from Rabbi Shlomo Carlebach)

How true it is that we often become more conscientious about our honoring of strangers or even friends than of the honor and feelings of those closest to us. Many cultures do indeed practice zealous hospitality toward their guests, often sacrificing the emotional and physical dignity of their family members. The Torah certainly makes a big thing out of hospitality to the stranger, though not in the vacuum that some people perceive it, but rather in the context of a much larger teaching about dealing gently and sensitively with people generally, not just strangers. Your spouse is your guest. Your child is your guest. Your Self is your guest:

> Each day when Hillel the Elder (first century B.C.E.) would take leave of his disciples, they would ask him: "Where is the rabbi going?" and he would reply: "To perform a deed of lovingkindness for a guest in the house." One time they asked him: "But do you have a guest every day?" Replied Hillel: "Yes, is not the soul a guest in the body? After all, today it is here, and tomorrow it is gone." (*Leviticus Rabbah* 34:3)

Conscientious relationship-ing, however, whether with Self or Other, whether with family and friend or stranger, is more than a process of moral and humanistic furtherance. It is also a process of self-ennoblement and personal spiritual growth. In wholesomely relating with Other, our own persona gets stirred into wakefulness from otherwise dormant or stuck places toward actualization and fruition. We each draw forth from one another attributes of our Self that would otherwise collect dust and mildew. Your relationship with me will mirror back to me my most illuminated parts as well as my darkest shadows. The reactions you trigger in me by your words or actions will put me more clearly in touch with what is OK inside me and with what is unresolved and needs healing. Taught the second-century Rabbi Nattan: "Do not rebuke your friend for faults that are really your own" (Babylonian Talmud, *Baba Metzia* 59b). Or as the third-century Rabbi Shmuel put it: "One who is always condemning others, probably sees in them his own faults" (Babylonian Talmud, *Kiddushin* 70a).

We each carry a key capable of unlocking the Other, and buried inside every one of us are clues to someone else's mystery of Self. How we choose to engage in relationship with one another, therefore, will determine whether each of our Selves gets shoved farther back into dormancy or gets drawn forward into personal Aliveness. In every man, for instance, there are attributes that are feminine, and in every woman there are attributes that are masculine. As the Torah puts it: "Male and female did God create them, and called *their* name Adam" (Genesis 1:27, 5:2). The fourth- century Rabbi Yirmiah ben Elazar understood this to imply that primordial man and woman were one and the same being before they were split into two separate persons, each manifesting separate gender qualities (Babylonian Talmud, *Berakhot* 61a; Genesis 2:21–22). In a healthy relationship, each honors the Other and the Other's process and coaches forth from themselves qualities that they see realized in the Other. And each then grows into more and more wholeness of being. For it is in woman that man sees the reflection of his own femininity, and, conversely, it is in Man that Woman connects with her masculine self.

It should not be misconstrued, however, that relationships with members of the same gender would lack the benefit of self-actualization. The biblical story of David and Jonathan is but one such example, as is the story of Ruth and Naomi. In both instances, there is a deep attraction of personalities down to the soul level. Of David and Jonathan it is written: "And it came to pass that the soul of Jonathan became interwoven with the soul of David, and Jonathan loved him as his own soul" (1 Samuel 18:1, 3). In the story of Ruth and Naomi, it is clear that Ruth was drawn to Naomi very intensely, and saw her not only as a mentor but as a very intimate friend: "And [Ruth] cleaved unto [Naomi] . . . and said, 'Do not ask me to leave you and to desist from following you. For wherever you will go, I will go. And wherever you will rest, I will rest. Your people shall be my people, and your

God shall be my God. And where you will die, so, too, will I, and I shall be buried there as well. . . . For nothing but death itself shall separate us'" (Ruth 1:16-17).

A similar quality of relationship is described in the Bible between the matriarch Sarah and her "maid-servant" Hagar (Genesis 16:1). Clearly Hagar was no maid-servant, a blatant mistranslation of the Hebrew word used, which is *shiff-khah*, akin to *mish-pakhah*, or family. Both words are spelled exactly alike but for the *M*, which prefixes the word for family. Hagar, then, as well as Bilhah and Zilpah, the *shiff-khah* of Leah and of Rachel, the wives of Jacob, were not servants but friendship-sisters who agreed to be surrogate mothers when their sister-companions were unable to bear children (Genesis 30:3, 9). No wonder, then, that when Sarah complains to Abraham about Hagar and asks him to send her away, Abraham's response comes across as: "Listen, this is about you and her, so it is up to you two to work it out, not me" (Genesis 16:5-6). The sistership between the two in that story obviously got sabotaged after Hagar had entered also into relationship with Abraham at Sarah's request (Genesis 16:2-4). Nothing of the sort, however, is recorded about Leah and Rachel's relationship with their sister-companions Bilhah and Zilpah after they, too, entered into relationship with Jacob for childbearing purposes. Everyone, the biblical stories demonstrate, is very different from the next, and their dances with various forms of relationship differ as well. Note, then, how the fracturing of the sister-companion relationship between Hagar and Sarah resulted in thousands of years of animosity between the descendants of both (Jews and Arabs), whereas the relative harmony of the relationship between Rachel, Leah, Bilhah, and Zilpah resulted in the forging of a single nation that exists to this very day (the Jewish people).

The institution of heterosexual marriage, too, is not considered by Judaism as the sole context even for sexual forms of intimate relationship. The eighteenth-century Rabbi Jacob Emden, for example, notes how nowhere in the Torah does it say that one must marry (*Sheilot Yaavetz*, vol. 2, no. 15, end of para. 10). Marriage, he writes, is recorded in the Torah only in passing and in contexts that imply it to be optional (e.g., Deuteronomy 22:13; 24:1—"*when* a man takes a woman to wife . . ."). Nonmarital living together is therefore not forbidden in Judaism and the offspring of such unions have full inheritance rights and rights to the priesthood if the father was a Kohen (Rabbi Jacob Emden, *Sheilot Yaavetz*, vol. 2, no. 15, end of sec. 10; letter of the thirteenth-century Rabbi Moshe ben Nachman to Rabbi Yonah, quoted in *Teshuvot HaRashba*, no. 284; sixteenth-century Rabbi Moshe Isserles [Ramma] and seventeenth-century Rabbi Shmuel ben Uri [Beit Shmuel] on Karo's *Shulchan Arukh*, *Even HaEzer* 26:1). Marriage is of course recommended across the board in mainstream Jewish teaching, but it is not necessarily based upon the infrastructure of Torah. Mortal religious leaders will insist that marriage and procreation are biblical imperatives, but the God-Word to "be fruitful and multiply" is written as a blessing, not an imperative (Genesis 1:28, 9:1). In fact, the fourth-century Rabbi Hiyya taught that not only is a woman not required by the Torah to bear children, but she also has the right to medicinally sterilize herself (Babylonian Talmud, *Yevamot* 65b; *Tosefta Yevamot* 8:2).

Where Judaism stands on sexual intimacy between members of the same gender is not as clear-cut as mainstream Jewish orthodoxy makes it out to be. Lesbianism, for example, was indeed tabooed by the rabbis throughout history but is not included among the prohibitions of the Torah. It is not even proscribed in talmudic literature and is mentioned there solely by the third-century Rabbi Hunna in the context of those women who are disqualified from marriage to a High Priest. In the final ruling the rabbis vetoed Hunna's stance and permitted lesbians in marriage to a *kohen*. But never was female homosexuality forbidden outright by Judaic law (Maimonides' *Perush L'Mishnayot* on *Sanhedrin* 54a: "It is neither a biblical nor a rabbinic prohibition"). Attempts to legislate against it resulted in little more than a passing value judgment about it being "merely immodest behavior" (Babylonian Talmud, *Yevamot* 76a). But as the fourth-century Rabbi Abbaya put it: "Since when did the Torah ever prohibit immodest behavior?" (Babylonian Talmud, *Yevamot* 55b; *Sotah* 26b). Others tried to link it to the Torah's prohibition against emulating the practices of ancient Egypt (Leviticus 18:3), one of which they alleged was marriage between two women (*Sifra* on Leviticus 18:3). Even if there was indeed marital sanction of lesbian relationships in ancient Egypt and Canaan, the practices forbidden to the Israelites were those associated with cultic rites alone, certainly not social customs (Babylonian Talmud, *Avodah Zarah* 11a; thirteenth-century Rabbi Nissim Gerondi [Ran] on Babylonian Talmud, *Avodah Zarah* 11a; Ramma on Karo's *Shulchan Arukh*, *Yoreh De'ah* 178:1), and, anyway, we do not derive religious legislation from homiletical or any other form of interpretive speculation (Jerusalem Talmud, *Pe'ah* 9b; *Kohelet Rabati* 6:2).

The proverbial religious prohibition against male homosexuality, however, appears to be spelled out more conspicuously in the Bible in the contexts of laws forbidding the ancient Jews from emulating the cultic practices of specific nations (Leviticus 18:3, 22; 20:13, 23; Deuteronomy 23:18). Yet it is wrong and antithetical to Judaic moral and legal process to weave blanket applications out of homophobia and personal value judgment. It is wrong for us to judge its implication for anyone. Certainly the Torah has as much room for the homosexual as for the heterosexual. Certainly is God indiscriminate, caring for all of us (*Exodus Rabbah* 21:4) regardless of our sexual orientations. What God is

described again and again as despising is when we hurt one
another, when we reject someone, when we make judgments
about Other. That is the greater abomination of the two. How
quick religion is to cry out in torment at the "sin" of homosexuality and yet give out hardly so much as a whisper against
the violent crimes of abuse against wife, girlfriend, and child,
for example, which pervade a significant segment of the
goody-goody "religiously correct" heterosexual population.
If we want to earnestly wrestle with interpreting the Torah's
teachings about sexual morality in relationship to contemporary real-life issues, then we need to do that wrestling with
the same authenticity and practical down-home blend of
compassion, reasoning, and assessment with which all other
issues were dealt through the ages. This involves fending not
only for the Torah but also for people who because of their
sexual orientation may find the Torah an obstacle. It involves
not only extending ourselves for the perpetuation of the God-
Word, but also for the God-Will. The God-Word has been
confined to finite texts and largely frozen creed; but the God-
Will flows freely through our hearts, both from the place of
creed and also in spite of it. Perhaps that is why the ancient
teachers dared to play at all with interpreting biblical capital
offenses, especially around the prohibitions against certain
nonviolent, consensual sexual acts such as adultery and male
homosexuality. To qualify for the capital violation of these
acts, for example, there had to be actual genital intromission.
Anything short of that was still disallowed but was not considered a violation of the biblical offense (Babylonian Talmud, *Yevamot* 54a–56a; *Sotah* 26b; *Niddah* 13a; see Maimonides' *Perush L'Mishnayot* on *Sanhedrin* 54a).

Sadly, religious orthodoxy across the denominations has
still not dealt with the issue of homosexuality except to
judgmentally condemn the whole kit and caboodle lock,
stock, and barrel with a zealousness that is far more deviant

from Jewish living than is homosexual behavior. Throughout Jewish history, the rabbis have repeatedly wrestled with biblical writ when in certain situations and periods it blocked rather than furthered human physical and spiritual aliveness. "At times," the second-century Rabbi Shimon ben Lakish taught, "the violation of Torah is its very preservation" (Babylonian Talmud, *Menachot* 99b). Even a nonemergency issue such as necromancy, which—like male homosexuality—is recorded in the Torah as a capital offense (Leviticus 20:27), managed to get reinterpreted enough so that certain forms of occult practice were exempted and allowed (Babylonian Talmud, *Sanhedrin* 67b, 101a; *Eruvin* 43a; *Pesachim* 110a; *Numbers Rabbah* 11:5; *Ecclestiastes Rabbah* 2:6; Meiri on *Sanhedrin* 67b; Maharal in *B'er HaGolah*, treatise 2, pp. 29–30). If ways were found to circumvent the prohibition against invoking demons, there must also be ways to make peace between the Torah's prohibition against male homosexuality and those whose lifestyles are inevitably at odds with that prohibition. A number of contemporary rabbis who are acclaimed also as medical-ethics authorities have written books and articles on homosexuality, declaring it inexcusable since it is a curable "pathology." The label inexcusable, however, belongs not to men whose sexual orientation is male, but to rabbis who render judgments about them without understanding them. How many of these rabbinic "experts," for instance, have actually befriended a gay or lesbian person and endeavored to understand their world? To sit behind a desk laden with sacred writ and legal codes will not bring us an iota closer to reconciling religious idealism with mortal reality.

Mirroring, or *partzuf*-ing, is therefore, again, a process intrinsic to the dynamics of wholesome human relationshiping in any context. It constitutes the subtle, underlying, sometimes unconscious intent of choosing to and implementing an encounter with an Other. Whatever it is that draws people together, and that might extend also to include physical intimacy or the desire thereof, needs to be acknowledged and honored as a particular manifestation of a specific yearning of the soul. We may not always understand what it is about the Other that draws the Self to him or her. Perhaps the Other offers something that complements something in the Self that beckons for completion, or perhaps the Other offers a unique opportunity for learning something, realizing something. Whatever it is, it is not always readily clear, and usually not at all clear. For example, it is not uncommon that we are drawn to someone, either for friendship, play, or romance, only to become bitterly disappointed later that what seemed at first to be compatibility was not. However, we might want to entertain the more positive possibility that the compatibility we assumed was in fact true and real, though perhaps not as experientially complete and all-encompassing as we imagined it to be. Deep down, something inside of us *was* attracted to qualities of, or experiences with, the Other that felt and, indeed, *were* complementary. Instead of only decrying what might have been, or judging ourselves for having chosen wrongly, we might rather want to take inventory of what advancements were made in our personal growth nonetheless, and of which pieces of the puzzle of our lives we have come away with. In other words, it might be a healthy exercise when we have to let go of friendships or relationships to focus not so much on what we have lost but on what we have gained; not so much on what we feel was taken from us, but also on what was given to us.

However, in our quest to complement the black holes in our Selves, the voids, the missing pieces, what we should be looking for in the Other are not solely the attributes, the particular ingredients we feel missing in our own lives, but, more importantly, the possibility of their processes. Whether an appliance *features* all its necessary equipment and accessories, for example, is not nearly as important as whether they actually function, and whether the quality of that functioning is compatible with our particular needs. Much frustration in relationship-ing is a result of assumptions about people, and assumptions, equally as mistaken, about ourselves, about what we are really needing, wanting, and looking for in an Other.

The key word again is *process*. In other words, we are not here to achieve wholeness, but to engage its process. As the first-century Rabbi Tarfon taught: "The work is not upon you to complete; but neither are you exempt from trying" (Babylonian Talmud, *Avot* 2:16). And so the world is set up so that no matter how "whole" you might get, you can always take yet another step, and another. Wholeness is not an objective but a process. Perfection is not a goal but a process. Life is dynamic, dynamism is life, and when it gets static, something has died within. Achieving a static state of wholeness in life is counter to life and living. It has no place in this reality. It is literally counterproductive. As the ancient rabbis put it: "One who says 'I have nothing but Torah,' has not even got Torah" (Babylonian Talmud, *Yevamot* 109b). Rabbi Zalman Schachter-Shalomi has a slightly different way of saying it: "When people start telling you they've got only Light in their lives, it's probably time to light a match for them" (conversation with the author).

Relationship-ing, too, needs to be seen as a process, not a goal. The term *settle down*, for example, is a poor one, even a dangerous one, for people deciding to get married. It is born out of the romantically ideal illusion that getting married is the culmination rather than the onset of a process. The end of the process of finding a partner is only the beginning of the process of living with them. Instead of saying, "I've found someone, so now I can finally settle down," we ought to be saying, "I've found someone, so now I can start yet one more chapter of my life process."

Basking in the bliss of communion with God, Abraham was in Nirvana, was whole as ever could be, yet he is portrayed as jumping to his feet in the middle of it all and running to tend to three wayfarers walking in the distance (Genesis 18:1–2). His sense of priority is not lost in the euphoria of God-ing. The gift of meeting God in another creature is great enough that it is not lost on a man orbiting the Godhead itself. Interestingly, the three strangers turn out to be angels. Angels are described in Judaic thought as earthly manifestations of God's will (e.g., eighteenth-century Rabbi Moshe Chaim Luzzatto in *Derekh HaShem* [*Way of God*] 2:5:3). The lesson then is that in our life processes we need to stay as grounded as possible, we need to be involved with our God, our spirituality, through the gift of the life we experience here and now in our day-to-day relationships with Other, through the "angels," the earthly manifestation of the God-Will that spirits each of us.

As seed in the world of ideal we are all that we *are*, but not all that we can *become*; we are encased in all our potentials, but remain barren of their fruition until we become implanted in the garden of the living, in the whirlwind of interactive dynamics that is life. The distinction, too, is made between the oneness of God *before* Creation, and the oneness of God *after* Creation. Before Creation, God was One, and since Creation, God has been One-ing. Before Creation God was unity, and after Creation God has been unifying. Before Creation God was self-contained singledom; and since Creation God has been all-inclusive collectivity, the One Creator of the many Creations that all share a single origin (sixteenth-century Rabbi Yehudah Loew of Prague [Maharal] in *Derekh Chaim* on Babylonian Talmud, *Avot* 5:1, paras. 4, 5). Likewise, in any relationship each party should remember about their Self and about the Other that prior to the relationship each existed in spite of and separate from the Other, and that the oneness both experience through the vehicle of their relationship should therefore not dismiss the quality of complete and separate individuality of each. If, on the other hand, neither party has an idea of where the Self ends and the Other begins, little process can occur, and the aliveness of each gets lost in the glob.

In the Torah, God is described by many different names, each name born in the moment of an experience of the Creator by the created, each name a momentary snapshot of someone's split-second glimpse of what God is. Idolatry, then, takes root when that momentary experience gets etched in stone, when a glimpse of the infinite gets locked in the finite and trapped in time and space; when we start worshiping the snapshot itself. But God, Judaism teaches, is forever dancing, forever in Aliveness and Flow. "And the Spirit of God is sweeping across the face of the waters" (Genesis 1:2). And so when Moses asks God for the dynamic name, the is-ing name, when God is asked the God-Name from the earthly, organic world of Free Will, the response is no longer a noun such as God or Almighty, but in the verb "*Ehyeh Asher Ehyeh*" (Exodus 3:14), which in its most raw form means simultaneously "I Was What I Was," "I Am What I Am," and "I Will Be What I Will Be." In other words: "Don't peg Me. I am fluid. I can't be pinned down."

Likewise, we need to beware of sculpting "graven images" of those with whom we establish relationships, of becoming stuck on momentary glimpses of who they are in the moment, without also leaving infinite space for their unfoldings, for who they are becoming, whether that fits our original snapshot of them, or not. This is the paramount challenge in any relationship, to see the Other truly as everflowing, evergrowing, everchanging; not to impose staticness on the

Other, whether in our illusions or in the framework of relationship that we establish with them.

We all yearn for some sense of security in our lives, whether it be in our careers or in our personal relationships. But we cannot nurture this yearning at the expense of someone else's Aliveness and sense of being. We cannot create others in our image. The proverbial Ten Commandments have for long been left etched in stone, its broader, everdynamic lessons petrified in lifelessness. If we free the words "Thou shalt not murder," for example, we will discover the broader application which the ancient teachers employed, such as: "One who shames another person in public, it is as if they had murdered them" (Babylonian Talmud, *Baba Metzia* 58b). "Do not commit adultery" was also translated as "Don't undress someone in your mind" (Babylonian Talmud, *Kallah* 1; *Leviticus Rabbah* 23:12)—in other words, don't even so much as entertain the notion of using someone for your personal gain or pleasure. Free the words "Thou shalt not steal," and we might find them in a pizza shop where a couple on a date are robbing each other of crucial information each needs to make some vital judgments and choices, something the ancient rabbis labeled *geneivat daat*—"thievery of information" (Babylonian Talmud, *Tosefta Baba Kamma* 7:3). "Do not bring false testimony against your fellow" can easily include bad-mouthing someone as in Exodus 23:1. And "Do not covet what your neighbor has" could mean: "Get a life of your own."

Perhaps we can take this even further, recasting the entire decalogue as it would apply to relationships (we will use the word *beloved* here to imply anyone with whom we are in relationship, whether child, parent, sibling, lover, or friend):

"You shall have no other gods before My Face"—Don't neglect your beloved by placing a higher priority upon your career, your hobby, or social responsibilities and expectations. Don't become oblivious to your beloved's presence in the company of others, for example, so that you end up seeming absent to them.

"Do not sculpt for yourself an engraved image"—Don't imprison your relationship in set imagery, in a set notion of what it is, leaving no room for what it can become. Don't drain your beloved of their dynamic life flow, of their internal changes and processes, even when you fear that their journey might possibly move in a direction other than your own. "For I am God who has taken you out of Egypt (*mitzrayim* in Hebrew, which means "constrictedness") from the house of bondage"—in other words, to keep someone trapped in one place when their soul calls out for unfolding is to enslave them, and is in opposition to what God is and does: liberation from our stuckness.

"Do not submit to an alien god"—Don't create a relationship standard that is alien to one or both of you, that is contrary to your or your beloved's sense of aliveness and rightness. Make sure your definition of relationship is shared by your beloved, and that it is a definition established by what resonates as true for you both. Do not follow after the ideals of relationship instituted by societal dictates or religious dogma when those ideals are alien to your or your beloved's rightness of being. Moreover, don't introduce into the relationship people or things that are detrimental to it, that would threaten it or betray it, such as unwholesome social liaisons, or a satellite dish at a time when you and your beloved are experiencing problems in communication.

"Remember the Sabbath day to make it special"—Remember to take time off from your life routine to hang out with your beloved. Remember every several years to sit down

with your beloved and reexamine your respective definitions of the relationship and whether or not it needs re-
defining or reformatting to more closely fit where both of
you are in that moment and where both of you are headed
tomorrow. In other words, every now and then take time
out to get an oil change and check the air pressure, change
the filter and grease the axles, check for leaks and examine the brakes. Worst of all, we don't want anyone over-
heating, so go over the cooling system as well and make
sure all the hoses are intact. Every seven years or so, Rabbi
Dr. Zalman Schachter-Shalomi cautions couples in particular, "redo your vows, rewrite your covenants and review
your relationship definitions" (in conversation with the
author).

"Honor your father and your mother"—Honor your past, the
birthing phases of your life process, even if you are today
in a whole different place. And honor this in others, too.
Moreover, don't expect your beloved to be always how
they were in the past. Honor how it was and make room
for how it has changed. After all, the wording is not—as
people commonly read it—"Obey your father and your
mother," but "honor them." We need to honor our past
processes—our father and our mother—which ultimately
gave birth to our present processes, but without either
blind or guilt-driven obeisance to other definitions and
other paradigms.

"Thou shalt not murder"—Don't kill the Aliveness of your
beloved by depriving them of the personal space and honoring they need to be fully themselves, or by putting them
down for choices and wishes that are important to their
Self.

"Thou shalt not commit adultery"—Don't sabotage whatever
your beloved has acquired for their Self that they hold as

personal in the space they consider their private domain and that is separate from and inconsequential to the relationship. Don't read your beloved's private diary or mail. Do not assume, in other words, that just because you are in a relationship there are no "secrets" between you. There are. Or at least there should be space for it. Remember that each of you is who you are not only because of, but also in spite of, the relationship you share together. Both parties are entitled to their personal space, to their secrets, to maintain a sacred corner of their life that is theirs and theirs alone, and that distinguishes their Essential Self from that part of their Self that is in relationship with Other.

"Thou shalt not steal"—Don't hold back from your beloved what they ought to know about your own needs and hopes, from life and from them, for your personal Aliveness and for your shared relationship. Don't deprive them of such information and then blame them for not guessing or figuring it out or knowing all along. Don't steal from them what they needed to have in order to be in relationship with you more wholesomely.

"Thou shalt not bear false witness"—Don't keep from your beloved praise or criticism, thereby leading them to think less of themselves or to think they're doing right by themselves and by you when they are not. Don't allow them to go on thinking that you're OK in the relationship when you're not. And don't allow them to think you aren't when you are.

"Thou shalt not covet"—Don't hate your beloved for being in the limelight at times more than you, or for attaining status or things you haven't been able to attain, or for seeming more skilled than you are at a particular task or profession. Rather, look into yourself and figure out what is blocking you from celebrating their moments of glory; what is clogging the plumbing that your love for them has trouble circulating to this particular arena, of rejoicing for your beloved's happiness; and what is blocking *you* from discovering and gardening your own potentials.

In the Jewish mystical discussion of Creation, the Creator's act of *tzimtzum*—making space in the All-God Presence for the existential possibility of Other—was followed by *shevirat hakelim*, or the shattering of the vessels (the big bang?). As the God-Will to create filled the space formed by the vacuum of stepping back, of *tzimtzum*, the resulting universe became a vessel that was capable solely of receiving but not of giving. And so it became filled with so much God-Light that it exploded, and in so doing became a vessel capable of receiving as well as yielding, of containing as well as pouring forth. It is in that universe that our world was conceived. A world of give and take, of inhaling and exhaling, of to and fro, of back and forth; a universe in which there could be dance, where life could be dynamic rather than static. In such a universe there is room for receiving only when there is also the capacity to give, of feeling loved only when there is also the capacity to love.

Shevirat hakelim is experienced by the average person at least some of the time. When you are the recipient of potent dosages of loving from someone and it is coming from a place of authenticity and altruism, you may experience an "explosion," a bursting-forth transformation in your heart that leaves in its wake amoebic stages of evolving love for the Other, the very beginnings of a wholesome *partzuf* process. Likewise when you are the recipient of abundant gifts from the wellspring of Life, from the planet, from the stock market, or from hanging out in the Chiracahua Mountains of New Mexico, for example, you may feel the *Shevirat hakelim* that happens in your gut as you are filled beyond your finite mortal capacity with blessing or with wonderment. And from that explosion will come forth a desire to give something back to the earth, or to share of your fiscal fortune with those less fortunate than yourself, or to return the partzufic gesture with a "halleluyah!" No sooner does David cry, "My cup runneth over [with God's benevolence!]" than he undergoes a microcosmic *shevirat hakelim* and explodes with desire to do something in return, to *partzuf* back to his Creator: "[I will be] Good [to my Self] and [will practice] benevolence [toward others. The desire to be in the world this way] shall pursue me all the days of my life" (Psalms 23:5-6; bracketed interpretation based on commentary of the twelfth-century Rabbi Abraham Ibn Ezra on Psalms 23:6, quoted in *Mikraot Gedolot*, Psalms 23:5-6).

New universes of love between people, graduating plateaus of relationship quality, do not happen from one solitary *shevirat hakelim* explosion in the moment of a marriage proposal, or of a commitment to move in with someone, or of bringing a child into the world. They happen rather in repeating again and again the cosmic dance of Creation played out in the microcosmic theater of relationship dynamics between lover and beloved, and between parent and child. And the choreography goes something like this: Step back a few steps to see the Other as truly a completely separate being from your Self (*tzimtzum*), then move in to manifest your will for the relationship to be from a place of altruistic honoring and loving (fill the vacuum with your presence), and then step back to leave space for response from the Other to what it is you are giving (*shevirat hakelim*).

Easily the most common impediments to the fluidity of a relationship are the assumptions and expectations with which people engage each other in relationship. Expectations are programmed into the software of our relationships and emotions either by societal definitions or by our own personal needs and hopes. Unfulfilled expectations and hopes in a person lead to instant resentment not of the situation but of the other person. When we expect an Other to respond to our *partzuf*-ing, to make responsive moves in our relationship dance, it is almost like collecting on an unwritten emotional IOU. When this happens it is time to *tzimtzum* again, but this time not for the purpose of creating relationship universes but rather to get back to the place of honoring the other as a distinct and separate Other whose hopes and desires in the moment may not necessarily correspond to our own, regardless of whether they did in the past. We must realize that we cannot receive all that we need and want in life from any one individual. If we try to do so we end up overloading the circuits and blowing the fuse that sparked the relationship/friendship to begin with. We ought indeed to want to have what we wish for, but it is the expectation of its fulfillment that often gets in the way of its attainment. In general, this is true with all of life: though you want it all, expect little and you will appreciate more and will be disappointed less. As an old cowboy saying goes: "Though I want everything—I expect nothing and appreciate anything."

If in a relationship with Other we find ourselves stuck, and experience our vessel as empty, as lacking the nourishment we had hoped to receive or once received but no longer, then we need also to check whether the blockage might be from our having too many expectations and assumptions of the Other, or perhaps from an obsession to receive.

Often it is the all out will to *get* that blocks the universe from giving us richness in the moment, and which therefore blocks *us* from giving, and which consequently blocks our life process from unfolding.

Much of the frustrations brought on by expectations and assumptions in a relationship can be avoided through clear and open communication. It is important to spell out what it is you expect from a relationship with someone, and to spell it out not with your diary or your confidant but with your relationship partner. It is also a wholesome practice for relationship partners to share openly with one another their respective definitions of the flavor of relationship they are looking for. Too often what happens instead is that people assume compatibility across the board once they've "fallen in love," that each shares the same culturally formatted definitions of relationship. And so all the questions and discussions that should be articulated before marriage, for example, get conveniently swept under the red carpet leading to the wedding canopy, only to emerge as betrayed feelings during marriage counseling several years later. Relationship partners are frequently also stricken with amnesia around the notion of asking for something. The idea of asking our partners outright for something we want or need from them for our Aliveness in the relationship gets easily buried in the weed-infested garden of assumptions:

> The foundation of good communication is conscious listening. No matter how articulate you or another person might be, if one or both of you do not adequately understand what the other means to be saying, communication is impaired. Also important for good communication is making clear and effective requests. Many of us are taught that the parties of a relationship ought to "just know" what each wants or needs "without either having to say so!" It is a combination of both these skills—conscious listening and clear request—which formulate the most essential ingredients for effective conflict resolution. (Lakme Batya Elior in a presentation at the Chicago Counseling and Psychotherapy Center Summer Institute, Chicago, 1990)

From ancient times forward, Judaism stressed the importance of conscientious engagement of relationship in any form, whether business or romance. Judaic law therefore permitted the annulment of either if they were engaged under false pretenses or by misinformation. If you bought a diamond because you were led to think it was from India and it turned out it was from Nova Scotia, the purchase agreement would become null and void and you were entitled to your money back (Babylonian Talmud, *Betzah* 7a). If you entered a marriage with someone you believed to be emotionally sound and he or she turned out to be psychotic, you were entitled to an annulment because the marriage was founded upon erroneous assumption, or *mekach ta'ot* (Babylonian Talmud, *Kiddushin* 48b-50a; *Iggrot Moshe, Even HaEzer*, vol. 1, nos. 79, 80; ibid., vol. 3, no. 46). The ancient rabbis therefore discouraged blind marriage arrangements prevalent then—and even now in some communities—and instead urged people to make sure they first met and liked someone before they married them (Babylonian Talmud, *Kiddushin* 40a). The rabbis even heaped praise upon women who delayed their marriages for however long "until they found men who were worthy of them" (Babylonian Talmud, *Baba Batra* 119a). In all matters of acquisition, they taught, the general rule was: "One does not negotiate about something which has not yet come into the world" (Babylonian Talmud, *Baba Batra* 79b; *Baba Metzia* 33a), which has not yet become a part of your life experience. That includes as well the unspoken expectations and assumptions with which we tend to negotiate our relationships. Another adage taught in the context of business relationship, which is equally applicable to personal relationship, is: "If you seek to claim something from an Other, the burden of proof is upon you" (Babylonian Talmud, *Baba Kamma* 35a [Mishnah]). In other words, if you feel your partner owes you something in the relationship that you felt was promised, it is up to you to verbalize your feelings rather than assume it will be spontaneously forthcoming. In a great many instances you might discover that your

partner was not withholding from you that which you needed
from them, but that you were withholding from your partner the information *they* needed from you to bring you the
gifts of relationship that you had been expecting from them.

Assumptions and expectations can also sabotage a relationship when there is conflict or when the relationship is
stalled and neither party is making a move because each assumes it is the responsibility of the Other to take the first
step. Hillel the Elder (first century B.C.E.) taught that in a situation where there is no Other taking care of what needs tending to, "then you yourself shall endeavor to become the *ish*,"
to become the one who is doing what needs to be done
(Babylonian Talmud, *Avot* 2:5). *Ish* literally means "man," and
ishah means "woman," but both words are rooted in the word
esh for "fire." Another rendering, then, would be: "In a relationship where there is no *esh*, no spark, no aliveness, then
you yourself shall endeavor to become the *esh*," the fire. Thus,
each of us, rather than wait for the Other, should initiate the
peace making or healing when there is an impasse or conflict; both share the responsibility of rejuvenating the relationship when the romance has gone flat. "They say of Rabbi
Yochanan ben Zakkai (first century) that no one was ever
able to preempt his greeting them, for he was always the first
to initate greetings to all people—believers in God or worshipers of the stars—wherever he ventured" (Babylonian
Talmud, *Berakhot* 17a).

We need, however, to recall here once more that while
there is compromise in a relationship, which can be noble
and foster healing, there is also self-compromise in a relationship, which can be destructive and emotionally waste-
ful. If after playing *esh* for a while there is no reactive com-
bustion but, rather, we are left burning ourselves out trying
to fix a relationship, then it is time to pass the torch to the
Olympic runner and direct our energies elsewhere.

The ancient Jewish prophets describe their visions of the God-Presence in the physical world as if their visualization took place through a sapphire stone (Exodus 24:10; Ezekiel 1:26). Each of us is like a sapphire stone. And in our soul-deep yearnings to image and merge with the Wellspring of Life from which we originate, we dance with each other like the sapphire stone dances with light—for we are each a prism of the common light we share together. And like the sapphire stone we both absorb and reflect our experiences of Other and transform them into a variety of colors as we spin. And as we turn and stir in the dynamic kiln of life, we flex our manifest Selves to accommodate in unique ways distinct sorts of relationships, be it romantic friendship, platonic, intimate, sibling, parental, soul, and so forth; our behavior is directed and affected in varying ways by our interaction with different personalities and under differing circumstances.

Therefore, when people are relationship-ing—whether starting a new level of Aliveness, or initiating a new project together, or simply fostering friendship—a sacred space is created in that moment for dynamic relationship-ing between the Creator and the Created, between God and the physical universe. The *Shekhinah*—the dwelling place of God, the metaphoric sapphire image reflection of the divine—is then drawn more and more into the human experience through the longing of cosmic unification played out in the mircrocosmic arena of relationship (Babylonian Talmud, *Avot* 3:6). When two people make love with one another, the first-century Rabbi Akiva taught, and their union is coming from a place of mutual longing to become in the moment one with each other and with their shared cosmic origin, "the *Shekhinah* is drawn to them" (Babylonian Talmud, *Sotah* 17a, based on Rabbi Moshe ben Nachman's interpretation in *Iggeret HaKodesh*, chap. 2, para. 4). The quality of sacred space created between two people determines the extent of the presence of God in their interaction, in their relationship. That space is created by the kind of respect and honor that each gives to the other and by the degree in which each steps back, so to speak, in order to allow for the other to emerge further, a reenactment of the Creation process during the initial phase of *tzimtzum*. The sanctification of this space is also determined by how conscious each is of the Otherness of the other person, of the Other's individuality and total separateness.

In counseling couples—marriage partners, siblings, parents talking about their children, or adults talking about visits with *their* parents—some of the most common complaints have been: "He spoiled my mood!" and "If she hadn't been such a grouch, I could have had a wonderful time!" and "Couldn't they see I was depressed?! They kept right on walking around singing and laughing!" Applied in such situations, *tzimtzum* means, get your Self place back off the Other's shoulders onto your own. Find a way to keep your own moods legitimate while at the same time making space for others to keep theirs. When people experience themselves as totally not heard unless the world around them behaves as if it feels identically as they do, there is barely room for even an I-It relationship. Then they lose sense of their right to be Self and of the Other's existence as separate and unique. But since the fact is that each Self and Other does exist, friction becomes inevitable. In such a situation, step back and declare, "This is *my* space and in that space I feel sad/happy/bleak and so forth. And over there is *your* space and you seem to feel bleak/ happy/sad and so forth. Now I'll listen to you, or you'll listen to me, and then we'll trade."

The phrase in the Torah, "flesh of my flesh, bone of my bone" (Genesis 2:23) applies to lovers and family members alike, for the time being or for a lifetime. But it does not say "thought of my thought, feeling of my feeling." So when it is your turn to listen to the Other, take a deep breath, and set your complete strivings, thoughts, and feeling to the side. Bring only your essential humanness and deep honoring of the Other to the listening arena, and keep them company. Do not dismiss your Self in the process by thinking: "As soon as I understand you, of course I'll agree and forget all about what I've been feeling just now." Rather, listen with the certainty that your psyche will continue to hold your point of view fully intact, and just listen to the magic, the weird and wonderful newness that is this Other person.

An integral part of the consciousness of honoring someone else as an Other is the realization that you can never know all of the Other as you can never know all of God, only those attributes which are revealed. As more of God's attributes, for example, become revealed to you in the experiences of your life through time and searching, so, too, do the attributes of the person you are trying to know. But the awareness that you will never fully know the other (any more than the other fully knows him or herself or, indeed, than you can know yourself) is important especially in a relationship since it maintains a check on judgment, and judging the other person is a common and disruptive facet of relationships. The closer we are to someone the more inclined we are to judge them as well as to project our own failings onto them or to assault our own failings by assaulting them. Honoring the Otherness in the Other is therefore crucial to the formation of the sacred space between two people, the space in which God is then manifest.

Honoring the Otherness in the Other also means being aware that the Other has a distinct Soul Other as well, here for a whole different purpose than yours, no matter how similar your circumstances. Similar circumstances, sharings, and experiences do not always spell sameness, for two people can experience the same thing in very different ways: in other

words, two people can come away from a single experience
with very different memories. Two people can experience the
same form of suffering, for instance, and feel very different
degrees of pain; what is painful to one can be experienced
as insignificant to the Other, and so forth. It is precisely when
two people are convinced that they are soul mates that they
must endeavor all the harder to maintain this kind of awareness in order to create the Sacred Space for each to be fully
who they are in relationship with and separate from one
another. We are all soul mates of God, for example, yet God
gives us plenty of room to be us.

In fact, the closer two people are to one another, the easier
it is to build up reservoirs of expectations, or for each to
assume that the Other is on their psychic wavelength and
knows exactly what is on their mind without having to be
told. This is due to deep investment of energy and trust in
the other person. And when that energy is usurped or that
trust shattered, the more intense the investment the more
intense the pain.

Moreover, the closer two people are to one another, the
greater is the tendency to take each other for granted, or to
take for granted the little routine things they do for one another, even to the point that these little routine things become subject to great expectations, become chores, demands.
If A serves B breakfast each morning and B takes it for
granted, then B may be very disappointed or outright demanding if A fails to serve it on time or at all one morning.
No one owes anything to the Other in a relationship. What
we do for one another should be what we want to do out of
our sense of rightness, love, and responsibility for our Self
and for Other. A person who is served a meal by another in
a relationship should be at least as grateful each time as he
or she would be were the server a total stranger, even a room-
mate at college. "Why thank you! You didn't have to do that!"

should be a daily exclamation in every household the moment the plate hits the table. If we begin to take these things for granted, we shall likely take the big things for granted in the end. We shall start to take the blessings of God for granted, the planet, life. "If one's love is contingent on an ulterior motive, then when the motive is gone so is the love" (Babylonian Talmud, *Avot* 5:16).

When you do a favor for someone, then, it may be a natural inclination to expect a favor in return at some point, but here you need to learn two things: 1) how to let go when you give, and therefore not expect anything in return, to give without intent to barter, without imposing a kind of unspoken IOU upon the other; and 2) how to at least recognize that since we are all very different in our needs, our likes and dislikes, we should not expect returned favors fashioned according to *our particular* requirements or likings. Perhaps the one to whom you've given is unable to return a similar favor or the kind of favor you may need at a given moment, but is able to do something else for you at some other time or in some other way. "Judge all people with the benefit of a doubt," taught the first-century B.C.E. Rabbi Yehoshua ben Prakhya (Babylonian Talmud, *Avot* 1:6):

> Once a Galilean hired himself to a man in the south as a laborer and worked for him three years. On the afternoon before Yom Kippur [Day of Atonement], he said to the man: "Pay me for my labor so I can return home and tend to my wife and children." The man replied: "I have no money." Said he: "Then give me some land instead." Replied the man: "I have none." Said he: "Then give me some cattle." Replied the man: "I have none." The laborer gave up and went home empty-handed and disappointed. After the festival, the landowner gathered three donkeys, loaded them with food, drink and a variety of delicacies, brought them to the laborer as a gift and also paid him his full wages. When they had finished dining together, the landowner said to the laborer: "When you asked me for your wages and I told you I had no money, what did you think?" Replied the laborer: "I figured

perhaps you had made some purchases and spent all of your money." Said the landowner: "And when I told you I had no oxen either, what did you think?" Said he: "I thought that perhaps you had rented them out to someone." Said the landowner: "And when I told you I had no land, what did you think?" Said he: "I thought that perhaps it had not yet been tithed." The landowner praised him and said: "Indeed it was exactly as you said it was! And just as you have judged me favorably, so may God judge you!" (Babylonian Talmud, *Shabbat* 127b)

Still, even if we do our best to heed all the wisdom about relationship-ing, there will be times when we are hurt by Other, or when Other is hurt by us. When that happens, when a relationship has been upset by betrayal of trust, of feelings, of honor, the Torah bids us to "have it out" (Leviticus 19:17). This counsel may seem to be in conflict with the more commonly espoused counsel to "turn the other cheek" (Isaiah 50:6; Lamentations 3:30), which most of us have been led to believe is the proverbial biblical way, but this is only because of our unfamiliarity with the have-it-out adage in the Book of Leviticus. However, the language of the Torah—the five Books of Moses—are nearer to everyday human reality, while the Books of the Prophets address us with metaphoric prose about idealistic hopes. "The Torah," declared the ancient sages, "speaks to us in the language of mortals" (Babylonian Talmud, *Berakhot* 31b). Indeed, how much turning of the other cheek was actually done in human history, especially by those who claimed to live by the Bible?

Judaism is interested in ideals and aspirations, and envisions a world one day at peace with itself, when armies will beat their swords into plowshares and their spears into pruning hooks, and when nation will no longer lift sword against nation, nor shall they learn war anymore (Micah 4:3). At the same time, Judaism also recognized that the journey toward such ideals is not as glorious and demands conscious work with our Selves and with our relationship with Others. Not to bear a grudge or to take revenge or to hate when you have been hurt by someone (Leviticus 19:17-18) is therefore only the half of it. The missing piece is *hokhe'ach tokhe'ach* (Leviticus 19:17-18), which most standard English translations render "rebuke," but which literally means "rebuke, rebuke." The ancient teachers interpret the double wording to lend emphasis to the teaching, that "if the one who has hurt you will not respond to your initial rebuke, then rebuke them again and again" (Babylonian Talmud, *Arakhin* 16b), but "do not take the failure thereof upon yourself," the Torah continues (Leviticus 19:17). In other words, if you try to talk it out with them and they do not want to hear it, or by the time you are ready emotionally to have it out with them they are dead, do not add further to what they did to you by now also beating yourself up for not succeeding, or for waiting until it was too late. Likewise, the sages taught, "Do not expend yourself admonishing those who refuse to listen to you, altogether, for scripture states: 'rebuke rebuke'—meaning those who are open to correction" (Babylonian Talmud, *Yevamot* 65b; see commentary there by eleventh-century Rabbi Shlomo ben Yitzchak [Rashi]). The warning against vengeance in the Torah (Leviticus 19:18) that follows "rebuke, rebuke" then warns us that if we go too far in our rebuke of someone who has wronged us, we could easily turn the tables and make them the victim and us the abuser. Indeed, the same rabbis who encouraged repeated attempts at reproving also cautioned against overdoing it (Babylonian Talmud, *Arakhin* 16b), for example, by embarrassing the Other in public, or jabbing at their feelings far beyond what was necessary in order to make them aware of their wrongness.

"Rebuke, rebuke" could also mean that while talking out a conflict with someone also be prepared to listen to the Other's rebuke, to what it was in the experience of the Other that led them to behave the way they did. In other words, "rebuke, rebuke" implies that in resolving conflict both parties need to alternate in allowing each the space they need to rebuke. In most conflicts, although not all, there are usually at least two sides to the story, at least two versions of the situation.

At times, however, "having it out" is not enough, does not feel finished, even if it elicits an apology. Sometimes people do things to each other that are plain cruel, that are violent, that feel to the victim unforgivable. Again, the Torah tells us "do not take the failure thereof upon yourself." If we find ourselves unable to forgive because of the intensity of what was done to us, or because the pain of it still lingers in us, we should not add to all this the burden of guilt as well, guilt over not being able to forgive. All of its idealistic teachings to forgive and forget and turn the other cheek notwithstanding, Judaism also acknowledges our right to our pain and sees forgiveness as sometimes a metahuman task that cannot always be accomplished overnight but may take a lifetime or two of processing. Many of us are raised to see forgiveness as instantaneous, but it is not always so, and is often a lengthy and difficult process. We might utter the words, "I forgive you," but sometimes the hurt from what was done to us will gradually resurface at the core of our being, and the words "I forgive you" will then become obsolete. To deny this when we are really hurting inside, and to cling tenaciously instead to the words of forgiveness we have already declared can easily lead to resentment toward the Other whom we forgave, sometimes to a degree far greater than that which we felt before the forgiveness. And so the Torah wisely adds the clause: "Do not hate your brother in your heart." In other words, if you still bear resentment, your attempt at forgiveness is not finished and you need to acknowledge that or you will bear a grudge and hate in ever-swelling dosages, if not toward the one who hurt you, then toward those who did not, or toward your Self. Rather, go back to that person and talk about it with them again: "Rebuke, rebuke your fellow, but do not take the failure thereof upon your self." As King Solomon put it: "Do not be so overly righteous" (Ecclesiastes 7:16). Find out where you are, be authentic to your feelings. If you feel so transcendental so that whatever wrong someone does to you is like oil on water, then you might be able to respond to the situation as Isaiah the Prophet did: "I gave my back to those who smote me, and turned my cheeks to those who plucked out my hair; I hid not my face when they shamed me and spat at me. For God will help me; therefore have I not been confounded; therefore have I set my face like a flint, and I know that I shall not be ashamed" (Isaiah 50:6-7). If not, then you need to go back to the more down-home realm of Leviticus and take up your rebuking once again.

The Talmud, too, is replete with teachings about how we ought to humble ourselves before those who hurt us:

He who hears himself cursed and is silent, is a partner with God Who is silent though the Holy Name is blasphemed. (*Shochar Tov* on Psalms 86:1)

Mar Zutra (fifth century) used to say daily: "If anyone has wronged me, they are hereby forgiven." (Babylonian Talmud, *Megillah* 28a)

They who are insulted but insult not back; who hear themselves reproached but answer not; who serve out of love and rejoice in their affliction—of them is it written in Scripture: "They that love God are as the going forth of the sun in its might" [Judges 6:31]. (Babylonian Talmud, *Yoma* 23a)

The world is not sustained but in the merit of the one who remains silent during an argument. (Babylonian Talmud, *Chullin* 89b)

Many more such teachings across the length and breadth of classical Judaic teachings are often taught as unqualified statements about how we need to be wimps, to take whatever comes our way and file our hurt away under martyrdom. But, again, these teachings need to be examined in context or they risk becoming a theology for how to be a victim and remain that way. That is not the God-Will.

Mar Zutra's daily declaration of forgiveness to those who wronged him clearly refers to situations of which he himself was unaware and therefore unhurt by, else, why the need for a general one-size-fits-all declaration of forgiveness as opposed to forgiving people on the spot in each instance. In other words his remark could be read thus: "Just in case somebody did something to me that was wrong, and which I did not catch in the moment, though God knows about it, I hereby forgive that person." This is not any different from the generic prayer of forgiveness the ancient rabbis instituted for daily evening recitation:

> Master of the Universe, I hereby forgive anyone who has angered me or insulted me or has wronged me whether in matters pertaining to my body or my property or my dignity or whatever I have, and whether it was unintentional or deliberate, accidental or conscious, whether by speech or by act, and whether in this lifetime or in a previous lifetime—and anyone. And let no one be punished on my account. (Devotion before Retiring for the Evening)

Mar Zutra, then, was not speaking of a situation in which someone came up and kicked him in the groin and called him a *meeskeit*, a "repulsive-looking person." And though it would appear that the other teachings quoted above encourage passivity in the face of insult and assault, the rabbis themselves applied these aphorisms to situations in which the recipient of the insult, for example, is in so strong an emotional or spiritual state that they do not take it to heart. But if it is taken to heart and there is pain, the perpetrator needs to be confronted and the conflict needs to be aired out. Further, they taught, these idealistic teachings about not feeling anger and vengeance toward someone who has wronged us refer to circumstances where we have been monetarily inconvenienced, for example, not when we have been hurt physically or emotionally (Babylonian Talmud, *Yoma* 23a; see also Meiri on same). In more severe instances, such as someone coming at you with a knife, the ancient saints had no scruples about suspending the other-cheek rule: "If someone comes at you to kill you, rise [to your defense] and kill them first" (Babylonian Talmud, *Yoma* 85b). The anonymous author of the fifteenth-century ethical treatise, *Orchot Tzadikim* (*Ways of the Righteous*) also addresses the importance of not being passive when people are antagonizing you: "The wrong kind of humility, however, is bowing to the assaults of the wicked. . . . On the contrary we are to admonish them for their deeds" (*Shaar HaAnivut*, toward end). After all, the Torah implores us not to "stand idly by the blood of your neighbor" (Leviticus 19:16). If we are to run to the defense of an Other, we must certainly be zealous on our own behalf.

Finally, the teaching about how the planet exists by the merit of those who remain silent in the moment of dispute does not necessarily imply passivity but can just as easily imply wisdom. Sometimes it is wiser not to talk back in an argument, not to react impulsively to conflict. Often, instant reactions lead not to resolution but to verbal or physical Ping-Pong, and the conflict spirals rather than dissipates. "The key to wisdom," taught the first-century Rabbi Akiva, "is silence" (Babylonian Talmud, *Avot* 3:13), which means knowing when to hold your peace. If we are advised not to *console* our friends in their moment of grief or rage (Babylonian Talmud, *Avot* 4:18), how much more so should caution be exercised when we want to have it out with them.

Of course, these idealistic teachings of having it out and reconciliation—of sharing and clearing—do not always work in the real world. Some of the people who have hurt us and with whom we would like to engage in conflict resolution are dead, or have left us no forwarding address, or live nearby but refuse to talk to us about the tabooed "it." And while we may not be obliged to "take the failure thereof" upon ourselves, we are still left with the pain.

There is no easy answer or any one answer to absentee resolution. Perhaps we could do a bit of psychical accupuncture on ourselves and explore what pressure points were affected by the words or actions of the absentee rebukee. What did their behavior toward us *partzuf* in us, reflect back to us about our Self? Or what self-image got twisted out of whack by their deed that from that point altered our person from what it was, and from what we had hoped it would become? Where amidst our inner audience are they seated, still booing or throwing tomatoes at some part of us? If we cannot confront and work things out with an external Other, then we may need to try and do it with the psychic imprint of that Other that lingers on inside of us, and cast it out. This can be done with a good, conscious *mikveh*, or ritual immersion in a natural body of water. It can be done in the motions of sweeping out crumbs before Passover, or during spring cleaning. Or by having a friend sit in for the absentee rebukee while we tell them off. Most importantly, however, we need to remind ourselves again and again that we are not a part of that which has hurt us. We are affected by but separate from anyone who has stomped on our sand castles. We are not attached to anyone and therefore do not have to schlepp them with us across the length and breadth of our personal life journey. In such situations, then, we need to shift from "You have hurt me" to "I have been hurt."

Covenanting with Other is therefore tricky. It is a dance

unlike any other we do in the play of Life. We are to relate to Other by leaving, within our situational experience of relating to them, ample space for their Self to manifest as fully as they need, while in the very same moment also maintaining the sacredness of the personal space for our own Self to manifest as fully as we need. Each of us should feel ourselves to be guests, not hostages, of one another's Self space, our respective Selves fully our own.

As in a dance, partners in a relationship need to learn to alternate stepping back for the Other to be fully Present and heard, and then also making sure they, too, have the space to be fully Present and heard. We are to celebrate our children's being in the world, our parents' being in the world, our friends' and lovers' being in the world, but also our own being in the world. Each of us has a right, a voice, and are entitled to our feelings and our eccentricities or *meshugaas*, our strengths and our weaknesses, our powers and our vulnerabilities. And as we would hope that others would honor our right to be who we are, so should we honor their right to be who they are and celebrate the "magic," the weird and wonderful newness that is this other person.

> Once during the celebration of Simchat Torah, the festival of rejoicing with the Torah, Rabbi Mendel of Kotzk (early nineteenth century) sat uninvolved in the corner of the synagogue as his devotees danced fervently with Torah scrolls in their arms. Noticing that their teacher was not participating, they asked him to explain. "Because you are not dancing properly." They then tried dancing even wilder and more rhythmically than before, but the rebbe remained in his chair. When they approached him again, he gave them the same excuse. They tried a different way of dance and still he refused to join them. "You just don't know how to dance," he shrugged. This time, however, the congregants asked him to show them how to dance properly. He replied: "Shut your eyes and imagine you are standing perfectly balanced atop the edge of a sword. Then dance." (Heard from Rabbi Shlomo Carlebach)

Covenanting with Other can indeed be so challenging a dance. But then it becomes that much more exhilarating.

The Sefirot in Love and Relationship

The *sefirot* represent an ancient Jewish mystical formula for esoteric gymnastics and God-shuttling. They are based on the ancients' understanding of the attributes of God, the qualities of the Creator revealed within the fabric of Creation. The *sefirot* are symbolized in the human form, each attribute corresponding to a particular sector of the body. What follows is a loose adaptation of this ten-point kabbalistic formula for a clearer understanding of relationship dynamics. The Shadow side of each is described as well.

KETER

PSYCHE

Keter means "crown." A crown symbolizes representation. Before engaging in a relationship encounter, make sure you are wearing your personality where it can be seen. When engaged in relating to an Other, be fully aware of your own greatness, your own uniqueness. You, too, count. You, too, wear the royal crown because you, too, are the child of the Cosmic Sovereign. Do not lose yourself in the Other to the point where you feel inferior to them, or less adequate or talented, or that you must conceal some part of yourself from the Other to win their favor. The Shadow side of *Keter* is staying so clear you are actually unconnected and functionally rigid.

CHOKHMAH

RIGHT SIDE (LEFT BRAIN)

Chokhmah means "knowledge." Knowledge means yesterday's consciousness. All that you know, in other words,
comes from your past. In entering the arena of relationship,
get in touch with your knowledge, your consciousness level
as it has been up to the point of the encounter with the Other.
Your past will need to be prepared for attunements and adjustments if it is to merge with the knowledge/conscious-
ness of another, if you are to have a future with another. The
Shadow side would be staying so logical and immersed in
what follows from before that you cannot see the innovations,
transformations, and surprise gifts that the universe is offering through yourself and others.

BINAH

LEFT SIDE (RIGHT BRAIN)

Binah means "understanding," "intuition," from the Hebrew
word for "construction." And it connotes tomorrow's consciousness. It processes, builds upon, what you've known
until now. And this is the next stage of encounter, seeing
whether you can build a unit out of the merging of your past,
your knowledge, and the other person's past/knowledge;
seeing whether there can be a future, whether you can move
together, or whether you might not end up obstructing the
movements of one another's mind. The Shadow side is that,
without *Chokhmah*, *Binah* consciousness renders you too
fluid and in the moment so that you do not keep agreements
because they don't feel right anymore. The Other can see and
respond to your authenticity but can barely find you or count
on you for anything.

(These three processes take place in the initial *embrace* and therefore their acronym, in sound only, is *CHiBeK*, Hebrew for "embrace." But this acronym works in sound only, not in actual spelling, for the initial embrace is not clear, it only sounds good. It hasn't been tested. It is a social, rather than intimate, embrace. If the embrace, the greeting or meeting, has succeeded, the next three movements of the dance can begin.)

CHESED

RIGHT ARM

Chesed means "grace." Once there is a meeting of minds, a synchronicity of consciousness, there develops an innocent sense of trust that unleashes a sometimes overwhelming desire to express, to give to the other. The giving may take any variety of forms ranging from loving, caring, and giving gifts to sharing your innermost secrets, spilling your guts. Its Shadow side is oversharing, losing boundaries, engulfing the Other, swallowing them up. Or, on the other hand, sharing too much when the Other is not honoring you in your deepest places.

GEVURAH

LEFT ARM

Gevurah means "constriction." The initial unleashing of the emotion we call love often gets us into a lot of trouble, a lot of pain, because of the tendency to spill it rather than to pour it. The attribute of *Gevurah* helps one to direct the outpouring in such a way that it does not overwhelm Self or Other but leaves ample space for feedback, for the Other to respond, for the Other to choose either to receive the *Chesed* expressed or reject it or harness it toward alternate directions for the relationship. *Gevurah* checks to determine whether the love is real, or infatuation, or perhaps even psychotic and obsessive. Its Shadow side is harshness, inflexibility, and demanding of too much structure and restriction around how each emotes or even around what time dinner is served. It can also involve censoring your feelings too harshly so that the Other is left with uncertainty about how you are seeing them. Too much *Gevurah* leads to emotional as well as sensual frigidity.

TIFERET

HEART

Tiferet is feeling. It means "beauty," but beauty is determined by feeling. *Tiferet* is the end result of the processes worked out up to this point, a healthy, well-toned feeling. Love. Harmony. Clarity. Good—as in: "And God saw all that God had made and behold it was Good" (Genesis 1:31)—when everything comes together and clicks. The Shadow side is feeling so blissfully complete about the relationship that you leave little or no room for the possibility of change in either your Self or the Other. The notion of conflict, too, becomes taboo, and you end up suppressing your feelings if you are hurt by something the Other says or does, because, after all, you have the perfect relationship.

(This second three-part process is that of interaction, playing out the mind merging of the first stages. Its acronym is appropriately *CHuG*, which means "circle," as in a circle or intimate gathering of people. The "T" for *tiferet*, stands for the final letter in the Hebrew alphabet, *tuf*, for like the *tuf*, *Tiferet* is the climax of the merging. The relationship has begun. Likewise, so have the most challenging of all the dynamics in a relationship: the power struggle, the nature of the final three-part process.)

NETZACH

RIGHT THIGH

Netzach means "victory" or "mastery." It is the expression of assertive power, or commanding presence, in a relationship. Once the security of relationship has been established, either by marriage or other commitment, or merely by living under the same roof, the idealism of mind meeting and integration give way to soul-deep linking of each person's powerfulness combined with a drive to manifest personal ideals. It is a dance in powerfulness. There are times when one partner feels the need to take control momentarily due to a situation that calls for someone taking action. *Netzach* would be an aggressive way in which this would happen. Its Shadow side is aggression, domination, sometimes violence, and ego-deep competitiveness in which each partner strives for the most power in the relationship, for the leading role.

HOD

LEFT THIGH

Hod means "splendor." It, too, is mastery or victory, but in a more gentle sense. *Hod* consciousness emanates from a place of solid self-esteem, a quiet affirmation of Self and Other, and a peaceful determination to work things out. In doing *Hod*, you affirm your stance in the relationship but without intimidating the Other from theirs. Its display or exercise of power is in its majesty, as opposed to force, being moved to religiosity by the awesome beauty of God's Creation, for example, as opposed to the awesome voice of God commanding. *Hod* would be a balancing, more gentle way to take control when needed, or to act out the power struggle if there is too much of a dominating presence of the Other in the relationship. The *Hod* method of dealing with *Netzach* would be akin to the art of *Akido*, where the martial artist operates with, rather than against, the force of the opponent's movements. It is diplomacy. The Shadow side of *Hod* is an inexorable force unceasingly pushing the Other toward a resolution of a process or issue that the Other finds untenable in timing or form, a nonviolent but unrelenting compulsion of the Other. Or, in Yiddish, being a *nudnik*.

SOD

GENITALS AND CENTER OF LOWER ABDOMEN

Sod means "mystery" or "secret." It also means "foundation" and in talmudic terminology connotes "intimate council." On the *Sefirah* model, it is the genitalia. And, indeed, it is the sexual arena where the power struggle or power play forges its foundation. It is in the sex act where a couple engage in secret, intimate council to work out the dynamics of control, of whether the relationship is to become one of give and take or one of give and receive. The mystery, or secret, of relationship interplay is contained deep within the body, at the base of desire, of want, of need: the *Sod*. Here lies the test of truth, the proficiency test for the mastery of all the above processes. The body rarely lies. Here the couple is tested on whether they have truly been honest in their representation of Self to Other (*Keter*); whether their respective pasts are truly compatible for a mutual future (*Chokhmah* and *Binah*); whether they are truly capable of harmonious interaction

(*Chesed* and *Gevurah*) and have integrated enough to feel clearly whatever it is they feel toward one another and from one another (*Tiferet*); whether they are capable of balancing respective roles in the relationship so that there is a mutual respect for each other's presence and leadership rather than a competitiveness (*Netzach* and *Hod*). Its Shadow side would be a linking through passion when all or most of the above "tests" have proven negative: cementing two people in an innately destructive combination.

(The acronym for the final three-part process is appropriately HaNeS, which means "the experience," or "the miracle," and is related to the word *HaNesayon*, "the test." It is the revelation of the relationship, as the initial revelation of God to Moses at the *SeNaH*, the revelatory burning bush. Because Sod is where it all coalesces into the total experience of mind, emotion, and body: the climax.)

MALKHUT

SOLES OF THE FEET, OR THE EARTH-CONNECTEDNESS
OF OUR SOULS, AND BASE OF THE SPINE

Finally, there is *Malkhut*, which literally means "kingdom." *Malkhut* is where the downward spiraling of divine energy fully reaches integration between Ideal and Real. The Ideal relationship has not come about—each Self and each Other has had to learn, compromise, do *tzimtzum*, assert themselves, dance, get hurt, and heal in order to get this far. But if the *Keter* started out right and the Shadow of each movement forward was danced back to a sense of rightness and strength of each stage, then the Real expresses the Essence of the Ideal even if the form, character, and flavor are all innovations. The process is highly personalized, but in its authenticity reaches the completeness of the Divine Will for there to be Life in physicality. The Shadow side is that without manifesting the consciousness of the other *Sefirot, Malkhut* becomes gluttony for the gifts that God creates for physical beings, a gobbling up of the riches of Life without absorbing them. One then becomes insatiable, because even as the food, power, sensuousness, fame, creativity, and so forth, are experienced in their most condensed form, there is no Whole Self sharing in the experience. There is always emptiness but for momentary illusions of fulfillment.

Malkhut and *Keter* are therefore one and the same, the point where the two ends of a line meet in a circle of wholeness, and holiness. *Malkhut* is the realization, the actualization, of *Keter*, of the initial move between the couple to engage one another in the dance of relationship, in the embrace. The Hebrew letter *mem*, for *Malkhut*, is described in the *Kabbalah* as the womb, for it is in *Malkhut* that the relationship has developed from unformed potential into a fully formed Creation; from a seed, *Keter*, to a tree, *Malkhut*—one being the fruition of the other. The acronym for the two, *Keter* and *Malkhut*, is *KoM*, which means "rise," for here the relationship has risen and now stands erect as a tree, risen from its seed. *KoM* can also be received as sound advice for the couple to rise up to *Keter* again and periodically begin the processes anew; to proclaim a Sabbath every now and then. The Sabbath is a period of rejuvenation, of taking a deep breath and regaining composure and clarity. No task needs this more than that of making a relationship.

5

COVENANTING WITH CHILDREN

During the fast of Yom Kippur, Shammai the Elder [first
century B.C.E.] was wont to feed his young son with only
one hand [frugally]. But the sages decreed that he feed
him with both hands.
                    —Babylonian Talmud, *Tosefta Yoma* 4:2

Covenanting with children is problematic. Children do not
yet exist at the time the parent establishes the Covenant with
them. And when the child arrives into the world, they are
far too young to negotiate their end of the relationship, far
too young even to know there is one. Parents or guardians
need to realize that their young ward is not sufficiently
learned about life or adequately developed in their sense of
Self to bring to the relationship their side of the Covenant.
We cannot make deals with children. We can make but one-
sided agreements with them and the resulting imbalance
leaves them in a vulnerable and powerless position. It is therefore a crucial task for parents to help the child develop their
sense of Self and their awareness of relationship by creating
a safe space for the child to become ever-conscious of their
individuality and their right to be heard, to learn that their
voice counts and their feelings matter.

As parents, we are inclined to do a lot of decision making on our children's behalf. We elders, after all, "know what's best for them." In establishing a covenantal relationship with children, however, we need first to realize that we don't know what's best for them any more than we know what's best for anyone. Rather, we might do best to listen and guess what is best for our children so long as we also acknowledge that they are guesses at best. Enough honoring of the child's space needs to happen between parent and child, therefore, to allow room for the child to call forth what it is they need to live their life optimally. This is best achieved by doing a lot of listening to what they have to say and leaving them a lot of room to express their feelings about things. What children need from us adults is an open ear, not a critical mouth. Criticism does of course also have its place in covenanting with children, but, again, since they are in a vulnerable, dependent, and relatively unlearned and underdeveloped position, the adults need to relate to them with delicateness. Their hurt is triggered more easily and more intensely and often gets more deeply embedded, potentially scarring them emotionally for a lifetime, or sentencing them to a lifetime of psychotherapy. When you have to criticize a child to correct them or discipline them, "let your left hand do the distancing of them while your right hand draws them near to you" (Babylonian Talmud, *Sotah* 47a). Of course, this does not mean we should lovingly embrace the child, say to them, "I love you," and then proceed to slap them or shame them. Rather, it means that in disciplining our children we need to stick within the boundaries of Covenant, of "this is still part of our relationship and my love for you has not in any way been altered or severed, not by your misbehavior and not by my disapproval." The Torah warns us thirty-six times to deal kindly with the stranger, and a child is definitely a stranger, perhaps even thirty-six times more a stranger than the adult stranger. After all, the child has just arrived on the planet, has not yet learned their way around the world, has not yet learned their way around their everchanging body, and is at the mercy of their adult hosts. Children, the ancient teachers remind us, are special guests on the planet and are therefore to be treated hospitably. "Children," wrote King David, "are God's adopted" (Psalms 127:3)—or, as the first-century Unkelos interpreted it: "God's special guests" (*Mikra'ot Gedolot*, Psalm 127:3).

The role of parenting, according to the ancient Judaic teachings, is not the exclusive domain of the birth parents. A child's "parents" are those who welcome the young stranger into their shelter and guidance and who treat them with love and honor. Parents who treat their children like personal possessions or objects to do with as they wish are not parents according to the traditional Judaic definition. Biological parents are not considered anything to the child when the child receives nothing from them but abuse. Rather, Judaism considers as parent the adult who takes the child under their wing and nurtures the child, physically, emotionally, and intellectually: "It is the one who raises the child who is called their parent, not the one who gives birth to them" (*Exodus Rabbah* 46:6).

Birth, then, is not necessarily a biological phenomenon. "Anyone who raises and guides an orphan, or who teaches someone else's child, it is as if they had given birth to that child" (Babylonian Talmud, *Ketuvot* 50a; *Megillah* 13a; *Sanhedrin* 19b). The ripping away of adopted children or foster children from wholesome parental environments and placing them into the hands of neglectful and abusive biological parents is a no-no in Judaism. In such instances, we do not let our compassion for a biological mother and father override the best interests of the child. As the third-century Rabbi Shimon ben Lakish warned: "One who acts with compassion toward those who are cruel will ultimately act with cruelty in a situation requiring compassion" (*Ecclesiastes Rabbah* 7:33). Thousands of years prior to the only recently enacted Western laws for the protection of children from abusive parents, Judaism acknowledged the problem and legislated against it (Babylonian Talmud, *Tosefta Baba Kamma* 9:3). Parents who hurt or publicly shamed their children were obliged by the rabbinic courts to compensate the children exactly as they would be required to compensate an adult whom they had harmed physically or emotionally (Babylonian Talmud, *Tosefta Baba Kamma* 9:3). The recent phenomenon of children divorcing abusive parents is thus innovative only in the minds of contemporary Western society. But in ancient Judaic law it was assumed that real parenting and parental right are not defined by whether your sperm or ovum fashioned a child but by whether you cared for and guided that child with love and honor (*Exodus Rabbah* 46:6; Jerusalem Talmud, *Horayot* 3:4, toward end). If you did not, and someone else does, then your child rightfully honors them as its parents more than you (Jerusalem Talmud, *Horayot* 3:4, toward end). In fact, the Hebrew word for parent is *horah*, which literally connotes "one who shows/guides," and is related to *morah*, which is Hebrew for "teacher."

All of this might sound crude and unfair. After all, it's my kid, I invested time, pain, and money in that kid. On the other hand, if that is my attitude, I will raise that child not in an environment of affection, honoring, and appreciation, but in an environment of emotional IOU's where the child will be made to feel like they owe me constantly for every breath and step they take. And I will feel free to handle that child as I wish. I will, in short, be relating to that child in the I-It mode. Judaism then reminds me again and again that I-Thou needs to happen between myself and my child or I become stripped of the role of parent, of the assignment to welcome and honor "God's special guests."

The concept of ownership, the Torah admonishes, is not without its qualifications. I may claim ownership of a goat, but I am also then required to feed it before I feed myself (Babylonian Talmud, *Berakhot* 40a) and see to it that it is treated honorably and not discomforted in any way (e.g., Deuteronomy 22:10, 25:4; Babylonian Talmud, *Terumot* 9:3. See also Maimonides' *Mishneh Torah*, *Mishpatim*, *Hilkhot Sekhirot* 13:3). And if my cow needs to be milked, and it is the Sabbath, I must go out to the barn and milk her to alleviate her discomfort (Magen Avraham on Karo's *Shulchan Arukh*, *Orach Chaim* 305:20). Further, I am forbidden to derive any personal benefit from this milk because my only right to milk it on the Sabbath day is on behalf of the needs of the cow, not my own needs (Karo's *Shulchan Arukh*, *Orach Chaim* 305:20). And if I own land, it's not mine to work whenever I feel like it. The land, too, has its rights above and beyond my ownership, and I am obliged to leave it rest every seventh day (Exodus 25:10) and every seventh year (Leviticus 25:4). I don't own my wife and she does not own me. I can call her *my* wife and she can say *my* husband, but then along come the teachings that remind us each to honor our separateness (Babylonian Talmud, *Shabbat* 62a), that my wife does not have to perform chores for me (Babylonian Talmud, *Ketuvot* 58b) or make love to me if she is not in the mood (Babylonian Talmud, *Eruvin* 100b).

Likewise, we can proclaim *our* children, but they do not *belong* to us. And even if we consider parents as partners in the enterprise of bringing children into the world, the ancient rabbis reminded us that there is a third partner—the Creator (Babylonian Talmud, *Kiddushin* 31a; *Niddah* 31b). Rather, children are newly embodied souls that belong to no one but their own precious Selves and the Creator. And the Creator, who *owns* each of us, *honors* each of us with all the space we need to be fully *us*. From the perspective of the Judaic science of reincarnation, it is even likely that a lot of children—while they might be newly embodied—are very old souls, sometimes older than those of their parents. If we sometimes have trouble respecting those little unruly brats, we might invoke a little reincarnation theory and see it as a matter of respecting our elders.

With all its teachings about the delicateness of relationship-ing with children, Judaism is not oblivious to the frustrations often involved in raising them. *Tzar giddul banim* is virtually a household term among traditional Jewish parents. Originally coined by the ancient rabbis, it means "the pain of raising children" (e.g., Babylonian Talmud, *Sanhedrin* 19b):

> Rabbi Elazar ben Shimon (second century) said: "It is far easier to grow an entire orchard of olive trees in the Galilean wilderness, than to raise a single child in urban Israel." (*Genesis Rabbah* 20:15)

Children are indeed demanding at times, calling us out of our important and noble adult pursuits to descend into their "infantile" reality. But even extremely busy spiritual and communal leaders like the second-century Rabbi Yehoshua ben Korcha realized that few pursuits in this life are truly more important or more noble than the invaluable and nurturing gift to a young child of an adult's conscious attention:

> There was once a man who stipulated in his will that his son should inherit nothing unless he became a fool. When the matter was brought to the attention of Rabbi Yosi ben Yehudah and Rabbi Yehudah the Prince, they decided to consult Rabbi Yehoshua ben Korkha. When they arrived at his home they found him crawling playfully after his son on his hands and feet, with a piece of straw in his mouth. They quickly hid themselves so as not to embarrass him, and when he was

finished playing they asked him concerning the will. He laughed and said: "The matter about which you have asked has just now happened to me! For when a man has children, he acts like a fool [and the will therefore means that the son should inherit nothing unless he became a father]." (*Yalkut Shimoni* on Psalms 92:15)

But not all of us are as patient and as willing as Rabbi Yehoshua to unzip the canvas of our grown-up suits and join the child, and even fewer of us are patient enough to put up with the interruption of the flow of our lives by the child, especially when the child becomes difficult and unmanageable in the moment. The frustration wells up inside us and many of us are inclined to raise our voices, or our hands, or simply shut the child out of our consciousness altogether and retreat into a parental coma. It is in such situations that we need to review the teachings of and life examples of those who mastered the art of weaving harmoniously between remaining steadfast in their adult consciousness and being present in the world of their children, of remaining cognizant of the gift and responsibility their children represent, a realization void of any sense of ownership:

While Rabbi Meir (second century) taught at the House of Study one Sabbath, his two sons passed away. His wife Beruriah placed them in their beds and covered them with sheets. When Rabbi Meir returned home after the Sabbath, he asked her: "Where are my sons?" Said she: "They went to the House of Study." Said he to her: "I sought them there and did not find them." She then prepared for him the cup of wine for the ceremony of separation [of the Sabbath day from the pending weekdays]. Again he asked her: "Where are my sons?" Said she to him: "Sometimes they go to such-and-such a place. They will return soon." She then drew herself near to him as he ate his dinner. After he had eaten, she said to him: "My teacher, I have a legal question to ask you." Said he to her: "What is your question?" Said she to him: "Some time ago, someone gave me something of his to watch over and care for. And now he wishes to take it back. Shall I give it back to him, or not?" Said he to her: "My daughter! If you have something which belongs to another, should you indeed not return it to its rightful owner?" Said she to him: "I did not want to return it without your knowledge." She then took him gently by the hand and led him up to the children's room and drew him near to their beds. When she removed the sheets, Rabbi Meir burst out in weeping, crying: "My sons! My sons! My teachers! My teachers!" At that moment, Beruriah said to him: "Rabbi, did you not say before that we ought to surrender to its rightful owner that which was given to us to care for and watch over? Thus, 'God gave and God took back; may God's Name be blessed'" [Job 1:21]. Said Rabbi Hanina: "In the way that she handled the situation, Rabbi Meir regained his senses and became consoled. Of her is it written, 'A woman warrior . . .'" [Proverbs 31:10]. (*Yalkut Shimoni* on Proverbs, no. 964, para. 7)

Beruriah, the second-century female talmudic scholar, thus taught that children are our wards, not our property, and that each is entrusted to us by the Creator for caretaking and nurturing. Parents therefore do not wield any authority to punish a child if there is no immediate pedagogic need. For example, they may not employ the classic wait-until-your-father-comes-home threat. Rather, any consequence meted out must be educative, meaning it must be associated with the misbehavior as conspicuously and as spontaneously as possible (Babylonian Talmud, *Semachot* 2:6; *Sukkah* 46b). Their sole right to disciplining their child is confined to the context of guiding that child, and therefore excessive punishment is forbidden (Proverbs 19:18; Babylonian Talmud, *Gittin* 6b [7b in some editions]). And anything more painful than a shoelace is forbidden (Babylonian Talmud, *Baba Batra* 21a). And all physical disciplining is proscribed for children of adolescent age and on (Babylonian Talmud, *Mo'ed Katan* 17a). And following the punishment, the child must be embraced, must be shown that the chastisement was a lesson from a place of love, not an act of parental revenge, not the desire of the parent that they be hurt, nor an indication of any iota of change in the parent's love for and commitment to the child: "For whom God loves does God admonish, like a parent appeases a child" (Proverbs 3:12). Again, as the ancient rabbis spoke of disciplining children: "Do not push them away with both hands, but as your left hand distances them, your right hand shall bring them near" (Babylonian Talmud, *Sotah* 47a). It is important to add, however, that many children coping with a correction cannot bear to be hugged in the moment. They need to be able to sense that loving and honoring have not been disrupted, but they also need physical distance in order to process bodily and to learn.

Children are innately too small. And for the whole of life as children know it, they are too unskilled to do for themselves even that which may be essential to the preservation of an intact Self. They are drastically dependent on the whims, abilities, and intentions of Others—the adults. Therefore, when a small child is demanding, for example, adults too often hear this as if the child were intending to say, "I wield power over you to force you to do as I please." While in their forcefulness of will and uninhibited passion small children certainly have the power to knock adults out of the energy flow that may be so important to the adult in the moment, they do not have the power to take their own lives into creative, effective fulfillment. They need the adults for that, whatever the personal flow the adult is in at that moment. So actually, what the child is saying is, "I am stating my right to Self. And my Self needs such and such and I cannot do it and you can!" With all the intention a child Self can bring to the demand, it may feel to the adult as if they are indeed being coerced and it is in fact at this juncture that abuse may arise, precisely because the adult is free to react with total disregard for the child.

We need therefore to reexamine certain teachings that seem to authorize, and even demand, physical punishment of children. For instance: "He who spares the rod, hates his son; but he who loves him disciplines him early" (Proverbs 13:24).

The Hebrew word used for what is classically translated as "rod," is *shevet*, which means a scepter, or a shepherd's crook. The authors have lived for several years on a sheep farm in West Virginia. When the farmer and his family were herding the flock, they would run to stand in the way of the sheep to keep them from going the wrong way. Occasionally, they would pick up the flimsiest of sticks from the ground and hold it straight out sideways at eye level in front of the sheep. It then appeared as a fence of sorts and the sheep would turn back toward the rest of the flock. They never beat the wayward sheep with the rod, but readily barred their way to guide them.

The purpose of enclosing sheep in pastures is threefold: to protect them from predators, to prevent them from getting lost or falling into ravines, and to protect the land from overgrazing. Sheep have a tendency to adopt a favorite spot and graze the grass to extinction. Shifting them from pasture to pasture prevents this. This is especially important in arid regions like the Middle East, whence these proverbs originate. There, fencing in enough land for grazing is unpractical and thus the open range is preferred, requiring even more the presence of a shepherd with a shepherd's crook. The sheep are kept together by the diligence of the shepherd, who gently keeps them moving from place to place to preserve the grazing for later use. The sheep are never battered by the shepherd to terrify them into clumping together.

Likewise, teachings about using a rod on a child mean using it largely, as sheep herders would, to fish the really little ones out of trouble, to demarcate limits that are not obvious to them, to show them the line as they get close to it, to thump them if they really aren't getting it—but never to beat them up!

If you let your sheep or your children run about without guarding them from ravines, coyotes, rustlers, greed, and belligerence, they will be destroyed. If you let them run loose without care, they will destroy their own future sustenance, whether it be grasses to graze or the ability to follow through on the job, skills necessary to be in healthy relationships, or to be in good standing with the community and the environment. The rod is a shepherd's crook to rescue and to set limits. It is like the king's scepter, to be shown in times of need. However, neither is to ever become a battering ram.

The Hebrew word that gets translated as "discipline"—*mussar*—means ethics, morals, or the imparting of ethical values, depending upon the grammatical form used. A translation of the same verse above, sticking more to the Hebraic original, would go something like this: "He who won't use the shepherd's crook hates his son; but he who loves him will impart moral values early in his life." Or, instead of "If folly settles in the heart of a lad, the rod of discipline will remove it" (Proverbs 22:15), we might read the punch line this way: ". . . the ethics of the community will remove it" or ". . . the scepter of ethics will remove it."

To translate *mussar* as discipline is to strip the word of most of its nuance. For example, another context in which it is used is in the term for ethical will—*iggeret hamussar*. This sort of last will and testament was common among the great rabbis of ancient and medieval times. It was not a bullwhip they left behind for their children to beat themselves with, but a letter to them espousing the ethical values of living in the world that they felt important and wished to impart to their children before they died.

Mussar is also related to the word *mesorah*, or "heritage," because, in general, it is a *mesorah*, literally a "giving over," of values and learnings that parents have gained in life and that have helped them that they in turn want to *moser*—"give over"—to their descendants. To constantly read the worst and most violently possible connotation into this word is to deprive us of a most vital lesson in parenting, and—worse yet—is to use the sacred writ as license for parents to take out their anger and frustrations on their children.

King Solomon also said: "One excessively reproved may become stubborn; but he will suddenly be broken beyond repair" (Proverbs 29:1). It is important, then, to watch the child to see whether their failure to respond might be because they are "frozen," in which case the parent needs to back off. Any person treated too harshly will remember only the harshness and not the lesson. Shahabuddin Les, a Sufi teacher, once described how one of his children did not feel noticed or cared about unless his father expressed himself to him in a tone that was definite and strong. As a result, they often dealt with issues at high volume, but the child responded. Yet, another of his children would silently crumple up at so much as a disapproving look or a raised eyebrow from him. With that child, therefore, he did not raise his voice at all—and the child responded effortlessly. As Solomon put it: "Educate each child according to their respective way" (Proverbs 22:6). Again, the teaching is that each child is an individual and should not be cast into a uniform mold for child rearing. No one book on raising children should ever be employed as *the* guide to raising any one child. There is no one-size-fits-all formula for parenting, but rather as many formulas as there are children.

The seemingly contradictory aphorisms of Solomon about disciplining children are not at all unusual. One can find contradictory teachings throughout the *Tanakh* and Talmud, contradictory only when we see these writings as one long run-on-sentence. They are not. They are compilations over thousands of years of many different teachings born out of many different circumstances and in response to many different questions of situational ethics. For example, in Proverbs 26:4, Solomon writes: "Do not answer a dullard in accord with his folly, or you will become like him." In the very next verse, however, he writes: "Answer a dullard according to his folly, or he will think himself wise!" In Proverbs 23:13-14, he writes: "Do not withhold discipline from a lad; if you beat him with a rod he will not die. Beat him with a rod and you will save him from the grave." Contrast that with Proverbs 29:1: "One excessively reproved may become stubborn, but he will suddenly become broken beyond repair," or Proverbs 19:18: "Chastise your child for there is hope, but do not set your heart upon his destruction." It can easily be imagined that King Solomon was speaking one day with parents who were strict and overbearing with children who had become sullen and uncooperative or very rebellious. And so he warned them against too much harshness, that it can do permanent damage, "broken beyond repair." On yet another day, the king was confronted by parents who could not bear to be anything but passive in response to the unruly behavior of their children. In their situation, the king opined that the children needed to *feel* their parents' presence and concern in their lives, that they needed some reaction.

This brings us to a very important principle in Judaism regarding all physical punishment, of either adults or children. The ancient rabbis taught that all references to beatings, floggings, stoning, cutting off of limbs, putting out eyes, and so forth are designed to get our attention, not to be taken literally. At times they are purely metaphoric. Rather, the monetary and functional *value* of an eye or a limb is meant (Babylonian Talmud, *Baba Kamma* 83b) rather than literally an eye for an eye or a tooth for a tooth, as worded in the Torah (Exodus 21:24). Another example is the biblical case of "the rebellious unrehabilitative son," whom the parents—feeling helpless—bring before the community elders for execution! (Deuteronomy 21:18-21). The ancient rabbis, however, did not take it literally: "It has never happened and will never happen" (Babylonian Talmud, *Sanhedrin* 71a). The teaching inherent in this otherwise crude sounding law was that if your adolescent child was out of control and turning into a sociopathic criminal, and you found yourself at your wit's end, you owed it to the child and yourself to turn to the community for help. Nonetheless, the recalcitrant son was still your child and you maintained the right to change your mind and take him back home (Babylonian Talmud, *Sotah* 25a). In other words, if you completely relinquish your problem child to society to deal with, your child will be destroyed. If you stick with the child while the child is getting outside help, you will save their life. When all else fails, turn to others for help, but don't give up altogether on your parental skills and rights. A society might not want to have such a kid around and do him or her more harm than good. Surrender your *problem* to the authorities, not your *parenthood*.

In cases where the punishment outlined in the Torah was meant literally, the constraints around its execution were so demanding and deliberately bureaucratic that they were rarely carried out. A court that imposed the death penalty even so much as once in seventy years was considered a "bloody court" (Babylonian Talmud, *Makkot* 7a). Even in the event that a court decided that a person ought to be flogged for a trespass, a physician had to examine them first to determine whether they could tolerate the prescribed number of strokes, or only a small portion thereof, or none at all (Babylonian Talmud, *Makkot* 22b-23a), and the punishment was then carried out not by hooded goons with bullwhips but by the spiritual leaders themselves: "Someone with much wisdom and little strength" (Babylonian Talmud, *Makkot* 23a). More important than applying the pun-

ishment, then, was the admonishment "not to allow your
fellow human to become degraded in your eyes" (Deuteronomy 25:3).

Many of us study these teachings and other teachings
about sensitivity toward ourselves, our things, our friends,
but for some mysterious reason fail to apply them to our
relationship with our children. If, as noted earlier, our children are our students, then we need to apply the dictum:
"Let the honor of your student be as dear to you as your own
honor" (Babylonian Talmud, *Avot* 4:12).

Therefore, the ancient teachers had to spell it out for us,
that when it comes to children and discipline, the tools of
physical punishment should be limited to nothing more
severe than a shoelace (Babylonian Talmud, *Baba Batra* 21a).
And if a parent or other adult marks, maims, or publicly
shames a child, the community is required to seek restoration for the child in court exactly as if it had been an adult
who had been so injured; and the child is due all recompense
ordinarily due an adult (Babylonian Talmud, *Tosefta Baba
Kamma* 9:3).

Yet, there are times when we lose it. We are, after all, human. And if it happens, we need to apologize, to ask for
forgiveness, to assess what pieces of the child might have
gotten bent or lost in our explosion, and to do what we can
to restore the child to their wholeness of being. And if we
explode a lot, we need to get help, for our sake and for the
sake of the child. "One who shatters their dishes in a fit of
anger, or who tears their clothing in a fit of anger, . . . it is as
if they have . . . committed idolatry" (Babylonian Talmud,
Shabbat 108b). How much more true must this be for one
who shatters their child's self-esteem in a fit of anger, or beats
their child in a fit of anger "Do not create an atmosphere of
terror in your home," taught the third-century Rabbi Hisda
(Babylonian Talmud, *Gittin* 6b).

Sexual abuse, too, is not something we can smugly sweep under the protective rug of religious piety. Incest is not a fossilized concept, something that used to take place thousands of years ago among some "uncivilized" people. It took place among even the most well-meaning and—surprise!—it still does. There is a tricky boundary line that stretches across that potent sensation we call love, and at some point it can spill over into physical expression, into physical intimacy. Incest does not happen because a parent is so in love with their child they start wanting to have sex with them. More often incest happens because the parent has crossed the line and has started to confuse the sensation of love with that of power. A parent who truly loves their child will not act out that love toward the child in any way that is harmful to the child's emotional or physical well-being. It is quite natural and harmless for a parent to become sexually aware of a developing child, but if they become sexually attracted they need to seek help.

In ancient times, and even today in some countries, people lived in small one-room homes and everyone slept together. The Talmud does not brush this aside in its discussions of parents and childen. And while it was not considered wrong for a parent and child to sleep together in the same bed, even if their bodies touched, there was everything wrong with doing so when the child was so much as beginning to feel uncomfortable with it (Babylonian Talmud, *Kiddushin* 80a, 81b). At what age do I stop seeing my child as uninhibited? When he or she starts sending even the slightest signals of discomfort with me dressing or undressing them, bathing them or lying in bed with them while I tell them bedtime stories. And these signals go easily unheard if there is no covenantal quality in my relationship with them; if I have not all the while up until then given them ample room to say back to me what they are feeling; if I have not until then provided them with safe space for them to be fully who they are and what they are becoming.

It may sound crude or lewd to some readers that the ancient rabbis did not just simply forbid a parent from sharing a bed with their child altogether, or at least forbid them to sleep together in the buff! In lieu of the phenomenal number of incidents of child sexual abuse and incest going on across the world and across religious denominations and socioeconomic situations, even so much as quoting such a teaching might come across as dangerous and potentially misleading. Yet, there is invaluable psychological lessons in such a teaching as well. Many women, for example, suffer from a self-image gone bad. They simply believe they are unattractive and void of sexuality, when to the people who love them they are the most attractive and sexy people on the planet. And quite often, in counseling such women, the authors have found that many of these women experienced an abrupt and dramatic physical withdrawal by their fathers as they began to mature physically and as their bodies began to transform from that of girl to that of woman. Fathers are sometimes prone to react that way out of fear of becoming sexually attracted to their daughters. Similarly, fathers tend to hold back in expressing their affection physically for their sons as their sons mature, usually out of homophobia more than anything else. Acting on those feelings of attraction are certainly harmful and abusive, but going to the other extreme and abruptly withdrawing and withholding physical touch and embrace is also harmful, though not as abusive. The same applies to mothers and sons, and mothers and daughters. The wisdom in the above talmudic teaching is then in its honoring of the child as the one whose limits of physical proximity and intimacy should be the primary determinant, not the parent's fear and insecurity. Let the child indicate what is OK physical contact and what is not, rather than suddenly withholding and withdrawing because of your own fears about your own feelings. Otherwise, you leave the blossoming child with a shattered sense of physical and emotional Self.

On the contrary, the ancient teachers admonished fathers to be supportive of their daughters' physical development into womanhood (Babylonian Talmud, *Ketuvot* 59b). Do not become frightened of it or intimidated by it, but rather nurture it and celebrate it within the realm of what is wholesome for the child. For example, it would be detrimental to a sexually maturing child if their parent went overboard in noting their child's transition into womanhood or manhood, such as sending them Valentine's Day cards. Perhaps it is a challenge of overwhelming proportions for all parents, whether heterosexual or homosexual, to walk this fine line with their daughters and sons, but the lingering question is: How long will we go on fashioning our children's sexuality by our own insecurities? If we can sacrifice vacations so that our children can have a college education, can we also then not sacrifice lust or our fear of it so that they may gain the gift of wholesome sexuality?

Our attitudes in general, then, very much influence those of our children. In terms of religion, too, a parent's treatment of their child will determine the child's view of God—as rigid, demanding, vengeful, and antisensual, or as loving, negotiable, compassionate, and Creator of the sensual. This is one of the reasons given for the appearance of the commandment to "honor your father and your mother" (Exodus 20:12) on the stone that held the first five of the Ten Commandments, which concerned issues between the human and God (fifteenth-century Rabbi Yossef Albo in *Sefer HaIkkarim* 3:26; sixteenth-century Rabbi Judah Loew [Maharal] in *Tiferet Yisrael*, chap. 36). Through their relationship with their parents children gain consciousness of the

relationship between humans and God, the form and tradi-
tions of relating between Self and the Omnipotent Presence.
It should be made clear, however, that the oft-invoked precept to "honor your father and your mother" applies to those
mature enough *to* honor, not to those too young to compre-
hend the meaning of the word. And should parents presume
the right to violently compel their teenager to honor them,
the ancient rabbis warned against lifting a hand against a son
or daughter in their teens or older. Such an action at that
age, it was feared, would in turn provoke a *reaction* and the
child would strike back (Babylonian Talmud, *Mo'ed Katan*
17a). Rather, for a parent to strike a child in their teens was
considered a trespass of the biblical commandment "Do not
place a stumbling block before the blind" (Leviticus 19:14),
meaning do not place someone in a situation that might lead
them to transgress—in this case, hitting a parent.

The ancient teachers realized how sensitive a phase of child
development is that of adolescence, the turbulent, treacher-
ous moat children must cross to gain entrance to adulthood.
Adolescence is indeed a phase during which the child walks
an emotional tightrope, churning with unfamiliar passions, and
seeking increasing degrees of separation from their parents
while also fearing the risk of losing their parents' closeness.
The adolescent is no longer the adoring child they so recently
were, and parents can easily forget this and trample all over
their adolescent child's very raw, sensitive self-image at a time
when they do not yet possess the life experience to know how
to temper their passions and impatiences. To explode at a child
during this highly sensitive stage, the sages realized, was to
risk a far greater explosion on the part of the adolescent, leading them, and their parents, to carve a nearly indelible pattern of wrongness, disrespect, and violence in the relationship.
It is so crucial, then, that new Covenants be forged with the
child at each phase of their development, as the horizons of

the relationship with them expand. And what more important and opportune time for reestablishing this covenanting with a child than at the onset of adolescence, as they enter their *bat/bar-mitzvah* age—twelve for a girl, thirteen for a boy (Babylonian Talmud, *Kiddushin* 16b).

In recent times, however, the rite of *bar/bat mitzvah* has become a joke. What does the parent give to the child at this marker of the onset of physical and emotional maturity? What new responsibility is handed to them, or what restrictions are removed? What sign of trust, of welcoming that child into adulthood, happens? Usually none. Usually, the child is subjected to gruelling lessons in Hebrew and in how to chant words that buzz with unfamiliarity and complete irrelevance to Mutant-Ninja-Turtle consciousness and a reality supplanted heretofore with transformers and video games. The painful and thoroughly resisted *bar-mitzvah* lessons these days are not very unlike the so-called primitive rites of indigenous tribes who yank the child out of the comfort and safety of home and subject them to ceremonies in which they are inflicted with some kind of wound or are dispatched into the wilderness for a solitary rite of passage that catapults them into adulthood. The only difference, perhaps, is that the primitive child undergoing such rites understands their meaning and is thereafter treated fundamentally as an adult and is thereby transformed—while the average contemporary *bar/bat-mitzvah* child finds the whole thing a drag and worth tolerating only on account of the checks and lavishly catered parties that follow. But when it's all over, they are instantly dropped right back into the mode of child rather than coached into the new grid of adulthood training.

A father once asked Rabbi Zalman Schachter-Shalomi if he would do the honors of officiating at his son's *bar mitzvah*. Reb Zalman then asked the man what new thing he was going to allow his son to do which he hadn't before. The man looked at him in puzzlement and said: "What do you mean? He's only a kid!" To which Reb Zalman replied: "If you're still going to treat him like he's only a kid, then who is the *bar mitzvah* for?" (From a conversation with the author)

Sadly, more often than not the *bat/bar mitzvah* is for the parents and relatives, not the child.

Parents hold so much of their child's sense of values in their hands and play an almost godly role in determining their child's worldview and definition of reality. How a parent handles their child's *bar/bat mitzvah*, how they conduct themselves in their relationship with their Self, with Others, and with their spiritual practices, will largely shape the attitudes of their children. If it's all a joke to you, it will undoubtedly become an even bigger joke to your kids. If you belittle your children, they will in turn belittle theirs. You are their Rand McNally, their road map, and their only road map until they are old enough to chart their own course—provided they were gifted with enough self-confidence to do so.

This does not mean that you must be infallible. You can't be. But it does mean that if you punish, judge, exact from, demand of, and humiliate your child, they will in turn experience the universe as being that way. Parents have the power to destroy a child's free will.

Yet, on the other hand, parents should not hold themselves responsible for everything.

The Torah's teachings about child rearing through the stories of the matriarchs and the patriarchs are offered not only to impart to us what to do, but also what *not* to do. Doing things "right" doesn't always work out. How a child turns out is not always guaranteed, for better or for worse, by the effort or neglect invested by a parent in child rearing. There are no guarantees—this is what the Torah teaches us in those inspiring stories. Even the most noble and ideal of parents and of child-rearing techniques cannot guarantee a specifically desired outcome. Many teachers of Judaica both yesterday and today go to great lengths to justify and rationalize the parental conduct of the so-called biblical heroes. But if we justify their behavior then we will easily end up justifying our own and never learn from their mistakes. They were as mortal as any one of us, their intimate relationship with the Divine Glory notwithstanding. When Jacob favors his son Joseph over the other children, it is wrong (Babylonian Talmud, *Shabbat* 10b), and we need to learn from it as Jacob does after much consequential tragedy (Genesis, chap. 37). When Isaac and Rebeccah each favor one son over the other (Genesis 25:28), it leads to a dysfunctional family situation that casts the two brothers into unnecessary conflict lasting for decades (Genesis, chap. 27). The brothers, Jacob and Esau, aren't able to make peace with one another until they have both been away from home living their own lives, and only in a meeting place far from the home of their exalted parents (Genesis 33:3-4). When King David allows his love for his son Absalom to go untempered with discipline when called for, the results are an overthrown kingdom and a tragic loss of life, including Absalom's (2 Samuel, chaps. 15, 18). And his failure to guide his son Adoniyahu leads the lad to declare himself king "for his father had never admonished him, saying 'Why have you done such and such?'" (1 Kings 1:6). Noah cursing and rejecting his son Hahm for humiliating him was wrong (Genesis 9:20-24). Parents today who reject their children because they have intermarried or declared themselves gay or because they have changed religious affiliation are wrong. Elisha the Prophet was admonished for rejecting his assistant "with both hands" (Babylonian Talmud, *Sotah* 47a) even though his servant had committed a sacrilege against the sacred office of the prophet (2 Kings 5:20–27).

The stories in the *Tanakh* about parents and their children were not recorded for posterity, but to teach. Everyone, from a Moses to a Judah, is fallible, is human, is not free from errors of judgment or action. If we ignore this, we learn nothing from the rich heritage that is their story. For their story is our story, each and every one of us. From the *Tanakh*, then, we not only learn what we ought to do, but also what we ought not to do. From the *Tanakh* we learn covenanting, and that means: I express my wrath over what you have done against me, but I also leave enough room for you to have done it in the first place and to choose now to undo it. I do not throw a curse on you and your descendants as the great God-loving Noah did, thus causing centuries of Bible-authorized racism. No. In a covenantal relationship I do not damn you for an eternity for what you committed in the moment. I do not consider my intermarried children dead because they married out of their faith. No. In a covenantal relationship I do not judge and condemn you for choices that are outside the realm of *our* relationship.

The bottom line, Judaism reminds us, is that the onus of completing the work is not upon us (Babylonian Talmud, *Avot* 2:16). At some point, regardless of what we have given our children, they will find their own way of being in the world. As parents, we can only do as the Creator does every moment of every breath of every being: *tzimtzum*, step back and acknowledge the otherness of the child. Each child is here for a particular journey of soul-actualization that has less to do with us as parents than how our own life directions and life choices have created for our children the most opportune predisposition for the launching and unfolding of their own unique souls.

6

COVENANTING WITH THE EARTH

Rabbi Amorai (first century) asked Mar Rahumai: "Paradise—where is it located?" Said Mar Rahumai: "Right here on the earth."

— *Book of the Bahir, mishnah* 31

The Bible of the Jewish people (*Tanakh*) does not begin with the creation of the Jewish homeland of Israel, but with the creation of all land. Nor does it begin with the creation of people, but with the creation of Nature. Nor does it begin with the account of the first Jews, but with an account of the first humans. The lesson is clear: to be a Jew you need first to be a mensch; to be a mensch you need to acknowledge the priceless gift of the earth that God created. And finally, it is through your appreciation of the magnificence of Nature, of which you are an integral component, as well as a key beneficiary, that you approach a consciousness not of a consuming God but of a gracious God, not of a selfish God but of a benevolent God, for "the Earth is full of the loving-kindness of the Lord" (Psalms 33:5). By so honoring the earth, as a sacred gift of the Creator, you honor all lands, not only yours; you honor all creatures, not only humans; and you honor all peoples, not only your own.

Judaism teaches that the earth is more than something God handed over to us to use and to live off. Rather, the earth—no different from our bodies—is a necessary part of our physical life and our spiritual sojourn. It is through the tangible metaphor of the physical experience that we grasp and integrate the abstract nature of the spiritual. The thirteenth-century mystic Rabbi Isaac mon de Akko once remarked that without the sexual urge, for example, one would have as much a chance at spiritual enlightenment as a mule, and that "the physical senses determine one's spiritual growth" (quoted in *Reishit Chokhmah: Shaar HaAhavah*, end of chap. 4). All of our physical senses and all of our physical environment comprise the clues, the lessons, the very nurturance of our being, because we are, after all, comprised of both spirit and matter, spirit in essence and matter in manifestation. To frustrate our manifestation would be to shackle our spirit:

> In order to serve God, one needs access to the enjoyment of the beauties of nature, such as the contemplation of flower-decorated meadows, majestic mountains, flowing rivers, and so on. For all these are essential to the spiritual development of even the holiest of people. (twelfth-century Rabbi Abraham ben HaRambam in *HaMaspik L'Avodat HaShem*, p. 165)

No wonder that Judaism has therefore stayed clear of ascetic forms of discipline that required excessive abstinence from the pleasures of the body. There is even an ancient teaching in the Jerusalem Talmud that when we die we will have to account to God for all the pleasures of life we had wanted to enjoy, had the opportunity to enjoy, and did not (*Kiddushin*, end of chap. 4).

Covenanting with the earth, with what we call nature, whether with its larger external form, the environment, or with its more personalized, microcosmic form, our bodies

(*Tikkunei Zohar* 140), requires an honoring of it as Other. This means I do what I can to care for it but I do not purport to know all of what it needs, or all of what is good or bad for it. As in any relationship, covenanting with our physical universe without and within requires a stepping back every now and then and becoming cognizant of its own space, its own right to be, its own self. And as we would not usurp or misuse or overuse or neglect our bodies, neither ought we to do any of that to our earth. If we do, we destroy the essence of our Self, because the earth is the mother of our body: "For God took the Human from the soil of the earth" (Genesis 2:7) and "God called the Human Adam" (Genesis 5:2) from the word *adamah*, which means "earth" (*Pesikta D'Rav Kahana*, Buber ed., p. 34b). "When God created the Human," a first-century teaching goes, "God formed the Human out of clay gathered from all four directions; from across the entire earth" (*Genesis Rabbah* 8:1).

It is unfortunate that much of religion teaches that the earth as well as the body are but vehicles for spiritual empowerment and mere vessels for the betterment of the soul. From such theology, almost entirely patriarchal, it only follows that the horse exists for us to ride, the donkey to carry our burdens, the elephant to haul our timber, the child to carry on a man's name, the woman to bear his children, cook his meals, and satisfy his sexual cravings. It is a theology of hydraulics, of putting you down to raise me up; a theology that gave birth to human slavery and to chronic war and conquest; a theology based on the pursuit and preservation of the power—the lordship—of humans over land and animals, of men over women, of adults over children, of one race of people over another.

Yet, reaching far back to the earliest teachings of Judaism, for example, one discovers an entirely different attitude toward the environment that leaves little room for hierarchichal power structure, though, admittedly, room enough for it to have evolved into the monster it has become in our own times. Laws abound in the Torah that remind us we are stewards of the earth, not her owners; neighbors of the trees and wildlife, not their conquistadors; relatives of Creation, not its landlords. Even in the heat of battle, the ancient Israelites were admonished not to tear down fruit trees (Deuteronomy 20:19), and in the euphoria of constructing the sanctuary for the Divine Presence and its altar, they were only to use acacia wood, for the ark itself (Exodus 25:10), the table (Exodus 25:23), and the altar (Exodus 27:1).

Every seven years the land was to be left alone, unworked, and acknowledged as an Other, with the right to exist whether it was useful to humans or not (Leviticus 25:4) and all debts were canceled (Deuteronomy 15:1-2). Every seventh day, too, on the Sabbath, not only was your land suddenly not yours to work, but neither were your servants or your animals (Exodus 19:10). You could not ride your horse, and your cow owed you no milk. And this was true to the extent that although you were of course permitted to milk your cow to alleviate her discomfort, you could not partake of the milk, because in no way was your animal to be used by you on that one day out of the week. On the Sabbath, then, the Jews—especially during the periods of history when they were largely agrarian—were reminded that nothing and no one belonged to them. That nothing and no one owed their existence to whether or not the human could make use of them. And every fiftieth year all land reverted back to its original owner, and if there were slaves they went free (Leviticus 25:10), again to shake loose the human tendency of getting stuck in lordship. These sabbaticals, when observed in ancient times, were vivid proclamations to the possessive human creature that no one owes anyone anything: "For the land is Mine [says the Creator], and you are but strangers and settlers with Me" (Leviticus 25:23).

Although there are indeed ancient teachings that consider the earth exists for the sake of the human, there are also teachings that the earth exists in its own right, and that God provides rain, for example, not just for the sake of the human but also for the sake of the earth herself, its human inhabitants notwithstanding (Jerusalem Talmud, *Taanit* 3:3 [based on Job 37:13]), and sometimes for the exclusive sake of a single blade of grass somewhere on the planet (Jerusalem Talmud, Taanit 3:2). Simply put, "Unto God (not the human) is the earth and all therein" (Psalms 24:1). Period. Even according to the school that teaches the earth exists for the sake of the human, she is not seen as a gift with which we may do whatever we wish, but as a responsibility: "When God created Adam and Eve, God led them around the Garden of Eden and said: 'Behold My work! See how beautiful they are; how excellent! I created them all for your sake. See to it that you do not spoil and destroy My world; for if you do, there will be no one to repair it'" (*Kohelet Rabati* 7:28).

Like the Native American path, Judaism is essentially very much centered on the gifts of the earth and the cycles of nature and her seasons. The biblical holidays, though they are today celebrated inside of the insulated walls and carpeted enclosures of synagogues, were once celebrated in the mountains and valleys by worshipers toting seasonal fruits of the earth and the trees rather than prayerbooks. David's psalms are filled with awareness of how trees and snow and rocks and beasts worship the Creator no less than does the exalted, holier-than-thou human (e.g., Psalm 148).

When King David completed his composition of the Book of Psalms, he bragged to God and said: "Creator of the Universe! Is there any creature in Your world that has sung praises unto Your Name more than I have?" Suddenly, a toad leaped up on a rock in front of him and croaked: "Don't let it go to your head, for I sing far more praises to God in a single day than you could in a lifetime." (*Yalkut Shimoni* on Psalms 150:6)

Every blade of grass sings poetry to God without any ulterior motives or alien thoughts and without consideration of reward. How good and how lovely is it, then, when one is able to hear this song of the grasses. . . . It is especially precious to go out into the fields at the beginning of Spring, when nature awakens from her sleep, and to pour out a prayer there. For every fresh blade of grass, every new flower, all join themselves with the prayer, for they, too, yearn and long for God. (Eighteenth-century Rabbi Nachman of Breslau in *Likutei MaHaRan M'Breslau*, p. 306, and *Maggid Sichot*, p. 48; see also *Likutei MaHaRan Tannina*, no. 11)

As the author of the biblical Book of Job reminds us, all creatures have souls, not just humans:

But ask now the beasts and they shall teach you; and the birds of the sky, and they shall tell you. Or speak to the earth, and it shall teach you; and the fishes of the sea shall declare to you. Who amongst these does not know that God has brought all this into being—in Whose hand is the soul of every living thing. (Job 12:9–10)

The earth, then, is seen by Judaism as an organic and conscious Life Form. As the third-century Rabbi Shimon ben Lakish taught: "Whatever God created in the human was also created in the earth" (*Kohelet Rabati* 1:9). "All trees converse with one another," goes another teaching, "and with all living things" (*Genesis Rabbah* 13:2). It was a common belief that every single blade of grass, for example, was empowered by an angel (à la Findhorn) and "imbued with heavenly wisdom" (*Zohar*, Exodus 80b and *Genesis Rabbah* 10:7). The ancients tell of a man who razed his garden and then went to sleep "when a ferocious wind came and wounded him" (*Genesis Rabbah* 13:2). To be in relationship with the earth, then, means more than politically correct environmental responsibility. One can recycle, make mulch piles, boycott Styrofoam, and still not be in a covenantal relationship with nature. Only when you open up the shutters to your experience with your environment and allow it to move you, or even turn you off, do you begin to relationship with it.

Today we have to a significant extent lost touch with how to relationship with the earth. The consequence is an ailing planet. Healing her will take more than environmental activism. It will also take improving the quality of our relationship with her. You can send someone to the best medical facility available and hire the foremost physicians and therapists, but if you won't visit them they will feel neglected, uncared for, and may not heal. We can mope and kvetch about our ailing planet, but if we don't also celebrate her, be in relationship with her, appreciate her, we depress her further. Those of us who are doomsday environmentalists and who keep harping on how the planet is dying, contribute to her deterioration. As long as even one person believes in this planet, the Torah reminds us, and celebrates and honors the Creations, the planet will survive the deluge, whether that deluge is the Flood of the Bible in Noah's time, or the reckless abuse of the earth's resources in our own time:

> Abraham asked Malkizedek [who was believed to be Shem the son of Noah]: "How did you survive [the flood] in the ark?" Said Malkizedek: "Through the merit of the charity we performed there." Said Abraham: "And what kind of charity was there for you to do? Were there poor people in the ark? Were there not solely Noah and his family?" Said Malkizedek: "We performed these acts toward the birds, the beasts and the animals that were there. We did not sleep all night but were preoccupied at all times with feeding each species their particular kinds of nourishment. . . ." (*Shochar Tov* on Psalm 37)

Part of why we are stuck in a dysfunctional relationship with the earth today is because we are so far removed from experiencing her as organic, as living, as macrocosmic of our own personal beings. Superscientific and technical advances in our era have all but obliterated our sense of wonder and awe at the Life Force of our planet. What our ancestors would consider miraculous, we today dismiss as humdrum routine, as the mechanics of nature, as if Nature were but one more machine to reckon with. What was once mystery has today become fact, so that little is left to the human imagination but to imagine what it was once like to imagine. Human relationships, too, grow sour when the mystery fades away, when the excitement of Other-ing ebbs because one or both partners have slipped from I-Thou to I-It and are under the illusion that they have the other figured out. When that happens, it is time to step back and *tzimtzum*, withdraw from presumptions about the Other, and re-create the sacred space that once was in which each partner was total Other—awesome, mysterious, fresh—and in which the relationship constituted newness and aliveness.

The dynamics of our relationship with our environment are no different. If we don't Other it, we will smother it. It is alive, the Torah forewarns us. And if you don't respect her, she will either "withhold her fruits" (Deuteronomy 11:17) or "vomit you out" (Leviticus 18:25).

In his classic, *HaMaspik L'Ovdei HaShem* (*Guide for Those Who Serve God*), the twelfth-century Rabbi Abraham ben HaRambam (son of Maimonides) demonstrates how the most ancient of the Jewish teachers and prophets deliberately chose lifestyles that would put them more in touch with the earth and with Mother Nature:

> Our ancestors specifically chose to become sheep herders and nothing else, only because they found it more conducive to their medita-

tion practices to be in the meadows and in places far from urgency. . . .
Our father Jacob herded sheep for fourteen years (Genesis 31:41)
though he had been offered by Laban, his father-in-law, the livelihood
of his choice: "Choose your livelihood and I shall reward you with
it" (Genesis 30:28). He forfeited the opportunity of earning gold and
silver or any other reward for his preferred choice of remaining a sheep
herder (Genesis 30:31). . . . And Moses, the master of prophets and
servant of God, too, was a herder of the flocks of Jethro his father-in-
law, and would frequent the wilderness when he would herd, as it is
written: "And he led his flock toward the wilderness, and he came to
the Mountain of God in Horeb" (Exodus 3:1). And he did not lead
his flock there because there was a lack of other places for them to
graze in the surroundings of Midian, but he went there with his flock
for the purpose of meditating and in his yearning for divine revelation. . . . And Elijah and Elisha meditated frequently on Mount Carmel
(e.g., 1 Kings 18:42; 2 Kings 2:25, 4:25). And Elijah in his meditation in the wilderness achieved divine revelation, as it is written: "And
he went into the wilderness . . . and came to the Mountain of God in
Horeb. . . . And behold a Voice came unto him . . ." (1 Kings 19:4
ff.). . . . In fact, all of the descendants of the prophets did their medi-
tations in isolated places like the Tomb of Rachel, and at Beth-El, and
Jericho and at the Jordan River, as indicated in Scripture (e.g.,
1 Samuel 10:2; 2 Samuel 2:15, 18, 23, and so forth). (Chapter on
Hitbodedut [p. 178 of *Keren Hotza'at Sifrei Rabbanei Bavel* edition—
Jerusalem, 5733/1973])

An even older ancestor of the Jewish people, Isaac the son
of Abraham, is described in the Torah as going out "to meditate in the field" (Genesis 24:63). As the eighteenth-century
mystic Rabbi Nachman of Breslau taught: "It is preferable to
meditate in the meadows outside of the city. Go to a grassy
field and the grasses will awaken your heart" (*Sichot HaRan*,
no. 227; see also *Likutei MaHaRan Tannina*, no. 11).

Historically, the Jews' attraction to urbanism was not by
choice but because of forced expulsion from the very agrarian lifestyle that once characterized them. Forbidden to own
land and eventually herded into urban ghettos, the Jews have

spent a good part of the last several centuries adjusting to the urban life of business entrepreneurship and merchandising. Their ties with the land have by now been all but severed, hanging on by the thread of ancient traditional celebrations of religious festivals once rooted in a lifestyle of earth consciousness and environmental honoring. Much like the Native Americans, the Jews were driven not only from their national homeland but also from their sacred connections to the earth mother.

The ancient tradition saw the universe not only as a Creation of God but also as an actual manifestation of God wherein the mortal can experience the Divine Presence. The Hebrew for "universe" or "world" is *olam*, and since the word *olam* also connotes "hiddenness," the ancient rabbis taught that God is concealed within the universe (*Book of Bahir, mishnah* 10); that God fills the universe as the soul fills the body (*Deuteronomy Rabbah* 2:26); that the Creator is Present in the very fabric of the Creation—"Do I not fill the heavens and the earth?" (Jeremiah 23:24); that it is through the physical universe that one experiences the Great Spirit. The earth, then, is as much a divine revelation as the Torah. And so is every element of Creation, whether a rock, a goat, or a person.

The Bible, too, or the Word of God, was understood by the ancient rabbis as a finite form of the infinite God-Will. And as the Torah is a textual manifestation of the divine will, so is the earth an organic manifestation of the divine will; as the Torah reflects its Author, so does the earth, too, reflect her Creator. Because, like Torah, the earth, too, reflects the Word of God: "For God spoke, and [the Earth] came into being" (Psalms 33:9). What occurred at Mount Sinai one moment some 3,000 years ago, then, was in essence no more a revelation of God than the Grand Canyon has been every moment *throughout* the past 3,000 years:

Said Rabbi Tanchum bar Hiyya: "A much greater event is the falling of rain than the Giving of the Torah, for the Giving of the Torah brought joy to the Israelites alone, but the falling of the rain brings joy to all peoples, and to all beasts, both wild and domestic, and to the birds." (*Shochar Tov* on Psalm 117)

Both, then—the Torah and the earth—are the Word of God, revelation of the same divine intent. And it is therefore through our awareness and appreciation of the earth that we can experience an immanent glimpse of the transcendant God, for "the entire Earth is filled with God's Glory" (Isaiah 6:3). The earth, therefore, is a form of Torah, yet another form of manifestation of divine will: "God looked into Torah and realized Creation" (*Zohar* on Exodus, p. 161a). Conversely, the human can look into Creation and realize Torah: "For the Human is placed on the earth to observe her and to thereby come to know God; to thereby come to know the Torah" (*Zohar* on Exodus 161b).

"Whatever The Blessed Holy One created was created solely for divine glorification [i.e., awareness and appreciation]" [Babylonian Talmud, Avot 6:14, based on Isaiah 43:7]. This means that . . . everything which, as a creation of God, bears the Name of God, has no other purpose but to serve the glorification of God, its Creator. . . . The nature with which every creature is endowed at the time of its birth, and all the influences that affect it under God's own guidance, both have the ultimate goal to guide all things and all peoples along that path which leads to the glorification of God above, on earth. (Rabbi Samson Raphael Hirsch [nineteenth century] in his commentary on Avot 6:14)

The ancient rabbis proposed, for example, that "Abraham fulfilled the entire Torah" (Babylonian Talmud, *Yoma*, 28b). How could he have known the Torah when its text was not yet in existence, not to mention the fact that he ate dairy and meat together (Genesis 18:7-8), a violation of later Torah law?

The lesson is probably that he knew the intended Torah, as opposed to the manifested-form Torah; that he knew the soul of the Law, the Spirit of the God-Will that pulsated behind the Letter of the God-Word—which he came to know after he observed the wonders of Creation and deduced that there must be a Creator (*Yalkut Shimoni* on Genesis 12:1; *Tanna D'Bei Eliyahu Zuta*, chap. 25). And even after Abraham had discovered God (not that he was the first to do so), God reminded him to remain grounded, to stay conscious of his physical environment just as he had during the process of his search for the Great Mystery: "And God said to Abram: 'Arise, walk through the land, across its length and breadth . . .'" (Genesis 13:17–18).

Judaism reminds us that religious practice is a dead-end road to God and to spiritual consciousness if we attempt to confine our worship exclusively to organized religion, to designated altars and directives of practice; if we sever the spirit of the Creator from the matter of Creation; if we try to separate our experience of God from our experience of the earth. On the contrary, consciousness of the Creation is taught as a prerequisite to consciousness of the Creator—a preface, not a mere footnote, to religion: "You are the God Who made heaven and all that is there, and the earth and all that is thereon; You are the God Who chose Abram . . . and established with him a covenant . . ." (Nehemiah 9:6-7).

Some might argue that marveling at Nature is unrelated to spiritual practice, to Torah. They employ the following teaching of the third century Rabbi Yaakov: "One who is walking along the way and studying, and then interrupts their study and says, 'What a magnificent tree that is!' Or, 'What a beautiful field that is!' scripture regards it as if they owe their life" (Babylonian Talmud, *Avot* 3:7). The seeming conflict of this teaching fades when we reread the lesson and

focus on the words "interrupts their study." Yes, I do negate
life if, during my meditation on Torah, I experience Nature
as interruptive; as non-Torah, and therefore interruptive.
Were I rather to experience Torah and Nature as interwoven—
corresponding one to the other like a structure and its blue-
print—both as the Word of God, then merely shifting my attention from the form of one to the form of the other is
anything *but* interruptive:

> Rabbi Hunna (third century) asked his son Rabbah why he did not
> avail himself of the opportunity to study under the great Rabbi Hisda,
> who was acclaimed as exceedingly wise. Replied Rabbah: "When I
> attend his discourses he speaks primarily of mundane subjects, such
> as the workings of Nature, and how one should behave in relation-
> ship to them." Said Rabbi Hunna: "All the more reason why you *should*
> study with him, for he occupies himself with the life of God's cre-
> ations; and you call that a mundane subject?!" (Babylonian Talmud,
> *Shabbat* 82a)

Having established the place of earth consciousness and
sacredness, what form of relationship need we create with
the earth to bridge these understandings? Are we lords of
the earth, or guardians of the earth? After all, does not the
Torah quote the God-Will for our relationship with the earth
in the words *v'kivshuho*—customarily translated as: "And you
shall subdue her"? (Genesis 1:28).

V'kivshuho as implying subjugation and conquest is more
likely a socially influenced interpretation emanating from the
patriarchal mind-set of war and ownership than the divine
intent behind the Word. For while the word *kevush* is indeed
used quite commonly in literal contexts of "violation," "sup-
pression," "oppression," "conquest," "force," and "restraint,"
it is also used to connote "honoring," as in: "When the sages
gather for discussion, (*v'nikhveshin eylu l'eylu*) and humble

themselves [in respect] for one another, God participates"
(*Midrash Tehillim* on Psalm 30 [end]). The biblical *v'kivshuho*,
then, could just as well imply the establishment between the
human and the earth of a relationship that is mutually hum-
bling; a relationship based on dialogue and cooperation in
which there is an honoring of one another's otherness. In
another instance, the Talmud defines a mighty person as one
who *kovesh* their inclination (Babylonian Talmud, *Avot* 4:1).
If *kovesh* here means to "conquer" or to "control," then the
teaching would imply that a mighty person is one who is an
obsessive-compulsive anxiety-ridden neurotic. Rather, the
meaning intended is of course one who directs their inclination, one who tempers their emotions. Even God is quoted as
saying, "May My Compassion temper (*yikh'vosh*) My Anger"
(Babylonian Talmud, *Berakhot* 7a).

These alternate choices of translation of *v'kivshuho* would
also be more in line with the context of the verse in which it
appears, which is recorded as blessing rather than command:
"And God *blessed* them, and said to them, 'Be fruitful and
multiply and fill the Earth *v'kivshuho'*" (Genesis 1:28).

The fact that the so-called injunction to be fruitful and
multiply and tend the earth is garbed in divine Blessing as
opposed to Commandment is indicative of a relationship
between the Creator toward us that is compassionate, gracious, and honoring of our humanity: "When God gives, God
gives according to divine ability; when God asks of us, we
are expected only to give according to human ability" (*Numbers Rabbah* 21:22). God, then, is not out to subdue us. Religion might be, but not God. Religion mandates that we
should have babies and dominate the earth; God, however,
blesses us that we endeavor to emulate that very attribute of
God that resulted in Creation, the attribute of Grace, the
desire to give, to nurture, to share, to bring joy and pleasure
to your Self and, in turn, to an Other:

Moses said to God: "Show me the attribute by which You govern Your world." God replied: "I owe no creature anything, yet I give to them gratuitously." (*Tanchuma, V'Et'chanan*, para. 3)

Rabbi Judah the Prince taught: "See how great is peace, that even if we were to worship idols, but there is harmony amongst us, then God would say, 'I cannot judge against them since there is peace amongst them,' as it is written: 'But Ephraim is taken up with idols only [as opposed to infighting]; he shall be left alone' [Hosea 4:17]. But if there is disharmony between us, then does God hold us accountable, as it is written: 'Their heart is divided; now shall they bear their guilt' [Hosea 10:2]." (*Genesis Rabbah* 38:6)

Rabbi Baruka of Huza frequented the market of Lapet. One day Elijah the Prophet appeared to him there. Asked Rabbi Baruka: "Is there anyone in this marketplace destined for a special place in The World To Come?" Elijah then directed his attention toward two men walking nearby, and said: "These two have a special share in The World To Come." Rabbi Baruka approached them and asked: "What is your occupation?" To which they replied: "We are jesters. When we see someone who appears downcast, we cheer him up. And when we see two people quarreling with one another, we try to make peace between them." (Babylonian Talmud, *Taanit* 22a)

God seeks the kind of relationship that is personal and organic rather than cold and nonnegotiable; a relationship of Covenant, rather than of contract; of open dialogue, rather than of totalitarianism. The covenantal quality of relationship, however, is not only for relating to God, but to the earth as well, to all of God's Creation. The biblical intimation for the human to *kovesh* the earth, then, implies more a responsibility of *tending* to the earth than of subduing her; more a directive to *garden* rather than conquer her.

If we choose to read *v'kivshuho* as responsibility to care for the earth, she is more apt to nurture us in turn; if we choose to read *v'kivshuho* as license to subdue the earth, we are more apt to destroy her:

There was an episode regarding a certain man who was clearing stones from his field and dumping them onto public land when a rabbi happened by and admonished him: "Fool! Why are you removing stones from land that is not even yours and casting them onto land that is yours?" The man laughed at the rabbi and continued his project. Several years later the same man was forced to sell his field and found himself wandering about on public land where he soon tripped and fell over those very same stones. "Alas!" he exclaimed, "the rabbi was right when he said 'Why are you removing stones from land that is not even yours and casting them onto land that is yours!'" (Babylonian Talmud, *Baba Kamma* 50b)

The rabbi's admonishment to the man in the story implied that the land he lived on was *his* only if he could relate to it as ownerless—as sacred and organic—which was certainly not possible as long as he was dishonoring even public land by dumping his stones there. His behavior clearly demonstrated that he perceived the earth as under his domain, to behave toward without regard for anything about it but what personal benefit he could derive from it. With that kind of attitude, the rabbi reproached him, the land owed no relationship with him and was therefore not his. As long as he saw the land as his own, it wasn't. And in that context of relationship, any land that was not his, like the public land where he was illegally dumping, was more his than his own land, if for no other reason than his diminished sense of personal entitlement to it.

The rabbi's admonishment is also a lesson about the planet being like a ship: whatever an individual does on the vessel, even in the privacy of their paid-for personal space, will affect everyone else on the ship. If I own 500 acres of rain forest, in other words, I cannot go about chopping those trees down without considering the adverse consequences for the planet in general, for the wildlife dependent upon those trees and their ecosystem, and for the people whose air quality will be radically altered by what I choose to do in the privacy of my space:

> There was a man aboard a ship at sea who was found drilling a hole in the floor of his quarters. When the others aboard reproached him, he retorted: "What business is it of yours; am I not drilling in the privacy of my own room?" Said they to him: "Indeed, but your foolishness will sink us all!" (*Leviticus Rabbah* 4:6)

When we assume that we own earth in the sense that it is ours to do with whatever we please, then the land is not ours. The earth has no capacity for this form of relationship, to become our property, our tool. Our ward, yes. Our responsibility, yes. But it is ours only when we engage it as an organic life force with which we share a vital relationship that nurtures our being in this world, physically, emotionally, and spiritually. Even as the earth is our ward, then, we are its ward as well.

And if we are to learn about the integrity of our privately owned lands, we need to step out onto public lands and readjust our sense of *all* land as organic and under no one's domain. In other words, only when we relinquish our sense of dominion and ownership over the land, does it truly become ours.

> With Ten Utterances did God create the world. But could God not have created the world with a single utterance? Rather, it is to teach the preciousness of creation by its complexity, and therefore also the severity of consequence for those who abuse the world that was created with ten utterances, and the great merit for those who honor the world which was created with ten utterances. (Babylonian Talmud, *Avot* 5:1)

In other words, the unfathomable details and complexities of our natural world—from the structure of an electron-microscopic organism to the pulsation of a living heart to the unfolding of a yellow daffodil out of a green stem—tells of a universe created with deliberation, consciousness, and tender loving care. Each pine cone, each bumblebee, each and every blood corpuscle teaches us clearly that to the Creator, Creation was more than an incidental afterthought, or some insignificant means toward a far more significant end. Rather, our physical life, and the earth upon which we live that life, is infinitely precious and beloved by the Creator. Else, we could just as easily have been made out of mattress stuffing and the earth from Styrofoam. Else, the universe could just as easily have come about from a single utterance of God rather than ten.

No wonder that the Torah does not concern itself at all with a spiritual world, with the hereafter, with what Judaism itself taught as the ultimate purpose of our physical life (Babylonian Talmud, *Avot* 4:16). Whether or not there is a hereafter, a World-to-Come, is not the emphasis of ancient Judaic teaching, though it is essential to its doctrines. Rather, what it does highlight is the magnitude of both the gift and responsibility of being in *this* world. And it is toward a more wholesome appreciation of and relationship with that gift, and that responsibility, that this book is dedicated.

BIBLIOGRAPHY

Buber, Martin. *I and Thou*. New York: Charles Scribner's Sons, 1958.
Dawidowicz, Lucy. *The War Against the Jews*. New York: Bantam Books, 1976.
Fromm, Erich. *You Shall Be as Gods*. New York: Ballantine Books, 1983.
Heschel, Abraham J. *God in Search of Man*. New York: Farrar, Straus, & Giroux, 1990.
Hirsch, Samson Raphael. *The Pentateuch*. New York: Judaica Press, 1971.
———. *The Psalms*. New York: Feldheim, 1966.

INDEX

About the Authors

Gershon Winkler is a circuit-riding rabbi of the rurals, serving the Jewish communities of Durango, Colorado, and Farmington, New Mexico. He is also the author of *They Called Her Rebbe, The Sacred Stones, The Soul of the Matter, The Secret of Sambatyon, Dybbuk, The Hostage Torah,* and *The Golem of Prague.* Originally ordained Orthodox by the late Rabbi Ben Zion Bruk, Dean of Yeshivat Beit Yossef-Novoredek in Jerusalem, Rabbi Winkler now considers himself "Flexidox." He has guest lectured and served as scholar-in-residence at colleges and universities across the United States as well as at Jewish and ecumenical retreats from coast to coast. He is married with coauthor Lakme Batya Elior, and the couple reside amid the Nacimiento Mountains of northwestern New Mexico.

Lakme Batya Elior is a psychotherapist in private practice who, prior to joining with Gershon, worked as a full-time therapist for the Chicago Counseling and Psychotherapy Center. She is also a certified focusing trainer and has conducted workshops nationwide on communication skills and focusing (developed by Dr. Gene Gendlin of the University of Chicago). A popular teacher of feminine spirituality and Judaica, Lakme has been a regular guest lecturer and workshop facilitator at Jewish and ecumenical retreats from coast to coast. She is currently writing a feminine interpretation of the Torah and serves as publisher and editor of *Pumbedissa Journal,* an open forum for uninhibited discussion of contemporary Jewish issues.